Meaning and Linguistic Variation

Linguistic styles, particularly variations in pronunciation, carry a wide range of meaning – from speakers' socioeconomic class to their mood or stance in the moment. This book examines the development of the study of sociolinguistic variation, from early demographic studies to a focus on the construction of social meaning in stylistic practice. It traces the development of the "Third Wave" approach to sociolinguistic variation, uncovering the stylistic practices that underlie broad societal patterns of change. Eckert charts the development of her thinking and of the emergence of a theoretical community around the "Third Wave" approach to social meaning. Featuring new material alongside earlier seminal work, it provides a coherent account of the social meaning of linguistic variation.

PENELOPE ECKERT is the Albert Ray Lang Professor of Linguistics and Anthropology at Stanford University. She is author of *Jocks and Burnouts* (1990) and *Linguistic Variation as Social Practice* (2000), co-editor of *Style and Sociolinguistic Variation* (Cambridge, 2002) with John R. Rickford and co-author of *Language and Gender* (Cambridge, 2003, 2013) with Sally McConnell-Ginet.

Meaning and Linguistic Variation
The Third Wave in Sociolinguistics

Penelope Eckert
Stanford University, California

CAMBRIDGE
UNIVERSITY PRESS

University Printing House, Cambridge CB2 8BS, United Kingdom

One Liberty Plaza, 20th Floor, New York, NY 10006, USA

477 Williamstown Road, Port Melbourne, VIC 3207, Australia

314 321, 3rd Floor, Plot 3, Splendor Forum, Jasola District Centre, New Delhi - 110025, India

79 Anson Road, #06-04/06, Singapore 079906

Cambridge University Press is part of the University of Cambridge.

It furthers the University's mission by disseminating knowledge in the pursuit of education, learning and research at the highest international levels of excellence.

www.cambridge.org
Information on this title: www.cambridge.org/9781107122970
DOI: 10.1017/9781316403242

© Penelope Eckert 2018

This publication is in copyright. Subject to statutory exception and to the provisions of relevant collective licensing agreements, no reproduction of any part may take place without the written permission of Cambridge University Press.

First published 2018

A catalogue record for this publication is available from the British Library

Library of Congress Cataloging in Publication data
Names: Eckert, Penelope author.
Title: Meaning and linguistic variation : the third wave in sociolinguistics / Penelope Eckert, Stanford University, California.
Description: Cambridge; New York, NY: Cambridge University Press, 2018. | Includes bibliographical references and index.
Identifiers: LCCN 2017060362 | ISBN 9781107122970 (hardback)
Subjects: LCSH: Sociolinguistics. | Language and languages – Variation.
Classification: LCC P40.E28 2018 | DDC 306.44–dc23
LC record available at https://lccn.loc.gov/2017060362

ISBN 978-1-107-12297-0 Hardback
ISBN 978-1-107-55989-9 Paperback

Cambridge University Press has no responsibility for the persistence or accuracy of URLs for external or third-party internet websites referred to in this publication, and does not guarantee that any content on such websites is, or will remain, accurate or appropriate.

Dedication

My senior year in high school, my French class had a substitute teacher for one week. He told us he didn't know any French, but that he was a linguist and could help us with whatever we were working on. We said we were struggling with irregular verbs. He had us read him the paradigms and then said, "Those aren't irregular." That day I learned about stress-based vowel alternations, and from then on my dream was to be a linguist. I will never know who he was. I've tried to find out, but I will never forget him. The principal told me that on his way home after his dissertation fieldwork on an Apache reservation, an automobile accident had killed his wife and his child and destroyed his notes. He was substitute teaching as he tried to get his life back together, but he gave up and committed suicide soon after. This book is dedicated to his memory, and to the life that he and his family never had.

Contents

List of Figures	*page* viii
List of Tables	ix
Preface: The Ant's Eye View	xi
Acknowledgments	xiii

Part I Beginnings — 1

1 Gascon — 3
2 Stigma and Meaning in Language Shift — 15

Part II My Participation in the Second Wave — 29

3 Jocks and Burnouts — 31
4 Jocks, Burnouts and Sound Change — 40
5 The Local and the Extra-Local — 66
6 On the Outs — 80
7 Foregrounding Style — 109

Part III The Third Wave — 123

8 The SLIC Generation — 125
9 The Nature of Indexicality in Variation — 143
10 What Kinds of Signs Are These? — 165
11 The Semiotic Landscape — 186

Postscript	193
References	195
Index	205

Figures

3.1	Average jeans leg width at lunchtime	*page* 36
4.1	(uh) values according to parents' socioeconomic status	59
4.2	(uh) values according to category affiliation	59
4.3	(uh) values in Redford and Livonia	61
5.1	Backing of (uh) by Jocks and Burnouts in urban and suburban communities	77
5.2	Raising of the nucleus of (ay) by Jocks and Burnouts in urban and suburban communities	78
6.1	Occupation coefficients for F2 of (aw) for men and women in Philadelphia neighborhoods (from Labov 1984)	93
6.2	Probability of Australian Question Intonation use by class and sex (from Guy et al. 1986:37)	94
6.3	The Northern Cities Chain Shift	102
6.4	Contrast between girls and boys and between Jocks and Burnouts as differences in percentages when calculated for the combined data in Table 6.1	103
6.5	Absolute differences of percentages for Burnouts and Jocks, calculated separately for girls and boys	106
9.1	Use of Detroit variables by gender and social category	149
9.2	Use of Beijing and international variables by managers in state-owned and foreign-owned businesses (based on Zhang 2005)	152
9.3	Indexical field of (ING) (based on Campbell-Kibler 2007a, 2007b)	157
9.4	Indexical field of /t/ release	161
10.1	The Northern California Vowel Shift	177
10.2	/ae/ nasal pattern (Rachel, Fields Elementary)	178
10.3	/ae/ non-raising pattern (Selena, Steps Elementary)	179
10.4	Individual (ae) means at Fields Elementary	180
10.5	Individual (ae) means at Steps Elementary	181
10.6	F1 (ae0) – F1 (aeN) in Hz	182
10.7	Stylistic variation for five kids	184

Tables

2.1	French borrowings in Soulatan. Three speakers' responses to word list	*page* 26
3.1	Average jeans width in the first floor halls	38
4.1	Social stratification of variables from Wolfram (1969)	43
4.2	Probability of use of extreme backed and lowered variants of (uh) by social category	60
6.1	Percentage of advanced tokens of the five vowels for each combination of social category and sex	103
6.2	Significance (yes or no) of social constraints on the vowel changes that constitute the Northern Cities Chain Shift	104
10.1	Range of F1 for /ae/ in Hz at Fields and Steps	179
10.2	F1(aeN) – F1(aeO) for 20 kids at Steps Elementary. (Shaded rows are crowd members)	183

Preface: The Ant's Eye View

I have always been an ant in an intellectual world that favors the bird's eye view. My development as a linguist has been a gradual recognition that this is not a deficit.

What follows is something like an intellectual autobiography, tracing the development of my engagement with the social meaning of variation and the emergence of the Third Wave of variation study. It is a somewhat personal account, because intellectual development is highly personal, intertwined with relationships and personal change. My academic life has not been easy, thanks to a great extent to a fairly paralyzing case of impostor syndrome. And if all my years of teaching have taught me one thing, it's how prevalent that syndrome is in academics, how much damage it does, and how important it is to talk about it. While I won't bare my soul or offer personal tidbits that are not clearly relevant to my linguistics, there will be some embarrassing stuff in the following pages and I hope it will be of use to some readers.

In a 2005 LSA plenary, which later appeared in the *Annual Review of Anthropology* (Eckert 2012), I traced the development of variation studies as a series of three waves: a First Wave of urban survey studies, a Second Wave of ethnographic studies of local dynamics, and a Third Wave in which the focus turned to the meaning of variation. I was trained in the First Wave, participated in the Second Wave, and found my center in the Third Wave. The Third Wave is not "a" theory but a theoretical perspective that puts the meaning of variation, in all its dynamism and indeterminacy, at the center of analysis. And it locates meaning not in the individual variable so much as in stylistic practice. The unfortunate aspect of the wave metaphor is that it has often been taken to mean that each wave supersedes the previous one. I would say that each wave refines aspects of the previous one, but it has always been clear that the basic ideas of each wave have always been implicit in the earlier waves. I have often said that the Martha's Vineyard study (Labov 1963) was the first Third Wave study, and certainly discourses of agency as well as of social meaning were around from the start, in conversations if not in writings. Trudgill's (1972) notion of covert prestige, based in notions of working-class male toughness, was certainly what one would call an example of indexical order (Silverstein 2003). And the accumulation of evidence in each wave made more work possible in the next. At the same time, while Labov's (1966) move to large-scale survey methods was the obvious next step (and, by virtue of its focus on class, pretty radical at the time), it ended up overshadowing – even suppressing – the insights of the Martha's Vineyard study. The Third Wave has picked up this thread.

The skeleton of this book is a series of papers that I think best illustrate my thinking over time. Some of these papers have been buried in obscure volumes, because I've never had a particularly effective publication strategy. Some of them were also written long after my thoughts had moved on, so the papers in this volume follow the chronology of my thought, not of their publication. I confess that the prose in the earlier papers makes me cringe. Too many paragraphs begin with *whereas, while, although* ... as if I was trying to be fancy by talking backwards. I think my writing improved along with my confidence that what I had to say was good enough that I could write it in my own voice. The book is in three parts, following what I see as three main phases in my development as a linguist: graduate school and my work on Gascon, my work in the Second Wave, centered on my study of Jocks and Burnouts, and my work in the Third Wave, which developed after I came to Stanford.

Acknowledgments

Since this book is about my entire career as a linguist, it is in itself a long acknowledgment. I've read acknowledgments that list dozens of people, and the more people one lists the more people one is likely to accidentally leave out. So while there have been many wonderful people in my life, each one bringing something different, I am keeping it simple.

I have a great and satisfyingly weird family, and I just hope that the world remains a reasonable place for the future of my wonderfully quirky grand-nephews, Owen and Noel Eckert. I'm grateful for the twenty-eight years that I shared with Ivan Sag, who was not only a wonderful life partner, but showed me how to believe in myself as a linguist. And although I no longer work on Gascon, my connection to Gascony is now forty-eight years old and deep, as is my love for four very special Gascons whom I consider my extended family – Gisèle, Bernard and Patricia Rumeau, and the late Sylvestre (Steve) Novak. Bill Labov has been in my life for fifty-four years, and I appreciate him more every day. His fascination with people and his love of fieldwork was what first drew me to him, and his friendship and kindness have drawn me closer over the years.

I became an ethnographer at Michigan, and it was at Michigan that I realized that my future lay in incorporating Anthropology into my work on variation. I'm grateful for the support and friendship of my colleagues in the Anthropology Department, particularly Rob Burling, Conrad Kottak and Skip Rappaport. Miyako Inoue is particularly special to me – brilliant and ridiculously modest, she has been my constant guide in the theoretical landscape of Linguistic Anthropology, and a most beloved friend. And Sally McConnell-Ginet's collaboration and friendship have been a complete gift. Now that we're no longer working together, I miss that sense of being part of a "with," but the closeness will always be there. Nik Coupland has always been both generous and inspiring from afar, and there are very few ideas in this book that he had not already had.

Fieldwork has always been my main inspiration, and I'm grateful to the many people who have allowed me into their lives – the people of Soulan, the administrators, teachers and students of Belten High and other high schools in the Detroit suburbs, and of Fields and Steps Elementary schools. And I'm unspeakably grateful for my years in the Stanford Linguistics Department, which is not only an unusually civil department, but the only Linguistics department I know of that has been truly serious about breaking down subdisciplinary boundaries. Where else could this community that has come to call itself the Third Wave have happened? I'm grateful to each and every one of the students that has contributed to this wave, both for the intellectual stimulation and for their trust, love and companionship. I've gotten to work with so many amazing students – in my twenty-eight years at Stanford, I've been on something like forty dissertation committees, of which I've chaired or co-chaired twenty-two. Each one of these has been an honor and an adventure, and many of these students remain close friends as well as colleagues. One of them, Rob Podesva, is now my very creative and wonderful colleague, and will carry on and continue to transform the sociolinguistics program at Stanford as I follow John Rickford into retirement. I've been very lucky.

I am grateful for the permission granted to reprint the following:

The Paradox of National Language Movements. *Journal of Multilingual and Multicultural Development* 4:289–300. 1983.

Diglossia: Separate and Unequal. *Linguistics* 18:1053–64. 1980.

Clothing and Geography in a Suburban High School. In Conrad P. Kottak (ed.) *Researching American Culture*. Ann Arbor: University of Michigan Press, 45–8. 1980.

Sound Change and Adolescent Social Structure. *Language in Society* 17:183–207. 1988.

Variation and a Sense of Place. In Carmen Fought (ed.) *Sociolinguistic Variation: Critical Reflections*. Oxford University Press, 107–20. 2004.

The Whole Woman: Sex and Gender Differences in Variation. *Language Variation and Change* 1:245–67. 1989.

Jennifer Arnold, Renee Blake, Penelope Eckert, Melissa Iwai, Norma Mendoza-Denton, Carol Morgan, Livia Polanyi, Julie Solomon and Tom Veatch. Variation and Personal/Group Style. Paper presented at NWAVE-22. Ottawa: University of Ottawa. 1993.

Vowels and Nailpolish: The Emergence of Linguistic Style in the Preadolescent Heterosexual Marketplace. In Natasha Warner, Jocelyn Ahlers, Leela Bilmes, Monica Oliver, Suzanne Wertheim and Melinda Chen (eds.), *Gender and Belief Systems*. Berkeley: Berkeley Women and Language Group, 183–90. 1996.

Demystifying Sexuality and Desire. In Kathryn Campbell-Kibler, Robert Podesva, Sarah Roberts and Andrew Wong (eds.) *Language and Sexuality: Contesting Meaning in Theory and Practice*. CSLI Publications, 99–110. 2002.

Elephants in the Room. *Journal of Sociolinguistics* 7:392–7. 2003.

Variation and the Indexical Field. *Journal of Sociolinguistics* 12:453–76. 2008.

Where Do Ethnolects Stop? *International Journal of Bilingualism* 12:25–42. 2008.

Part I

Beginnings

I was a crowd pleaser as a child, an attention-grabber. I was always nice, and I was "popular" in high school. But inside I was a quietly angry girl with a rich and obsessive fantasy life, because I felt that there was no place for me in the real world of serious people. How this came about is my business, but what might better have taken the form of healthy rebellion became resistance, and I became one of those students who got A's and D's. But I was good at standardized tests, so I managed to get into Oberlin, where I arrived with a sense that I didn't deserve to be there and continued to cultivate the occasional D.

I got at least some of my anger from my mother, who loved mathematics more than anything, and apparently was brilliant at it. But back in the nineteen-twenties, on her way to a PhD, the Columbia math department forced her to choose between her upcoming marriage and her fellowship. I'm a grateful and guilty product of that choice, and I've been living the life she should have had. I grew up on stories of my mother's clashes with the gender order – how her mathematical triumphs were attributed to my father, how as a decoder during World War II she had to put up with a roomful of male colleagues talking about how stupid their wives were. I heard much of this from my father, who had a hard time living with his complicity in this cultural script, and did everything he could to keep me from falling victim to sexism, institutional or otherwise.

Although I knew in high school that I wanted to study linguistics, it wasn't very available as an undergraduate subject. So during the summer between my freshman and sophomore year in college, I went to Columbia to take William Diver's Introduction to Linguistics. Diver was an inspired teacher, and I was in heaven every single day of that course. But although I was determined to be a linguist, I had no picture of myself as a real academic. Or a real anything for that matter. Approaching graduation, I became increasingly afraid of the future, as I struggled with the contradiction between my academic ambitions and my inability to do school. I had a very nice boyfriend, and for a while I thought I could get married and get a job, and gradually weasel my way into graduate school. But at Christmas his parents gave me an ironing board, an iron, and a set of cutlery with stars on the handle. I was overcome with terror, and I'm still ashamed of the cowardly way I backed into, and then out of, that engagement.

He deserved better. After graduation I went home to New York to find myself and a nine-to-five job. I ended up as a bilingual secretary at Rockefeller University (then The Rockefeller Institute) to Belgian Nobel Laureate Christian de Duve. De Duve was a wonderful person, a great boss and friend, but it was soon clear to both of us that I didn't want a nine-to-five job, that it was time to bite the bullet and become a linguist. I applied to Columbia but didn't get in. Uriel Weinreich advised me to take courses and try to prove myself, and reapply. So I got a job teaching high school and moonlighted taking linguistics courses at Columbia: two semesters of morphology and syntax taught by Bill Labov (a new Assistant Professor), and Romance Philology taught by Mario Pei. It was a very full year, and I loved both the linguistics and being in the high school. It was being around teenagers that I really liked, not so much the teaching, and I hated dealing with classroom discipline. When I left the high school at the end of the year, I told myself that I would find a way to come back. Little did I know that it would be under such great circumstances.

When I arrived at Columbia, Bill Labov was the coolest act in town. His MA thesis, the Martha's Vineyard study (1963), had been published, his dissertation, the New York City study (1966), was about to be published, and he was into his Harlem study. He was young, politically engaged, casual, outgoing, with boundless energy and excitement. Bill has been a central presence in my life ever since. He has been a mentor, an inspiration, on occasion an adversary, a frustration, and always a beloved friend. And he kept me alive through graduate school, where I was continually terrified and felt I didn't belong.

I never asked a question or volunteered an idea in class or even in conversation, for fear of saying something stupid. When I had a question in class, rather than asking it, I rushed off to the library to find the answer. I wasted huge amounts of time poring over books looking for answers to questions that I could have gotten in a second if I'd only asked. And of course I didn't always find the answers either. I didn't think I was stupid, just clueless. I loved collecting and working with data, and I knew I was good at it, but I always thought I didn't – or couldn't – really understand theory. Years later, after hearing me give a talk on the impostor syndrome at the LSA, my classmate Benji Wald told me he'd thought I never said anything because I was too cool. I'd felt anything but cool, but I'd probably tried to seem cool just to get by. For all I know, my defense may have intimidated other insecure people. Nowadays, talk of the impostor syndrome is everywhere, but back when I was in graduate school it felt shameful and private.

1 Gascon

I became a dialectologist in Marvin Herzog's course on Yiddish dialectology, during which I began a lifelong relationship with the French linguistic atlas (Gilliéron 1902–10). I have never revered books – I like reading them, but their object-hood has never meant much to me. I'm not one of those people who loves the touch and smell of books. This atlas, though, gives me the shivers. I couldn't and still can't get enough of it. The sheer wonder and eternal value of the work that went into it is overwhelming, as is the pleasure I've gotten from tracing sound changes as they wander and interact across the countryside. The paper I wrote for Herzog's course turned into my master's thesis, on morphological constraints in the raising of Latin unstressed *a to [o] in southern France. I found the phenomenon in the intersections of the spread of this change with the spread of the deletion of the plural marker. I thought it was interesting, but Bill had to point out its relevance to current theory. I didn't publish it (Eckert 1985) until sixteen years later, when its theoretical message was no longer timely.

My work with the atlas made me want to hear the southern dialects I'd been focusing on, and an exploratory trip in the summer of 1968 gave me a taste not only of what the dialects sounded like, but of the stigma attached to them. I'd never been a Francophile, so stigmatized peasant dialects were just what I needed to be comfortable with France at the time. I put an ad in the New York francophone newspaper *France Amérique*, hoping to find a speaker of one of these dialects. I got a response from a man who told me dialects didn't exist, and one from a young guy who figured I was trolling for a French boyfriend and claimed to speak all dialects. But sitting in a laundromat on Broadway one day, I met a woman who had seen my ad but hadn't responded because she'd thought it sounded suspicious – after all, what normal person would want to study a peasant dialect? She was Anna Cau, from Ercé, in the Gascon-speaking Pyrenees of Ariège, and she became my wonderful consultant for the months leading up to my fieldwork.

Ercé was the source of many of New York's French restaurants and restaurant workers. And lying in the midst of the isogloss bundle that separates Gascon from Languedocien to the east, it had the added distinction of sporting a particularly stigmatized dialect. Since Madame Cau had also lived for some time in the Languedocien dialect area, she often provided me with forms in both dialects, and it was clear that she thought the Languedocien versions were "better." It also became clear that some of the words she provided on the first pass were nonce borrowings from French. The Gascon equivalent she gave for the French word *fleuve* 'river that flows into the ocean' was *flobe*. Later as I read through my word list to check my phonological analysis, she balked at that one, and said she'd never heard that word and that main rivers and tributaries were both called *ribero*. There were several other items that she rejected on similar grounds, and it became clear that her bilingual competence included borrowing rules that essentially reconstructed several hundred years of sound change. This nonce borrowing, I decided, would be the topic of my dissertation.

In the fall of 1970, I landed in Toulouse with a Nagra and 100 five-inch reels of Scotch recording tape. In my early days in Toulouse, I found a warm welcome among participants in the regional Occitaniste movement. I was introduced to people in a community near Agen who were working to revitalize the language, and they arranged for me to live with a family with three generations of speakers – the only family I ever met with children growing up speaking Occitan. I was touched by these people's commitment, friendliness, and generosity, but I was interested in the dynamics that had given rise to language loss, not the potential cure. So I thanked them and headed south into the Pyrenees, in search of a rougher situation – a language without hot running water, so to speak. My search for a field site is to be told elsewhere, but I ultimately landed in Soulan, one valley and a couple of isoglosses over from Ercé.

Soulan is a commune of six villages arrayed over the south side of a mountain. I lived in St. Pierre, the main village of the commune, with a population of about eighty people. I lived with the family that owned the café, benefiting both from a family life and from a built-in excuse to hang out in the café, which was also the house's living room and kitchen. People came to the café not only to drink and socialize, but to buy wine, milk and cigarettes as well, so it was the ideal place to see the world go by. And André (Pépi) Vidal, the very colorful old man who had run the café for a generation, was a local, even regional, gossip clearinghouse. Pépi owned the physical café, but in order to collect his pension, he had to give up the café license. Joseph Rumeau, a plasterer from the higher village of Boussan, had bought the license from Pépi and moved in with his wife and three children ranging from two to fourteen years old. The older generations are gone now, but the three kids, Gisèle, Bernard and Patricia Rumeau, now middle aged, are like close family to me.

During my year and a half in Soulan, I maintained my friendships and connections among the Occitanistes, but felt increasingly at odds with their ideology. The stigma of "patois," and the greater stigma of the patois of the region around Soulan, was manifest in all things, and only exacerbated by the work of the Occitaniste movement. The movement was infected with the purism that had led to the language shift that they were trying to reverse, as the need to establish a standard language added a layer of stigma to actual spoken varieties. Kids from Soulan who took Occitan in high school learned only that their parents' language was not "Occitan" (or I should say not *even* Occitan). And while the Occitanistes celebrated my ability to speak Occitan, they thought the dialect I spoke was bizarre. Even Pierre Bec, the revered Occitan dialectologist whose book (Bec 1968) tracing the isoglosses in the region of Soulan was my bible, couldn't help correcting my Gascon to make it sound more "standard" – even though he himself had documented the very forms he was rejecting.[1]

Turning a peasant language into a regional standard required a lot of ideological work, and speakers of local dialects were being asked to cleave to a polity that had little meaning or advocacy for them. I was annoyed that the Occitanistes often referred to peasants with the condescending phrase *les braves paysans* 'the good peasants'. It had a similar ring to the common bourgeois way of referring to a fully adult woman who cleans your house: *petite portuguaise* 'little Portuguese'. I put my thoughts about this some years later into the following article.

THE PARADOX OF NATIONAL LANGUAGE MOVEMENTS

Introduction

A political movement that seeks to unify a large and diverse population needs to elaborate the construct of unity within and of the common threat from without, and to convince each segment of the population to identify its own experience and interests with that construct. The popularity of the movement depends not only on the severity of the problems it is designed to confront, but on its success in presenting the common interest of the entire population in such a way that all segments of the population can identify their own situation with it. A fundamental paradox arises when these considerations are put into the

---

[1] Specifically, he corrected the past participle in *n'ai cap comprenuch* 'I didn't understand' to *compreish*. (This was as if I'd said in French *je n'ai pas comprenu*, and he had corrected me to *compris*.) He said that while he knew that the Soulatan form was *comprenuch*, it was ugly and that the least I could do was say *comprenut* – the pronunciation of the next commune to the east (closer to Languedocien).

practical context of a regional or national movement. To aspire to any form of autonomy, a region needs to be large and diverse enough to comprise a viable economic unit. At the same time, the movement must be able to point to an underlying common heritage to justify unification of the region and its separateness from a larger political unit from which it desires to achieve autonomy. This is usually effected through the elaboration of a cultural, historical and/or linguistic heritage common to the diverse population of the region. But since the uniformity imposed by this elaboration will tend to be at the expense of local or sub-regional differences, the process of regional standardization may very well be reminiscent of the kind of external oppression that the movement is designed to counteract. A paradox arises, therefore, when the needs of unification require the submersion of authentic local or sub-regional differences. To the extent that the submersion leads to the belittling of local characteristics, segments of the population will not identify with the movement. This problem arises particularly in areas that are far enough from the regional center that there are extreme cultural and linguistic differences from what is considered the regional standard.

The following discussion will illustrate just such a case in a community removed culturally and linguistically from the center of a regional movement that intends to represent the community. The case in point is in Occitania (southern France), and illustrates not inadequacies in the movement, but the pitfalls in even the most carefully considered regional movement. For the force of this paradox is more a result of the conditions that the movement exists to counteract than of any serious oversight or elitism on the part of the movement. This community's alienation from the regional movement arises from the very problems that should create its solidarity with it. But the very problems that give rise to the movement become acute sooner in the poorer and more isolated areas of the region, and make such an area subject to apparent regional as well as extra-regional oppression. The symbols of the regional movement can bear, for a marginal area, meanings reminiscent of existing external domination. The discussion will focus on language, since language is the clearest and most powerful symbol in the movement. However, insofar as cultural variability affects geographically marginal areas in a way similar to linguistic variability, any discussion of local cultural features in relation to the regional movement will follow closely.

Occitania and Occitan

Fishman has pointed out (1973) that for language to be an effective symbol of a nationalist movement it must be the current common language of its population, or one must be able to trace that language back to an era when the population was united. Fishman's criterion of authenticity is ideally answered in Occitania and the language is perhaps the clearest issue in the movement.

That Occitania is a clearly defined linguistic region has been long established in the literature of Romance linguistics. The north and south of France are separated by a concentrated bundle of isoglosses running west from Bordeaux and fanning out to the east to define the region known as Franco-Provençal. The area to the south of this bundle of isoglosses is Occitania. Several bundles of isoglosses divide Occitania, in turn, into a number of regions, but the differences between regions within the South are not nearly as great as those that separate the south as a whole from the north. Dialect variability within the South has always been considered a source of richness, and pan-dialectal comprehension has traditionally been an important part of linguistic competence in this region. As a result, one does not have to go back in history to find authenticity for Occitan. But history does enrich Occitania's claims. The different regions of Occitania have yielded great rich literary traditions (d'Artagnan from Gascony, the troubadours of Provence) and the political and economic importance at various eras of different parts of Occitania contrast sharply with the region's current dependence on the north.

But Occitan's most important claim to linguistic authenticity is the fact that it remains to this day the predominant language among older people in rural villages, and an important linguistic presence throughout the South. It has only been in the past thirty to forty years that French has supplanted Occitan as the native language of most children in rural areas of Occitania, and virtually all of these younger people have at least a passive competence in Occitan. Occitan is symbolic of their villages, their families, their families' way of life. It is the language that surrounded them in their childhood, a language that has been absorbed by much of southern French popular culture, and many of whose expressions and exclamations they have incorporated into French. The language, therefore, is still alive enough for all Occitanians to be a prime symbol of solidarity throughout the region. But over the past hundred years, as the abandonment of the region and the acquisition of French has been the main means to economic survival for individuals in Occitania, Occitan has also become symbolic of the poverty and isolation of these villages. One cannot talk about the two languages of Occitania, Occitan and French, without invoking their opposing social connotations: connotations that have developed over the years of language shift.

The oldest Occitan speakers in many areas were the first speakers of French in their communities, and they have seen the replacement of Occitan by French as the predominant language in the course of their lifetime. This transition was not usually gentle, and the disgrace suffered at the hands of French national education (to say nothing of northern visitors) is an important bond among the wide population. Perhaps Occitan unity is based as much on common linguistic

8   Beginnings

experience as on common language. In fact, the Occitan movement bases much of its appeal on this common experience. The appeal of common linguistic experience stems from the process of language shift.

Language Shift in Occitania

While French was introduced as the administrative language in Occitania in the sixteenth century, there was no official desire to introduce it as a standard language until after the revolution of 1789 (Brun 1923). At that time, French became symbolic of democracy and national unity, and a long campaign ensued to rid the country of non-French dialects, considered to be a major barrier to mobility, unity, and participatory democracy. Free national education, actually implemented in rural areas of Occitania 100 years later, became a powerful agent of centralization and of the eradication of non-French varieties. As centralization and industrialization pulled the population out of Occitania and into the north, increasing numbers of Occitanians learned French in order to escape the increasing poverty of their region. In recent years, as forces in Occitania have mobilized against domination from the north, this abandonment of the Occitan language has served as a powerful symbol. Part of its power stems from universal and very personal experience of stigmatization of Occitan culture through its language.

The introduction of French into Occitania followed a pattern of gradually evolving diglossia, whereby French replaced Occitan in increasing numbers of domains progressing from the periphery to the center of community and private life.[2] In this process, French gained dominance, with the need for economic mobility as the main force, and through the interplay between the social statuses of the languages themselves on the one hand and of the domains they represented on the other. As a result, Occitan was not simply replaced in an increasing variety of domains; it was shamed out of existence in domain after domain, reaching from outside the village eventually into the home and into relations within the family. Linguistic shame was exercised in a series of social oppositions associated with the domains of the languages: French was the language of the outside, the rich, the educated; Occitan was the language of the home, the poor, the uneducated. This series of oppositions eventually entered the Occitan language itself, leading to considerable borrowing from French in a constant effort to make Occitan "more acceptable" (Eckert 1978). In the course of language shift, the dialects of Occitan became increasingly localized. One of the earliest social oppositions between French and Occitan stemmed from their

---

[2] The process of language shift in one Occitan community is described in Eckert (1980a).

association with the outside and the inside respectively, as the strangers who entered the villages tended to be Francophone and to be representatives of the government or of French institutions. Therefore, as French became the language for dealing with the outside, Occitan dialects retreated into local obscurity, to be used only with natives of one's own village. Thus people stopped thinking of their native language as the language of the region and began to think of it as a "local" language. This localization had several major effects on regional solidarity: It decreased awareness of the unity of the various varieties of Occitan, and the traditional pan-dialectal competence of the speakers throughout the region, and it quite simply transferred all extra-local communication into the French domain. This localization of Occitan was intensified by the establishment of French as the written language: For the size of the Occitan-speaking population, Occitan has been virtually invisible in public media. The dialects, therefore, lost prestige not only insofar as they were politically subordinated to French, but also insofar as they were fragmented and reduced in status from a gradual dialect continuum to a miscellany of apparently disconnected local varieties. Because of the clear genetic relation between French and Occitan, it has been easy for the dominant, French, society to label all non-French Romance varieties as "dialects of French." The popular notion that the various forms of Occitan are "perversions of French" is still widespread. The considerable regional and local variability of varieties of Occitan is invoked as evidence of a process of decay, and the comparative homogeneity of French is taken as proof of that language's superiority.

The Occitan movement is comprised of efforts of various degrees to reverse the process of economic, linguistic and cultural colonization from the north. Since language is a key to the unity of Occitan, the language policy of the movement is of crucial importance – in fact, for some, language is the primary issue. As mentioned above, the great authenticity of Occitan's linguistic claims stems from three facts:

1. A considerable segment of the population still speaks Occitan.
2. The fundamental relation between all dialects of Occitan is overwhelmingly apparent.
3. The populations of Occitania have had similar experiences with linguistic oppression from the north.

The exploitation of this authenticity, however, presents many pitfalls, for the reintroduction of Occitan as the language of the region can be conceived of in one of two ways: It can be an undoing of the process of language shift that has accelerated over the past hundred years, and thus reinstitute Occitan in its original role, or it can simply replace French as far as possible with Occitan. The former assumes time and considerable means. The latter is more realistic in a practical sense, but less realistic in its aims to establish authenticity in modern terms.

The Need for Standardization

Fishman has pointed out the contradiction in the claims of authenticity and the need for standardization. For although the pragmatic and symbolic functions of the regional language are closely interconnected, they can also be contradictory. For Occitan to replace French in its public domains requires:

1. Putting Occitan into intraregional communication. This must be done through the selection and imposition of a standard variety or the reestablishment of global pan-dialectal competence.
2. Putting Occitan into written communication through the extension of French orthography to Occitan, or through the development of a standard Occitan orthography.
3. Putting Occitan into technological and educational use, through broad-based lexical innovation. This can be done either through regular borrowing from French, or through the development of new Occitan vocabulary.

In cases 2 and 3, the first option is the one taken informally over the past generations as speakers of Occitan have adapted to technological development in its bilingual context. These "natural" options, insofar as they are responses to, and institutionalizations of, French domination, are symbolically unacceptable for a regional language movement. The other options, though, however appropriate they may be for the movement, create other difficulties, for establishing the regional authenticity of a language and connecting that language to the speech of individuals are frequently separate problems.

The original, authentic linguistic unity of Occitan lay in the gradual differences of its geographic varieties (and in the speakers' corresponding pan-dialectal competence) and in the common differences between these varieties on the one hand and French on the other. For several reasons, however, it is difficult for a regional movement to exploit this "unity in common diversity." First of all, native pan-dialectal awareness is one of the aspects of Occitan that has been damaged to some extent in the process of language shift. But far more important, as a symbol, Occitan must be a language that can be opposed to French and that can compete with French on the latter's own terms. For French, as the current standard, has acquired the right to set the requirements for "language-hood" even for the regional language. One such requirement is homogeneity. The association of variability with "irregularity" has dominated linguistic thought over the years, and has had its role in the denigration of Occitan varieties. Particularly in the purist climate associated with French, a symbol cannot be variable. The compromise has been to establish several regional standards, each chosen from the cultural and linguistic center of the region, providing a standard that is fairly close to every living dialect.

Given the proximity of dialects within the sub-regional scheme, the development of a pan-dialectal orthography can help to reduce dialect differences in the written language. In the earlier days of bilingualism, it was common to write Occitan in French orthography. The spelling was completely phonetic – thus localized – and cumbersome, but available to all who are literate in French. This orthography is felt to be unacceptable for these and for symbolic reasons, for needless to say, the subjection of the language to a relatively unsuitable French orthography is reminiscent of French domination.

By the same token, the more difficult solution to the third problem – the development of new Occitan vocabulary – is the only acceptable one. Habitual borrowing from French is not only a constant reminder of French domination, but it is indeed part of the process of disintegration of the division between the two languages. Lexical revitalization, therefore, must be accomplished independently of French.

It must be emphasized that all these decisions taken about codification of a regional language are necessary, given the role of this language in a political movement. The paradox to be discussed below, therefore, is a true one; it is not created by the linguistic decisions themselves, but by the very exigencies of a political movement. Establishing the regional authenticity and usefulness of a language, and connecting the revitalization of that language to the current speech of the region can involve contradictory strategies.

The Regional Periphery

Regional centers have maintained linguistic and cultural traditions through institutional means, and speakers in these centers have been able to identify their own speech with that of a nameable and identifiable (if extinct) power. But in the outlying areas, people enjoy no such association between their local varieties and those "mythical" prestige varieties of Occitan. It is important to remember the differences between central and peripheral areas in discussing regional movements, for the two experience these movements in quite different ways.

It is worthwhile, therefore, to consider the Occitan movement from the point of view of a rural community far from the regional center.[3] This community, located in the Pyrenees of Ariège, is an ideal target for sympathy with

---

[3] The following discussion is based on eighteen months of sociolinguistic fieldwork in this community, supported by a dissertation grant from the National Science Foundation (NSF-GS-3211).

the regional movement, for the economy of the area was seriously damaged by centralization policies of the post-revolutionary government. The sheep herding economy of the region was destroyed when the post-revolutionary government withdrew peasants' grazing rights on domain lands in the Pyrenees (Chevalier 1956). Subsequent battles against the French authorities (Baby 1972) set a strong tradition of revolt against the central government, and resistance to government efforts to install a new economy indicates a long-lived alienation (Chevalier 1956). Local dialects of Occitan are still relatively vital in this area: People over the age of fifty still regularly speak Occitan among themselves, and younger people have at least a strong receptive competence. A few people currently in their twenties still speak it as their first language.

Situated within the isogloss bundle that forms the transition between the Gascon and Languedocien dialect areas, the dialect is contextualized by significant local variability. Differences among the dialects of surrounding valleys are internalized and part of the speakers' everyday competence. Speakers can enumerate and place lexical, grammatical and phonological isoglosses in the dialects of the surrounding area. It is significant that while linguists consider the dialect of this community to be unequivocally Gascon, the speakers are unaware of any relation. For according to local dialectological beliefs, there is an age-old distinction between central (named) dialects and "patois." The named dialects (Gascon, Languedocien, Provençal) possess a status close to "language," dignified by codification, literary tradition, and history. The (unnamed) dialects of non-central regions, however, are "irregular," as witnessed by intense local variation, and bear only a poor and degraded relation to the named dialects. There is a general feeling that rural people living closer to regional centers are culturally and linguistically "nobler." This is reinforced by the tendency, which predates the current Occitan movement, to consider the language and culture of regional centers as what is "Gascon," "Provençal," etc. A kind of elitism and purism characterizes virtually all efforts to publicize traditional culture, as one variety – a variety that has long had the means to elaborate art forms – is selected to represent a region. Thus people on the periphery of regions have always known that they are linguistically and culturally subordinate.[4] Rather than viewing central varieties as part of a continuum, they have come to see the center as homogeneous and systematic, and the periphery as a continuum.

---

[4] This sense of linguistic and cultural inferiority is immediately obvious to a fieldworker entering such a community, for residents cannot understand why a more central community was not chosen. It was frequently pointed out to me that if I really wanted to study the language, I should be in an area where they "speak better."

The Reperipheralization of the Periphery

The current and last generation of Occitan speakers in this community are self-consciously transitional. They have chosen to raise their children as Francophones, to provide them with the means to economic mobility, and to save them the disgrace of being speakers of "patois." At the same time, insofar as they comprise the population that did not emigrate, their loyalty to the region, their home and their language is considerable. This transitional generation is closest to the issues on which the regional movement is established, and they are the true link between Occitan history and the Occitan movement. In regional centers, this generation has been recruited to some extent. There are families that have decided to raise their children as Occitanophone after all, and there is a proliferation of public use of Occitan. But for a variety of reasons, this is more difficult in peripheral areas.

The Occitanophone generation in the peripheral community under consideration is aware of its transitional nature in two senses: The language of the community is and always has been transitional among Occitan dialects, and the language of the young generation is "bilingually" transitional insofar as it has been heavily influenced by French. This provides two sources for feelings of inadequacy in relation to the Occitan movement, for speakers in peripheral areas have little access to the accepted form of the language. It must be kept in mind that there are rewards within the French system for the revival of Occitan. The Occitan movement has managed to introduce Occitan in the schools as a means of satisfying the language requirement. Thus parents in the regional centers can for once teach their children their native language for educational reward rather than punishment. But in marginal areas, the parents' language is different enough from the standard that the parents' linguistic skills are considered (as always) to be only marginally useful in school. Thus the transitional nature of the local dialect in relation to other Occitan dialects is once again stigmatized.

But even if the local dialect were closer to the standard, intense French influence in the current generation's speech makes much of their speech unacceptable by movement standards, as well as by general standards within the community. Over the past century, speakers have come to rely increasingly on French for vocabulary, and have reached a point where they borrow lexical items from French that already have local Occitan equivalents. But while this French influence is valued neither by the community that implemented it nor by the Occitan movement, it remains an important part of local linguistic habits. Rejection of borrowing is in fact a rejection of the language in general precisely because borrowing is so pervasive. Lexical purism simply adds another source of stigma to the local language. The denigration of local language skills, therefore, is almost an automatic outcome of the standardization and purification of Occitan. The development of a standard Occitan thus creates a situation parallel to the one that existed between French and Occitan, but with a new, regional norm adding a new level to the local linguistic hierarchy. Now the local "patois" is inferior not only to French but to Occitan.

Conclusion

A political, and even a purely linguistic, movement is faced with some important choices. Different areas of a region will not only speak different regional varieties, they will show different relations to these varieties. Language shift occurred earlier in urban areas of Occitania, and many people that the regional movement represents are second and third generation Francophones. Very different linguistic measures are required to provide them access to the regional language. Insofar as nationalist movements generally rely heavily on an urban educated elite, it is important to provide this access. But the tailoring of a language to be accessible and useful to such an elite will alienate other segments of the population both linguistically, insofar as the language will be disconnected from their own linguistic base, and politically, insofar as an urban elite – Occitan or not – evokes the French urban elite that it endeavors to supplant. This is particularly true of the relation between the movement and the remaining native Occitanophones. They have already suffered enough linguistically, and for any linguistic revival to appeal to them it would have to effectively roll back the stigmatization process of language shift, and provide them with the confidence and motivation to resume public use of their native dialect. Their Francophone children pose a related but different problem, since they have inherited knowledge of the linguistic stigma, but have not personally suffered for it. These people have a strong emotional attachment to their parents' native language, and many of them experience deep regret at having to leave their villages to find work. Although these young people are prime targets for the movement, there is no direct link between standard Occitan and their parents' language as they know it. This is not just because of geographic difference, but because the movement, with its elaboration of standard Occitan in its politicized context, tends to stress the language as a vehicle of intellectual, political, and artistic communication. The language is, therefore, not the language of these people's personal experience, but a symbol of that language. It is paradoxical that while the real thing is more accessible to these people, only its symbol has value.

2 Stigma and Meaning in Language Shift

I had developed a rudimentary competence in the dialect of Ercé in my time with Madame Cau, and switching to Soulatan was not particularly difficult. What was difficult was getting people to speak it with me on a regular basis, because it was completely anomalous for them to speak patois with anyone they hadn't grown up with, and certainly with someone as young as I was. People cooperated, though, and I settled in to do my own version of sociolinguistic interviews. Since there were practically no Soulatan speakers under the age of forty, I was able to center my interviews on how life in Soulan had changed in their lifetime. And since it had changed a lot, the interviews were lively and interesting, and I developed a good sense of the social changes that had brought about language shift. The population of Soulan in the seventies represented the entire process of language shift: The members of the oldest generation had been the first to acquire French as a second language, and those born after World War II were the first monolingual French speakers.

The diglossia paper that follows grew out of a conversation with Bill Labov at the time of the Ann Arbor Black English trial in 1979. It was common wisdom for many linguists that encouraging African American kids to use standard language in school and AAVE (African American Vernacular English) "where it's appropriate" would result in competence in, and respect for, both dialects. It had become clear to me in Soulan, though, that diglossia sets up an opposition that stigmatizes the vernacular and the situations in which it is spoken. Bill told me I'd better publish the idea right away because, as he said, he would talk about it and people would think it was his idea unless he could cite me. I wrote it in a weekend, and gave it as my first ever conference talk at NWAV (New Ways of Analyzing Variation) in Montreal.

DIGLOSSIA: SEPARATE AND UNEQUAL

Terms such as code switching and diglossia are now becoming part of the vocabulary of politics, as the issue arises with increasing insistence in America

15

and abroad, of the accommodation or non-accommodation of government and institutions to vernacular languages. It is becoming increasingly noticeable, for instance, that sociolinguists hesitate to take a position on the issue of teaching standard English to speakers of non–standard dialects in the American public schools, and on what role English should play in bilingual education programs. Many people contend that the school should provide minority children with the linguistic means (standard language instruction) to enter the power structure, and concern for the loss of the solidary function of vernacular languages in the minority culture is allayed by a resort to well-known notions from the field of bilingualism. The most important of these notions is *diglossia*, introduced into American linguistics by Charles Ferguson (1959).

Diglossia refers to the use in one community of two languages: a superposed variety, referred to as the "high" language, which is reserved for use in more public, formal and learned domains; and a vernacular, or "low," language, used in more popular and intimate domains. Ferguson describes situations (in Arabic, Greek, Haitian and Swiss German communities) in which the high is spoken by an elite as a second language, but points out that the term could be applied in a wider range of situations. In its loosest sense, diglossia is an organizing principle in bilingual and bi-dialectal communities: a linguistic division of labor whereby each language is limited to its own domain. In current usage, the term *diglossia* is indifferent to whether or not the entire population commands both languages, and in most modern situations at least a portion of the general population does. These individuals organize their own bilingualism around the principle of diglossia: The individual bilingual is a microcosm of the community's linguistic organization. The notion of diglossia brings language choice into the framework of structural linguistics by providing a structural-functional account of behavior at the community level. Complementary distribution of the coexisting languages virtually eliminates the possibility of random choice, and structures behavior of the community and discourse level by means similar to those at work in the grammar of each language. It is generally assumed (e.g. Fishman 1971:87) that this division of labor allows the speakers to keep the two linguistic systems separate, and thus to retain the structural integrity of each language. Talk is frequently seen, therefore, as a structured means of reserving the vernacular for in-group use while speakers use the standard language for entrance into the wider society. In this perspective, therefore, diglossia appears to be a force of stability. It is important at this point to consider the full implications of phenomena like diglossia in relation to certain social questions: Is diglossia, in fact, an effective means of language maintenance?

Ferguson has pointed out that diglossia can be extremely stable, but only on the condition that the high language be restricted to a literate elite. In other words, this stability is dependent on rigid social stratification. In the subsequent literature, however, the notion of diglossia has been expanded to include a wider variety of complementary arrangements, and to be seen as not just a result, but a contributing force of stability.[1] Diglossia in its more general definition might be seen therefore as a democratic arrangement insofar as it allows the vernacular to coexist with a high language. The question must be raised, though, whether linguistic domains so defined can be separate but equal. It is this question that I will discuss in the next pages, and I will maintain that diglossia can be not only the very means of elimination of vernacular languages, but also a serious threat to the self-image and solidarity of the community.

The twentieth century has witnessed a trend for rapid language shift, generally accompanying two kinds of political development: the imposition of foreign languages by colonial powers, and the reversal of this action through the imposition of revived national languages in postcolonial situations. In either case, nation-building virtually always involves language legislation:

> An expanding state, e.g., a colonizing power, will tend to impose one language on all its new subjects, whereas at the time of independence the ex-colonies take their revanche and do likewise as regards the newly appointed national language: it is supposed to supersede the local languages. (Knappert, 1978:72)

The modern notion of one nation/one language focuses standardization on intra-linguistic regional and ethnic differences as well as on actual bilingualism or multilingualism, and in a broad sense the sociopolitical issues involved are the same no matter how great the difference between the vernacular in question and the standard language. Under rapid industrialization, the promise of socio-economic mobility has led masses of laboring people to abandon their vernacular languages in favor of the standard language associated with those in control of the means of production. Fishman characterizes a community undergoing this process of language shift as non-diglossic, since the social change has been too quick to allow linguistic accommodation on a community level:

> Under circumstances such as these no well-established, socially recognized and protected functional differentiation of languages obtains in many speech communities of the lower and lower middle classes. (Fishman 1971:87)

According to Fishman, this transitional situation can follow a period of diglossia (with or without bilingualism), but it is functionally separate from diglossia. This shift, therefore, generally results in the impoverishment and death of the vernacular. However, it might be well to consider the relation between diglossia and this kind of rapid shift. Are these developments so separate from

---

[1] This is my interpretation of Wexler's statement, "By stability, Ferguson probably means the resistance of diglossia to attempts to resolve it" (Wexler 1971:331, fn. 2).

18   Beginnings

the diglossia that precedes or are they a logical outcome of diglossia under certain (most current) sociopolitical conditions?

Martinet (1963) chooses to distinguish between community and individual diglossia, referring to linguistic complementarity within the community as *diglossia*, and within the linguistic habits of the individual as *bilingualism*. Whatever, community diglossia with bilingualism cannot exist unless the bilingual individuals themselves experience diglossia in their own speech habits. The fate of an individual's bilingualism, then, is closely tied up with that of the community, and diglossia has a very personal effect on bilingual individuals. The question of concern here is what happens to a community that is characterized at least in part by the sharing of the vernacular language, when that language is supplanted by the language of the wider society. The breakdown of diglossia in a community is associated with differing abilities among members of the community to enter the wider society, and the question of the importance of diglossia stems from concern for the community that remains. Insofar as it is desirable to retain the vernacular as an important component of the life of a solidary group within a larger community, we must examine with care the extent to which the loss of the vernacular can result in the loss of community.

Diglossia does not arise; it is imposed from above in the form of an administrative, ritual or standard language. By virtue of its political and economic status, this language becomes requisite for access to power and mobility within the society. Therefore, diglossia cannot be socially or politically neutral, and it is clearly in view of this that Ferguson (1959) refers to the languages in a situation of diglossia as "high" and "low." It is the availability of the high language to the masses (through free public education) that renders a language standard and thus democratic; but this does not render diglossia neutral. While the availability of the standard may provide opportunity for the individual who can master it through formal education, it has a different effect on the vernacular-speaking community as a whole. The functions of the standard language exist in opposition to those of the vernacular, and this opposition can operate as a powerful force of assimilation, by interacting with and reinforcing social evaluation of the domains in which the two languages are used.

The very existence of a high implies a low, and the imposition of the standard language creates an immediate social opposition between the standard and the vernacular. This sets up a situation that one might think would remain stable, but that under most circumstances will become dynamic through a continual redefinition of the standard and the vernacular, and of their domains. The notion of diglossia is probably as satisfactory to linguists as it is because it corresponds closely to our models of linguistic structure. This analogy can be taken a good deal further, for structure is both a force that allows speakers to store the system and a force that gives rise to shifts within the system over time. Structuralist studies of linguistic change attribute paradigmatic shifts to pressures within the paradigm (Martinet 1952). The same can be said of the structure of linguistic interaction governed by diglossia. This will be illustrated in the following pages by a historical account of a situation in which diglossia was a stage in total and rapid language shift, and in which one can say that diglossia actually organized the shift.

Until the turn of the century, the majority of the rural population in France still spoke non-French varieties as their only or first language. These varieties were either Celtic (in Brittany), Basque (on the southwestern border with Spain) or indigenous Romance varieties. Romance varieties spoken in the southern half of France (Occitania) are commonly referred to as Occitan varieties, or dialects of the Langue d'Oc. These Occitan varieties comprise a continuum of dialects, all mutually incomprehensible with French. This language group, which provided the earliest (from the twelfth century) of the Romance literary languages, are all now stigmatized as "peasant" dialects. Their literary and general public function has been taken over by French, the language of centralization. Although these varieties are all clearly separate languages from French, by any criteria, their inferior social status, combined with their clear genetic relationship to French, has given rise to a common belief that they are "dialects of French."

French was officially introduced into Occitania in 1539 with the edict of Villers Cotterets, which required that all official documents be written in French. Lafont's (1971) characterization of this development as the beginning of diglossia and the end of Occitan autonomy is only too apt. From this moment forth, French became the language of writing, and this early characterization of French and Occitan as respectively "written" and "spoken" has never been overcome. This has led to a powerful characterization of the ideas expressed in the two languages: one worthy and the other unworthy of publication. The official limitation of literacy to French has served in turn as an important barrier to intraregional communication.

Until the revolution of 1789, there was no official desire to teach French to the peasants; on the contrary, it was understood that if the rural population learned French they would be able to leave the land, where they were needed to guarantee the food supply of France. In the cause of the French economy, village schools were often discouraged (Brun 1923:432 ff.). With the revolution came the resolve to teach French to the entire population in the interests of democracy, to encourage popular participation in government. As part of the ideology of liberation through standard language, the local dialects were seen as symbols and agents of oppression, and as such were to be eliminated – supplanted rather than supplemented by French. The suppression of non-French varieties in France has been dramatically accelerated over the past century of rapid industrialization. Political and economic centralization has forced workers to leave their regions in pursuit of socioeconomic advancement, and has thus made the French language a necessary means to advancement and has denigrated regional languages in the linguistic marketplace. Regional languages, therefore, have become symbols of regionalist movements, which see the suppression of their languages as both a tool and a result of the "colonization" of the provinces of France by the central power structure. The history of the introduction of French into the large southern region of Occitania shows this to be true: language shift has been a means as well as a result of social change. Lafont (1971) has pointed to diglossia as the ultimate Occitan compromise, and it is clear that the effectiveness with which the shift has occurred can be attributed at least in part to the diglossia with which it began.

The French language was a "presence" for some time before it was actually introduced as a spoken language. It penetrated the region through the top of the social hierarchy, and through large communities, from which it then spread to rural areas. In the nineteenth century, rural dwellers encountered French when they went outside the village and when outsiders came into the village. But the average rural person was not called upon to use French, and one needed only Occitan to function and live inside the village. The language of the village (Occitan) was simply opposed to the language of the outside (French). But the outside was clearly where the power flowed from, and this association would serve in subsequent years to pull French into an increasing range of uses.

The following is a sketch of the advance of French in one Occitan community. This sketch has been reconstructed through interviews and discussions with the current population of the community.[2] Since practically the entire shift from Occitan to French has occurred during the lifetimes of the oldest current inhabitants, whose parents were monolingual Occitan speakers and whose grandchildren are monolingual French speakers, the history of this shift can be reconstructed on the basis of these people's recollections. The community in question is located in the Pyrenees of Ariège, within the bundle of isoglosses that separate the two Occitan dialect areas of Gascony and Languedoc. The language of the community is classified as Gascon (and I will refer to it as such from now on) because it shares features traditionally diagnostic of Gascon.[3] It is significant, however, that the speakers are not aware that their language is a Gascon variety. The stigmatization of the dialect of this area is no doubt heightened by the area's cultural and linguistic distance from central Gascony – a distance that renders their language and culture "non-standard" in relation to the accepted norms of the center of the region.

---

[2] These observations were made during eighteen months of participant-observation in this community in 1970–72, in the pursuit of a study of sociolinguistic variation. The research was supported in part by National Science Foundation dissertation grant NSF-GS-3211.

[3] *f > [h] (L. *focus* > *huk* 'fire'); Latin *-ll- > [r] (L. *bella* > *bero* 'pretty' fem.); the use of the affirmative particle *ke* (*ke boli aigwo* 'I want water').

The community, a small community made up of six villages, lost its main economic base after the revolution, when the government took over the domain lands for forestry – and thus denied the region its essential grazing land (Chevalier 1956). This resulted in a long period of guerrilla warfare (Baby 1972) but the ultimate result was the impoverishment and swift depopulation of the entire region. The total population of the villages that make up this commune has fallen to about 300, from a population of 2,000 a century ago. The remaining population consists of older people subsisting on a small number of cows, and those younger people who have either amassed larger amounts of land or who have found alternative livelihoods (in particular skilled and unskilled labor in the surrounding area). The adult population of the commune is consciously transitional – they have encouraged their children to leave the region to find work, and in preparation for this they have raised them as monolingual French speakers.

The elimination of Gascon was part of the elimination of the peasant economy; thus very directly, French has long been the means of economic mobility and Gascon has been stigmatized as both a barrier to mobility and a symbol of peasant poverty. The practical necessity of leaving the village led the population to stress school and acquisition of French for their children. The speed with which this has led to total language shift is striking, and attributable to the social relation between the two languages in the community. The following description of the evolution of this relation is intended as an illustration of the dynamics that a structured relation can give rise to. The structured coexistence that characterizes diglossia can create the dynamics for change as well as a means of stability. Particularly, since the languages are put into contact through social change, language choice can become a term in a paradigm defined by social roles. Within this paradigm, social and linguistic roles evolve in relation to each other. If we consider the community organization of language use in terms of speech events as put forth by Hymes (1972), diglossia can be roughly defined as the assignment of each language to its own set of events. The events of the community, then, are defined partially by the language they occur in, and each language in turn is defined by its events. Language shift, then, can involve the gradual encroachment of one language on the events of the other.

Setting up an Opposition

To some extent a high language brings its own speech events with it when it is introduced into a low-speaking community. These events, in turn, become part of the official justification for the imposition of the high on the population. The high is the language of its speech events, and participation in these events is seen as necessarily requiring the use of the high.

French actually penetrated the community in question in its own situations. Its major step in the community was with free public education, where it was the only language of the classroom. As the language of the classroom and of the government that had set up the school, French remained very much an outside language. For school comprised not only a small number of speech events, it affected a relatively small portion of the population at the start. But as social change brings in the speech events (school, conversations with outsiders, official consultations) it also eliminates old ones. Along with these events disappear the verbal genres that characterize them. Ghost stories lost currency along with the long events of communal work that had provided their setting, and ranking songs disappeared as their setting – the café – lost its intimacy and became an increasingly frequent setting for encounters with outsiders.

Even in its marginal capacity, French entered a structural relation with Gascon. With the introduction of French in its own domains, Gascon ceased to be adequate for all situations within the village. It became "inappropriate" in the school, and schoolteachers instilled in their pupils emotionally loaded constraints on the use of Gascon in school situations. This is typical of situations where the high language is being introduced in the schools, and it is not normally done by gentle means. Punishments for speaking the low language in school frequently embody the establishment's characterization of that language. In Occitania a common practice was to tie a wooden shoe (an albatross of peasanthood) around the offender's neck. In U.S. schools, children have been punished for speaking American Indian languages with whipping, having their mouths washed out with soap, and even (as recently as 1970) having their heads flushed in the toilet.[4] There can be no ambiguity in such messages. While the children are learning the appropriate use of the high in the classroom, there is no reverse temptation: no tendency to use the high in low situations. Any supposed onus on the inappropriate use of the high and low domains in such a situation is a purely theoretical construct. The low is in actuality the "trespasser," and this notion of linguistic trespassing puts the low always in the wrong.

Corollary to the inappropriateness of Gascon in the school situation is the popular notion of its "inadequacy." French teachers were trained to believe that a person limited by a peasant dialect could not pursue logical, abstract thought. This is similar to arguments put forth by Bereiter and Engelman (1966) in America for the necessity of teaching standard English to preschool speakers of the Black English vernacular. This notion of linguistic "inadequacy" can become somewhat of a self-fulfilling prophecy insofar as the disuse of the language in any domain will result in at least lexical impoverishment. Since the

---

[4] Gary Witherspoon, personal communication.

original domains of high, furthermore, are frequently new domains to the community, the low sets out in its relationship with the high with a built-in lexical deficit.

Bringing the Opposition into the Community

When the high and the low languages interact at the periphery of community life, the social oppositions associated with the opposition between the two languages are relatively simple and immaterial to the life of the community. It is when the high enters the actual life of the community that it enters into a more meaningful opposition with the low. The economic and educational association of the high makes the low uneducated and poor by comparison. As language differences come to be associated with social differences with increasing frequency and in an increasing variety of situations, the social meanings associated with each language become increasingly complex. This complexity is always along the same general lines – the high being opposed to low as powerful to powerless, and the social detail that accrues to this opposition only serves to bring this closer to home.

Where the community in question had been defined by its own language, the introduction of French events established an opposition within the community between French and Gascon events. From that moment, an opposition began to arise between individuals who had the means (whose parents could afford to free them from agricultural production) to participate in these events and those who had not. As education became more universal in the community, the community became more bilingual. This had the highly significant result that one no longer needed to speak Gascon to live and function in the community, and the government and the church could send representatives there who spoke only French. French thus entered certain public events that had previously been in the Gascon domain. The increasingly frequent participation of outsiders in daily life came to redefine many public conversations as French, and to make public places potential settings for French. The opposition between French and Gascon thereby moved from "outside/inside" to "public/private," and as those oppositions were encountered in more speech events, the social oppositions between the French- and Gascon-speaking participants were increasingly exercised in conjunction with language choice. French became associated with the widening variety of contacts with mainstream society, emphasizing the concomitant retreat of Gascon to events associated with decreasing power.

Bringing the Opposition Home

As members of the low-speaking community become more mobile, they find that they associate some of their own traits and aspirations with the high domains. Because of the linguistic division of labor, they cannot develop an adequate self-image in terms of the low, and they come to incorporate the high into their self-image. Thus the need to express different aspects of their own personalities in different languages leads to code switching. In this sense, code switching is an internalized diglossia.

As villagers armed themselves with French, they left the community with increasing frequency to join the economic mainstream. They themselves became associated with French in the minds of the villagers, and they returned to visit the village with monolingual French-speaking spouses and children. This led those still in the village to compare themselves on a daily basis with people once close to them who had become distanced through their use of French and their associated mobility. This moved the opposition between "outside/inside" people and "public/private" events to very personal oppositions based on differences between people who had "succeeded" and those who had been "left behind." Through constant juxtaposition in ever more intimate domains, the community continued to redefine the opposition between French and Gascon. French, always moving from above, brought with it its lofty connotations, and gradually replaced Gascon in its own loftier functions, leaving Gascon increasingly impoverished not only in use but in reputation. As the use of Gascon was associated with increasingly modest domains, the very use of French began to have the power of dignifying situations. This led eventually to code switching: an indication that the individual self-image had come to incorporate both languages. At this point, people began to raise their children entirely in French, so that they would themselves be associated with the positive values of that language.

The experience in Occitania is just one of many examples that show how diglossia can not only provide the means of organizing chronic bilingualism, but can actually organize language shift. The association of certain domains with dominant values creates a situation in which one language must disappear for the community to retain a positive self-image. The decision as to which language that will be is heavily weighted by economic considerations. In the case of this Gascon community, regional poverty had become so great that the adoption of French was seen early on as a simple survival mechanism, and only later as a relinquishing of local prerogatives. French was extended as the sole requisite for socioeconomic advancement, but as it turned out, acquisition of a second language from outside could not take place without the concomitant acquisition of the outsider's view of the community itself. It cannot be too strongly emphasized that the vehicle for the acquisition of a new self-image was the very division of linguistic labor that facilitated the entry of French into the community.

The process that this community underwent was a logical outcome of the assumption that use of a high language will provide access, acceptance and adequacy in the wider society. When a group speaking low is eager for socioeconomic advancement, and the group in charge of the means of production uses the high as a means (or barrier) to that advancement, the path of least resistance is to accept the high language along with the high speech events. Those speakers who have more opportunity to participate in these events will tend to be the more successful, and the opposition between their personal qualities and those of the rest of the low-speaking population will become associated with the social meetings of the two languages. The next step is for the speakers of high to extend the need for high into previously low events. This is concurrent with a growing tendency for speakers of low to elevate these very events by using high in them. This in turn reflects negatively on the events that remain low: The low gradually retreats into increasingly powerless domains, and, more insidiously, stigmatizes these domains by their association with the low language.

There is a wide variety of situations of diglossia throughout the world, each with its own particular history, and some apparently more stable than others. The abandonment of vernaculars is clearly a survival strategy employed with an intensity that varies from case to case according to a wide range of social and economic factors. But in any given situation in which linguistic labor is divided according to domain, any gain for the high must be, by structural definition, loss for the low. It is clear, then, that the only circumstances under which the use of two languages within a community can be "separate but equal" is when equal means the same domains, not the same number of domains. If the language of the community does not serve all the needs of that community, and express all the interests of its people, there is a serious danger of division and ultimate dissolution of the community.

* * * * *

Nonce borrowings surfaced regularly in my interviews as well as in everyday life and in elicitations, and they were commonly the result of a reconstruction of the differential phonological histories of Soulatan and French. The borrowings were often exactly what they would have been if they had emerged in Soulatan. I did sociolinguistic interviews with a variety of people, but I also spent a lot of time with a small number of people documenting the dialect, eliciting vocabulary and grammar. At some point I asked each of these people for the Gascon equivalents of a set of words that I was pretty sure had no Gascon cognates. The results suggest that borrowing had become more acceptable over time, and that in the process, conventions for this borrowing had set in. Table 2.1 compares the responses of speakers aged 76, 60 and 43 (the latter being one of the youngest speakers of Gascon). In the case of words clearly not part of traditional Soulatan life, the oldest speaker simply said there was no equivalent, while the youngest speaker never failed to produce a borrowing. In the case of terms that had a non-cognate equivalent in Gascon, the older man

Table 2.1 *French borrowings in Soulatan. Three speakers' responses to word list*

	French	Local Pronunciation	76 years	60 years	43 years	Gloss
1	vulgaire	vylgɛr			bylgari	vulgar
2	biographie	biografi			biografio	biography
3	antarctique	antartik			antartiko	antarctic
4	ébène	ebɛn			ebenu	ebony
5	anthologie	antoloʒi			antoloʒic	anthology
6	encyclopédie	ansiklopedi			ansiklopedio	encyclopedia
7	ambre	ambrə		ambre	ambre	amber
8	écluse	eklyz		eklyzo	eklyzo	canal lock
9	annuaire	anyɛr		anyari	anyari	phone book
10	écran	ekran		ekran	ekran	screen
11	humeur	ymœr	maw karatʃ	ymu	ymu	mood
12	salaire	salɛr	pago	salari	salari	salary
13	crémeux	kremœ	ka ỹ hloc de pinto	kremus	kremus	creamy
14	itinéraire	itinerɛr	kami	itinerari	itinerari	itinerary
15	supérieur	syperiœr	deʃyj de nuz awti	syperiyr	syperiyr	superior
16	accueil	akœj	pla resebytʃ	bun akyʎ	akyʎ	welcome
17	épineux	epinœ	kɛspigon	epinus	epinus	thorny
18	populeux	popylœ	puplatʃ	pupylus	pupylus	populous
19	honneur	onœr	awnu	unu	unu	honor
20	ancêtres	ansetrə	bjeʎi	yjeʎi	ansetros	ancestors
21	écrevisse	ekravis	rekylajro	ekrebiso	rekylajro	crayfish
22	éteindre	etendrə	amurta	amurta	amurta	extinguish
23	emphysème	amfizem	amfizem	amfizemu	amfizemu	emphysema
24	embouteillage	ambuteja ʒ	ambuteʎadʒe	embuteʎadʒe	embuteʎadʒe	traffic jam
25	pronostic	pronostik	pronostik	pronostik	prunostik	prognosis
26	suppositoire	sypozitwar	sypozitwar	sypozitwar	sypozi·wer	suppository

26

gave the equivalent, while both of the younger speakers provided a borrowing in ten (11–19) out of thirteen cases, and only one of them in two cases (20, 21). Both younger speakers gave the Gascon term *amurta* (22), which is very much an everyday word since fireplaces were still the main source of heat in the home. (It would also be difficult to provide an authentic-sounding borrowing for this word.) In the case of more common terms (24–26) that probably had no Gascon equivalent, everyone provided borrowings. The younger speakers, particularly the youngest, were more consistent in their reconstructions, having opted for one way of dealing with ambiguous correspondences. The youngest did more phonological adjustment, applying the Gascon rule that raises /o/ to [u] in word-internal unstressed and in post-nasal position with some consistency, applying Gascon morphology (e.g. 1, 13, 26) etc.

But what was even more striking was evidence that the peasant stigma had entered the lexicon itself, producing pairs of words that differed only in social connotations. I heard two words for barn – [bordo] and a clear borrowing from French, [granʒo]. When I asked the difference between the two, I was told that a *bordo* is a peasant barn, while a *grangeo* is a nice barn, like the baron's barn. I heard two words for rag – [tʃifun] and [pejot]. The *chiffun* is a nice rag that one washes and uses again while a *pejot* is a distasteful object – whether a terrible piece of clothing or the nasty stiff rag that hangs under the sink.

Before I pursued the actual use of borrowings, though, I had to have a clear way of identifying them. But since Soulan is located right in the isogloss bundle that separates Gascon from Languedocien, many Gascon sound changes died out as they were passing through the area. So several of the changes that differentiate Gascon from French (e.g. the deletion of intervocalic *n, and *f > h) affected only part of the lexicon. These two changes would have changed *fina 'fine f.' to [hio]. So how could I be sure that the actual modern form, [finu], was a borrowing from French *fine*, or a native Gascon word that had not yet undergone either of these changes? It was clear that in order to identify borrowings, I would have to reconstruct the phonological history of the dialect, with particular attention to the internal constraints on those sound changes that had stalled at the Gascon–Languedocien border. I worked on this reconstruction while I was still in Soulan, while I continued to gather data, intending it to be the first chapter of my dissertation.

Part II

My Participation in the Second Wave

When I came back to New York in 1972, a lot had happened in the world of variation. Variable rules had arrived on the scene, and Bill had moved to the University of Pennsylvania, where his students walked around with boxes of punched cards destined for overnight Varbrul runs on the mainframe. One of the box carriers was Ivan Sag, who was very friendly and scary smart. We didn't really get to know each other, and certainly the last thing either of us would have guessed is that thirteen years later we'd end up married.

As it turned out, I was not destined to hang out in New York and write my dissertation. Early on in graduate school, I had acquired a stalker, who was a major irritant in my life throughout graduate school. Irritant is putting it mildly – he hounded me at home and on campus. Campus security kept the Linguistics department apprised of "boogey man" sightings, and I had to phone before I came to campus to know which entrance was safe to use. For a time, I had police escorts to and from campus. My stalker was schizophrenic, and very smart. He even managed to get into someone's records to see the NSF proposal for my dissertation and pursued me by mail and telephone in France. Once I was back in New York, things got worse and his death threats led me to federal court. The FBI agent who reviewed my case told me and my lawyer that it was the worst case of aggravated harassment he'd ever seen. Nonetheless, the federal DA refused to prosecute. New York was full of women being harassed, he said, and he couldn't be prosecuting them all. A group of feminist lawyers wanted to use this as a test case, suing the federal DA for discrimination. They were sure of winning. But they were also sure that if the DA prosecuted him, he would be committed to a psychiatric hospital for observation but would then come out and kill me. They advised me to leave town if I could.

It just happened that at about that time, the Anthropology department at the University of Michigan wrote to Bill wanting to hire one of his students (that's how you got jobs in those days), preferably a female. I took the job in order to get out of New York, but also because I found the department exciting and thought I'd be productive there. In those days, it wasn't unusual to take a job before finishing the dissertation, but I had barely begun and wasn't even sure yet what it was about. This had consequences that followed me through a good deal of my career.

I arrived at Michigan a total babe in the woods, with no background in Anthropology and no clue about its theoretical issues. I was immediately swept up into a bitter conflict between the cultural materialists (i.e. Columbia) and the symbolic anthropologists (i.e. Chicago). Since I was from Columbia, I might be a materialist. But since I was a linguist, I might be more symbolically inclined. But then my kind of linguist counted things, so I might be a materialist after all, etc. This was pretty scary, particularly given my feeling that I didn't deserve the job in the first place.

Meanwhile, I worked on my dissertation when I wasn't being paralyzed by the feeling that I had absolutely nothing to teach my students. I didn't feel insecure about my dissertation though, but it started carrying me in a new direction. As I got deep into reconstructing variable processes in the history of the dialect as well as the changes in progress, it became clear that this was to be no small task. I also became obsessed with it. So the first chapter became the dissertation. It took me three years to finish it, and during that time I made regular trips back to Soulan both in summer and in winter. Soulan had become a second home, and I went there just to be there, but also to collect more and more data. I learned eventually that the belief that you never have enough data is endemic to fieldwork, but there was nobody to tell me to stop.

My dissertation was really good although I didn't quite know it at the time. But I didn't want to be a historical linguist. Living in the midst of a bundle of isoglosses in the Pyrenees had led to an obsession with how sound change spreads: where and why would someone pick up a new pronunciation? Did it happen at the monthly market in St. Girons, where people from Soulan socialized with people from farther into Gascony? In interactions with people from the next village? I was sure that the motivation lay somewhere in the meaning people attributed to the new sounds, but Gascon was dying, so change would no longer spread. Fortunately, there was a very nice chain shift going on right in my new back yard, in Michigan.

3 Jocks and Burnouts

Survey studies of variation had provided evidence that adolescents are the most advanced speakers in their communities. Yet all the discussions of social motivations for the spread of sound change were focused on adult participation in the class system. It made perfect sense to me that adolescent social life was the terrain through which linguistic change traveled. After all, if regular contact is a prerequisite, there's nothing like a crowded heterogeneous school to provide that. But more to the point, the intense identity work that goes on during adolescence provides mountains of motivation for linguistic influence. There was no question in my mind that sound changes carried social meaning, and that the meaning would be related to adolescents' orientation to social class. Counting on the received wisdom that sound change spreads outward from urban centers, I ventured to study the spread of the Northern Cities Vowel Shift outward through the suburbs of Detroit. My own adolescence in the New Jersey suburbs, along with my linguistic geography background in Soulan and the Linguistic Atlas of France, disposed me to focus on the nature of social contacts that led to the geographic spread of change. Some of my students at Michigan had attended Detroit suburban high schools, and I learned from them about Jocks and Burnouts, the dominant social categories in those schools. We did some exploratory work in my classes, and by the time I finished my dissertation, I was ready to jump into fieldwork. I got a seed grant from the Spencer Foundation for exploratory work, on the basis of which I then applied to NSF for a grant to fund a full ethnography in one school and shorter ethnographies in other schools around the suburban area.[1]

I had spent some time in 1978 with John Gumperz and Sue Gal at a small workshop where I was presenting stuff on Gascon borrowing, and I was deeply influenced by their discussions of social networks. Lesley Milroy was doing her work on social networks in Belfast as I put this project together, and her ethnographic orientation and her commitment to social agency made her a

---

[1] This research was funded by NSF grant # BNS-8023291. Lynne Robins partnered with me in the fieldwork during the Spencer-funded pilot phase, and Michael Jody partnered with me in the fieldwork in the schools other than Belten.

32   My Participation in the Second Wave

wonderful ally and inspiration. I was intent on studying class as a grid determining social contact, and sound change as moving upwards through that grid through networks of contact. I sought the motivation for that upward movement in the social categories that made up those networks, and in the social traits that distinguished those categories. The following theoretical introduction from this proposal is very much in the Second Wave:

Since Labov's study of New York City in 1966, sociolinguistic community studies have continued to underscore that the socioeconomic hierarchy provides a general grid for the spread of linguistic change. Correlations of linguistic variation with social categories other than socioeconomic class (ethnic identity, sex, peer group membership) indicate that socioeconomic class is only the larger context in which speakers respond to finer social categories in speaking more like (or less like) those close to them in the social network. Since sound change moves upward through the socioeconomic hierarchy, any hypotheses about the function of social identification in linguistic change must account for the fact that, at least in their unconscious linguistic behavior, most speakers identify downward in that hierarchy. Trudgill tried to approach an explanation of this downward identification in his discussion of sex differences in Norwich (1974b), but social traits have yet to be isolated from the larger context of socioeconomic class and ethnic membership and correlated with linguistic variation. While it may be unrealistic to hope to accomplish such a correlation, this study will pursue a systematic examination of the relation between linguistic variation and some finer social categories. This study will aim at both linguistic and ethnographic richness in its examination of the setting that provides contact between adolescents of different socioeconomic classes: the high school.

* * *

In this study special attention will be paid to the relation between social networks and parents' socioeconomic class, the extent and nature of social mobility within these networks, and the link between local high school networks and the larger networks in the community and the urban-suburban area. All forms of mobility play a role in the spread of linguistic change. Social versatility is facilitated by stylistic versatility in language, and it is probable that people who move through a wide range of social categories exhibit a wide range of sociolinguistic variation – that in fact they are historical "movers." This includes people who interact frequently – and particularly who have good friends – in a wide variety of groups, as well as classically upwardly and downwardly mobile people (in this context people whose peer group is of a noticeably different socioeconomic class than themselves.) But regular linguistic change is no doubt the result of more common behavior – not of the actions of the most mobile – and its force will be sought in the day-to-day interactions of social groups in adolescent society.

There was no mention of social meaning in this proposal, because after a conversation with Bill, I knew that such language was not likely to go over well with reviewers. My half-hearted caveat "While it may be unrealistic to hope to accomplish such a correlation…" was a way of letting critical reviewers know that I was not going overboard in my search for something looking like social agency. But I deeply believed in the importance of such agency.

I first walked into Belten High during lunchtime, and the opposition between Jocks and Burnouts was there in plain sight, as kids arrayed themselves across lunchtime territories. If I hadn't already heard of Jocks and Burnouts, I would have discovered them on my first trip through the school. From their hair to their jeans, from their posture to their movements to their voice quality, from where they stood to what they put in their mouths while they stood there, the Jocks and the Burnouts used every means at their disposal to construct mutual difference. This was the origin of my preoccupation with style, which began as a way into the social geography, and over the years became the central preoccupation of my linguistic work. It is not surprising, then, that my first paper on Belten High focused on the semiotics of clothing. (Oh God, the paper begins with a conjunction.)

CLOTHING AND GEOGRAPHY IN A SUBURBAN HIGH SCHOOL

While the character of the population of every community differs across both time and space, the structural feature of stratification is constant. In the same way, although student populations of no two high schools are alike, these populations tend to be organized by constant structural features. The most striking of these features is the development and polarization of a number of individuals into categories that represent the two social extremes of the population. These two extremes have been found to correspond to the upper and lower ends of the socioeconomic scale within the local population (Hollingshead 1949; Larkin 1979), and they represent to the school population differences in assimilation to the values of the school. Students whose lives center around involvement in school activities tend to be from the upper end of the local socioeconomic continuum. They cooperate with and share many social values with the school staff. As a result, they enjoy considerable favor and freedom in the school and they generally feel that the school is serving their needs. Depending on the era and place, these students will be referred to by such terms as *Jocks*, *In-crowd*, *Elite*, and *Rah-rahs*. In opposition to these students are those who do not feel that the school serves their needs or cares about them, and who are generally alienated from school-associated activities. These students, typically from the lower end of the local socioeconomic continuum, will be labeled by such terms as *Hoods*, *Greasers*, *Freaks* and *Burnouts*, again depending on their specific characteristics determined by era and locality. These two categories, representing local extremes, are the main foci of attention in the school: Virtually all students orient themselves to the behavior of the people in these two categories, and members of the two extreme categories define themselves to a great extent in relation to each other. Boundaries between the extremes are closely maintained, and salient characteristics of each group are terms in a series of oppositions: nonparticipation vs. participation in school activities; truancy vs. attendance; smoking vs. nonsmoking; and so forth.

In the school that provided the focus of this study, everyone recognizes the two major categories as the *Jocks* and the *Burnouts*. The Burnouts are described by all (including themselves) as the kids who smoke, who take drugs or at least smoke some marijuana, who hang out in the courtyard (smoking area) of the school, who are not interested in school, and who do not care a lot about clothing. The Jocks are described as the kids who are either abstemious or prefer alcohol to drugs, who are active in school activities, who go to class, and who dress fashionably. Although these two categories do not account for half the population of the school, their polarized behavior defines the extremes of behavior for the school. The large mass of the school population – called the *In-between kids* or the *regular kids* – while perceived by the two extremes as an intermediate mass, comprise a wide variety of groups, many of which overlap with the Jocks or the Burnouts. However small the actual number of "full-fledged" Jocks and Burnouts in the school may be, their significance in the school far outreaches their numbers. The quality of relations between Jocks and Burnouts governs aspects of behavior of virtually everyone in the school, for those who are neither Jocks nor Burnouts are nonetheless aligned or are struggling not to be. Since the Jocks and the Burnouts represent the two extremes of behavior in the school (with relation to the school and its values), it is a reasonable starting point to assume that the rest of the school population orients its behavior to that of the two categories. In this sense, the "In-between kids" are truly in-between.

Certain kinds of information about categories of people can only be obtained through observation of larger patterns of activity – through the movements of large numbers of members of each category. To do this, one needs a way of identifying the category membership of anonymous individuals. In a situation of extreme polarization, as between Jocks and Burnouts, the possibilities for observable physical differences between members of the two categories are great. As people are thrown into intensive contact in the small area of a school, boundary maintenance is increased through careful attention to overt behavior: Burnouts will not involve themselves in sports or school activities, Jocks will not smoke, Burnouts will not eat in the cafeteria, Jocks will not enter the courtyard. These behaviors, however, do not provide ever-present category markers, since they are limited in time or place. Personal appearance is the only form of marker that an individual displays at all times, and that can serve as a consistent means of identification. Therefore, physical adornments such as clothing and hairstyle make ideal category markers if such markers can be found.

The clearest feature of dress that correlates with category membership in this school is the cut of jeans. When asked to describe the two social categories, students will occasionally mention that Burnouts wear wide bells, and Jocks are occasionally identified as always buying the latest fashions. The ratio of the width of the bottom to the middle of the jeans leg has changed over the years as an important component of fashion. The width of jeans that one sees in the school spans the past ten years of fashion, from wide bells through flares and straight legs, to pegged legs. This decrease in ratio of bottom to middle of the leg corresponds to fashion time, and in the larger context of Euro-American fashion, the continuum from bells to pegs is a continuum of fashion – the pegs being "in" and the bells being "out" at the time when this research was being done. Following fashion requires considerable financial resources, and insofar as socioeconomic class is an important term of the opposition between Burnouts and Jocks, the salience of jeans width in this social context is clear. However, it would be misleading to imply that money is the direct and only cause of this difference in high school fashions, or that the Burnouts are consistently "out of fashion." Since leg width has become an important category marker, the difference in leg width is maintained beyond financial limitations, and Burnouts will choose not to replace their old bell-bottoms with new straight-legged jeans. And while Burnouts may frequently have fewer clothing alternatives to jeans than people at the wealthier end of the social continuum, their general dress is not so much "behind" that of the Jocks as it is in a different system. (The networks of spread of fashion change into and within the school population are themselves of great importance to study.)

The following discussion will demonstrate the usefulness of jeans width as a marker of category membership, by tracing some large movements through the observation of jeans width. Virtually all high school students own jeans, and on a given day, jeans account for more than half the lower body apparel of the student population (on one day, 52 percent of the girls and 64 percent of the boys were wearing jeans out of a sample of 190 students). Therefore, while jeans width will fail to account for about 42 percent of the students, the sample defined by the wearing of jeans is sufficiently representative for current purposes. For this study, jeans will be coded according to the relative width of the bottom of the leg to the knee. A value will be assigned to each style:

wide bells	4
flares	3
straight legs	2
pegged legs	1

And for any collection of individuals, the average jeans width will be an average of those width values for jeans worn by those individuals. All other kinds of lower body apparel will be ignored.

The first problem in this study is to establish that jeans width correlates with other aspects of category membership. As Robins mentions in her essay in this volume (Chapter 1), territory in the school is a prime category marker. Territories in the school under study are occupied primarily during lunch periods and to some extent before school. The Burnouts' territory was assigned, in a sense, by the school administration, when they declared the courtyard in the middle of the building as the only area in the school where smoking would be permitted. Since many Burnouts smoke cigarettes, they go to the courtyard between classes and during lunch. And since smoking is a Burnout category marker, the close association between the Burnout population, smoking, and the courtyard has made this territory very strongly marked. One cannot say that the Jocks have a territory in this school; it is the Burnouts who have the territory, and the Jocks' territory is defined residually by being as far from the Burnouts' territory as possible. Most Jocks report never having set foot in the courtyard during their entire time in the school, and virtually none of them ever go there. One can expect the average width of jeans therefore to be higher in the courtyard than in other areas of the school. In fact, this correlation is found in the data. The center of the Burnouts' territory – the courtyard and its entrance from the school – is inhabited at lunchtime almost exclusively by people wearing wide bells; while the furthest area from the courtyard – the area directly in front of the cafeteria – is inhabited primarily by people wearing straight legs (pegged pants are still rare in the school). This is shown in Figure 3.1, which gives the average jeans width in each territory and in the

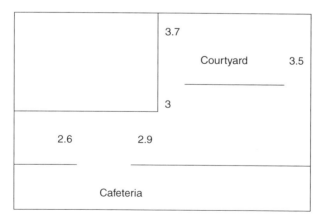

Figure 3.1 Average jeans leg width at lunchtime.

area between. The left side of the courtyard (average jeans width=3.7) is the center of Burnout territory, and In-betweens who smoke stick to the wall on the right, slightly reducing the average jeans width. The jeans width in the main area in front of the cafeteria (2.6) is greater than 2 because of the presence of some boys wearing flares. All girls in this area wear straight or pegged legged jeans. And the spatial transition between this area and the courtyard shows a gradual increase in jeans width. This transition is the result of two kinds of mixture: between the two territories there is some interaction between people in bells and straight legs, and there is also a greater proportion of flares. Thus the area is transitional not only in average width but in actual width, indicating that flares themselves may be a transitional or "In-between" marker.

Examination of groups of students in the halls at various times, furthermore, shows that there is relatively little interaction between people wearing straight legs and people wearing bells. The socially In-between status of flares shows up in the relative frequency of co-occurrence of the three kinds of jeans. If jeans width were random – that is, if people wearing all kinds of jeans mixed freely – one would expect to find all kinds of jeans co-occurring in proportion to their overall frequency of occurrence. Since there are the same number of bells as flares in the sample, one would expect a random mix to show straight legs co-occurring with bells as often as with flares. And while there are 50 percent more straight legs than flares or bells, flares occur about equally with other flares, with bells, and with straight legs. This confirms what was observed in the lunchtime territory dispositions: that flares are a socially transitional marker between bells and straight legs.

Once it has been established that jeans leg width correlates with category membership, one can use it in observing general behavior. During class time, there is a certain amount of student traffic in the halls. Freedom to walk the halls during this time is in some sense a privilege, since it requires the explicit or implicit permission of the school staff. It is important to know who is in the halls, therefore, in order to get an idea of freedom of geographic mobility within the school. Jeans width, therefore, was recorded for 400 students walking in the halls during the same half-hour class periods during one week, in order to get an idea of freedom of geographic mobility within the school. First of all, it is significant that whereas the average jeans width in the school as a whole is 2.8 (based on a sample of 711 students), the average width in the halls during class was 2.6. Thus it is apparent that Jocks are circulating more freely in the halls during class time. Table 3.1 shows the average jeans width of people circulating in each of the five halls that make up the first floor of the school. While the value hovers around the overall average of 2.6 in the back and central halls, it is considerably lower (2.3) in the front hall. This hall is the area of highest visibility in the school, running between the front entrances. It is also the riskiest area for walking without permission, for it is the hall that

Table 3.1 *Average jeans width in the first floor halls*

		Central Halls		
Front Hall	Back Hall	North	Middle	South
2.3	2.7	2.7	2.8	2.7

the administrative offices are situated on. Thus it appears that the Jocks are not only freer to move in the halls in general, but whatever Burnouts are in the halls prefer to stick to the relatively unmonitored back halls.

One additional correlation in these data ties together the relation between jeans width, geographic mobility in the school, and financial resources. The data used in this report were collected during the week that followed spring vacation. During spring vacation, large numbers of students traditionally go to Florida, and the Florida tan is an important status symbol in the school. Of the people recorded walking in the halls, 17 were unmistakably tan. All but one of them were recorded in the front hall, and their average jeans width was 1.9.

Of course an indexical feature like jeans width will not provide insight into the social structure of the school. It will only provide the means to observe correlations with other aspects of behavior that will suggest fruitful areas of inquiry. When one is doing research in a familiar setting, as a high school is to most of us, there is considerable danger of overlooking important phenomena. The use of an indexical device in quantitative observations may direct our attention to areas that we would otherwise have ignored.

* * * * *

While I was busy running around in the suburban schools, a group of amazing students[2] were at work in my lab doing orthographic and phonetic transcriptions. The orthographic transcription alone was a huge task, and transcribing and checking fifty tokens of each of the five variables of the Northern Cities Shift for 150 speakers (70 in Belten and 80 across four other schools) was pretty huge as well. The grant included money for computer time, which I ended up spending on the first model of the IBM PC. It arrived in pieces for me to assemble, and since there was no word processing software available, I taught myself Basic during a very fun weekend and wrote a little program to print out transcripts. It took time before I had data that I could actually analyze, so there was time to write an ethnography.

---

[2] Lynne Robins, Marcia Salomon and Mary Steedly transcribed the interviews into text files; Susan Blum, Jane Covert, Larry Diemer, Alison Edwards and Becky Knack did the phonetic transcription; and Leanna Tyler did all the data entry.

Before going into the schools, I had looked all over for good ethnographic literature on adolescents in school, and the shelf was bare. This came as a shock, and motivated me to commit to writing an ethnography before doing the linguistic analysis. I wanted to commit myself to a social analysis and to the assignment of speakers to categories before seeing the linguistic results. But I also thought it was important for people to understand how the institutional structure of the school encouraged social polarization and served as a social tracking system. I wrote the first draft of the ethnography *Jocks and Burnouts* (Eckert 1989a) towards the end of the fieldwork, and gave it to a number of students and the principal to read. The Jocks who read it thought it was accurate, the Burnouts felt vindicated. I was particularly pleased when the principal called me some time later asking my advice. He was under pressure from the community to close down the smoking area, but since he'd understood from my book that it was the one place where the Burnouts felt comfortable, he was inclined to resist the pressure. Over the years, people have tried to get me involved in school reform, but while I may be able to see and even analyze problems, other people are better at finding solutions, and are sometimes in a good position to carry them out.

4   Jocks, Burnouts and Sound Change

While the study began with a focus on networks, it became clear during this fieldwork that the usefulness of social networks as conduits for sound change decreases with social distance. While social networks clearly structure exposure to change between cities, this effect is minimized in a small and intensely co-present population like a high school. How much contact is needed to move a sound change or even a chain shift forward? Once the movement is already in the speakers' dialect, they do not need to interact intensively with more advanced speakers in order to move it further. The speaker is already implementing the internal constraints on the change, so what is new is a bit of ramping up or down. What is needed is enough exposure to the larger community to know the social patterning of the implementation. The friendship network I constructed for Belten High represented not so much the path of spread of change as the social divisions and contacts that motivated individuals to intensify or mitigate a process that they were already engaged in.

A sound change is not usually new when its use arrives in a new place. It comes with history and it's not so much exposure to the change that spreads as the motivation to adopt it. One might say that this motivation is the social meaning of the variable. This perspective showed up in the first major paper I wrote on this project. The paper focused on the backing of (uh), and if I avoided mention of social meaning in the NSF proposal, it leaked into this paper in the guise of "symbolic value." The paper maintained the view of the social network as a conduit for change, as the In-betweens (those who were neither Jocks nor Burnouts) mediated meaning between Jocks and Burnouts. But in fact, while some In-betweens fell between the Jocks and Burnouts in the social network, others fell at the opposite extreme from the Burnouts. Their In-between-ness was not geographic but ideological. (Damn – another paper beginning with a conjunction.)

SOUND CHANGE AND ADOLESCENT SOCIAL STRUCTURE

Introduction

Although there is ample reason to believe that major advances in regular sound change take place during preadolescence and adolescence, much of the speculation about the social motivations of sound change has focused largely on adult social structure. The following discussion is based on the assumption that the acquisition of local phonological variables in adolescence is intimately involved with the development of social identity and is structured by the development of a social structure within the age cohort. The discussion, based on several years of participant observation and sociolinguistic analysis among Detroit suburban adolescents, will put forth arguments about the social dynamics of two major patterns of society-wide sociolinguistic variation: the regular spread of phonological change (1) outward from cities and (2) upward through the socioeconomic hierarchy. Focusing on adolescent social categories and networks, I will demonstrate that class-related differences in orientation to society and geography among adolescents lead to differences in influence which in turn determine the flow of phonological change between and within communities.

Background

The study of phonological variation in Western industrial societies over the past twenty years has uncovered a set of regular correlations that indicate some constant patterns of the spread of phonological change through and between communities. The interpretation of these patterns has led sociolinguists to move from general demographic correlations based on survey techniques to participant observation in smaller groups and networks in an effort to uncover the social motivations for the kinds of linguistic emulation that lead to the spread of change through populations.

Regularly observed demographic patterns of phonological variation indicate that, at the bottom line, phonological change spreads between and through communities through networks of communication. Although phonological changes can begin anywhere, those changes that catch on and spread widely tend to originate in urban areas. The distribution of isoglosses in areas with long-term stable populations shows that change fans out from economic and political centers, creating linguistic regions around major urban centers. Recent work in linguistic geography shows that sound change, like other kinds of innovation, follows networks of communication and influence, spreading gradually to the outlying areas of urban centers and also spreading directly from larger to smaller urban centers (Callary 1975; Chambers & Trudgill 1980; Trudgill 1974a). Community studies have found, furthermore, a regular socioeconomic stratification of phonological variables within communities, in which the frequency of innovative forms decreases as one moves upward from the working class through the socioeconomic hierarchy, suggesting that it is the working class that brings changes into communities and that these changes then spread from the working class through local class-related networks (see Labov 1966 and Trudgill 1974b for classic studies of the social stratification of urban English). The progress of phonological change is further reflected in age differences within communities, with a general increase of innovative forms as one moves downward through the age continuum.

There are, however, discontinuities in both the socioeconomic and the age continua. Lower-middle-class speakers show a far greater stylistic range than those above or below them on the socioeconomic hierarchy, and in doing so they regularly show more conservative speech in formal style than upper-middle-class speakers and sometimes show more innovative speech in casual style than working-class speakers (Labov 1972a). This behavior reflects the precarious position of the lower middle class in the economy: a position that constrains them to maintain acceptability in the working class at the same time that they try to gain acceptance in the middle class. Of particular interest to the current discussion is a possible age discontinuity that is still difficult to document, that is, a discontinuity between preadolescents and adolescents. Since most age-graded data appear in community studies whose focus is on broad demographic categories, speakers under the age of twenty are generally grouped together, making it difficult to examine differences among finer groups of pre-adults. The grouped data show a gradual continuum through all age groups, with pre-adults showing the same social stratification as the adult population. Since pre-adults are classified according to their parents' socioeconomic status, these data suggest that patterns of variation are ultimately determined by childhood environment. Since it is well established that older children acquire the dialect of their peers rather than their parents, one might assume that it is the socioeconomic character of neighborhood-based childhood peer groups that accounts for pre-adults' linguistic patterns. However, if sound change spreads as a function of active social processes, one would assume that individual pre-adults would develop patterns of variation based on their choice of peer groups rather than on neighborhood groups. As they develop socially, adolescents may move out of their neighborhood networks into networks that may have a quite different socioeconomic character. Thus, one would expect that where individuals' emerging social identities conflict with those of their parents' or neighborhood peers' socioeconomic identities, their patterns of variation will adjust

Table 4.1 *Social stratification of variables from Wolfram (1969)*

	10–12 years	14–17 years	Adults
Word-final t,d			
Bimorphemic clusters	+	–	–
Monomorphemic clusters	+	–	+
Morphemic-medial and final θ	+	+	+
Syllable-final d			
[t]	–	–	–
ø	–	–	–
Postvocalic r	+	–	+
Suffixal -z			
3rd singular	+	–	+
Possessive	+	–	–
Plural	–	–	+
Multiple negative	+	–	+
Copula deletion	+	+	+
Total +s	8	2	7

+ perfect stratification
– not perfect stratification

accordingly. Heightened social mobility accompanies the passage from pre-adolescence to adolescence, particularly with entrance into secondary school, where a variety of factors provide greater social choice and motivation to make that choice. It follows that while children's and preadolescents' social identity and linguistic patterns are largely determined by family and residence, adolescents' identity and linguistic patterns may be somewhat independent of these. Data from the few studies that separate these two age groups suggest that this may well be the case. Romaine (1984b) summarizes the evidence of social stratification among preadolescents, arguing that awareness of the social value of linguistic variables does indeed begin at a fairly early age. The two socioeconomic stratification studies that systematically separate preadolescents from adolescents show different patterns. Macaulay's (1977) data show that both age groups exhibit fairly regular socioeconomic stratification and a fairly regular age stratification within the full community age continuum. Wolfram's (1969) study of black speech in Detroit, however, shows a cumulative difference between the patterns of variation of adolescents (10–12 years) and adolescents (14–17 years). Wolfram presents eleven variables according to age group and socioeconomic class. Table 4.1 shows, for each age group, which of these variables show perfect social stratification. As the table shows, the adolescent age group (14–17 years) shows regular stratification for far fewer variables than the older and younger age groups.

The difference between Macaulay's and Wolfram's data falls in with the frequent observation that there is less socioeconomic mobility and greater class loyalty in British than American society (see, for example, Trudgill 1972). Both of these factors would presumably lead to greater determination of peer group membership by parents' class in Britain than in the United States, at all age levels. It is possible, therefore, that the stratificational similarity between preadolescents and adults in Wolfram's sample results from the close fit between individual identity and class assignment in these two age groups, while the lack of stratification in the adolescent sample reflects the relatively smaller relevance of parents' socioeconomic class to adolescent social identity. This interpretation will be strengthened by the following discussion, which will demonstrate that where individual adolescent identity conflicts with parents' socioeconomic class, speech patterns will conform not to parents' class, but to the individual's independent social identity.

Adolescent Social Structure

If any one thing makes the adolescent age group stand out in U.S. society, it is the intensity of its social life. This intensity has been attributed to anxieties and conflicts associated with sexual, cognitive and social development, and indeed is, if anything, over-explained. The overriding theme of all discussions of adolescent intensity is that of separation from the nuclear family and the development of individual identity. As they enter secondary school, American youth recognize that they are making a formal transition into a life stage in which they are expected to accomplish a separation from the family and parental authority. For most, this separation is achieved communally with the age cohort as it develops a social structure that provides the means for the development of an identity independent of the family structure.

As adolescents move away from the family, they seek to replace an ascriptive identity based on place in the family with one based on their characteristics as individuals in relation to a broader society – on what Eisenstadt (1956) calls "universalistic criteria." In order to accomplish this, they need to enter a society that is sufficiently structured to compensate for the loss of the security of family structure and based on sufficiently broad social values to provide a meaningful basis for identity. Insofar as American adolescents are isolated during this period, the society in terms of which they must develop this identity is defined almost entirely in terms of their age group, hence the social forms that give rise to such constructs as "adolescent society" or "adolescent culture." Peer interactions are particularly consuming for the adolescent because these relationships represent the main alternative to the family, and the anxiety over separation from the security of the family contributes to the emotional investment in the evolving substitute. The resulting highly normative nature of most adolescent peer groups accounts for what is commonly (and disparagingly) referred to as adolescent conformity or "peer pressure" – a careful monitoring of all aspects of social behavior and an intense involvement in such systems of identity symbols as adornment and musical taste. The participation of language in the adolescent system of social symbols is popularly recognized in such consciously manipulated features as those associated with "Valley Talk" and in the general phenomenon of teenage slang, both of which arise within specific segments of the teenage population and have social group significance within the age group. It is reasonable to assume that the rapid development of social structure in preadolescence and adolescence is intimately associated with the development of patterns of linguistic variation, and that the social significance of variants for adolescents would be associated with the system of social differentiation arising within the cohort.

The following discussion focuses on the development of a basic social division within the adolescent cohort, which begins around the time of entrance into secondary school. The discussion is based on three years of participant observation in several high schools in the Detroit suburban area, in particular on two years in one school, in which one graduating class of 600 students was followed through their junior and senior years.[1] The schools, typical of Detroit suburban schools, have virtually entirely white student bodies, among whom the major social differentiation is based on socioeconomic class. While the picture developed here is complicated in ethnically diverse schools, the mechanisms of the fundamental division are common to schools across the country and interact variously with ethnic divisions as a function of the relation between ethnicity and class in any given community.

Secondary schools provide the major locus of contact among the various segments of a local adolescent population, and since the school represents an extension of parental authority, orientation to the school becomes the basis of social issues within the cohort as the cohort reinterprets familiar childhood issues within a broader context. In public secondary schools throughout the United States, the fundamental issue of acceptance or rejection of adult authority is played out in the opposition between two social categories: those who center their lives around the school and its activities on the one hand, and those who reject the hegemony of the school on the other. These categories, building on differential expectations, needs, and interests that are fed by class differences, represent a fundamental split over orientation to adulthood and over the basis of negotiation of a relationship with the adult world.

In the schools under study, as in schools across the country, working-class and middle-class students overwhelmingly separate into vocational and

---

[1] This research was sponsored by the Spencer Foundation, the Rackham School of Graduate Studies at the University of Michigan, and the National Science Foundation (BNS 8023291).

college-preparatory curricula, with middle-class students showing a greater rate of completion and academic success.[2] Furthermore, while middle-class students dominate extracurricular activities, working-class students pursue social activities independently of the school.[3] The present discussion will take as given the broad range of dynamics between students and adults that contribute to this differentiation and will focus on dynamics within the student cohort that organize these differences into a peer-based social structure that will eventually emerge as an adult class system.

The age cohort, upon entrance into junior high, undergoes an abrupt polarization into two opposed social categories that grow out of elementary school networks which, in turn, are loosely related to neighborhood networks. The "Jock" category, comprised primarily of middle-class students who have enjoyed prominence and faculty favor in elementary school, enter junior high with the intention of maintaining this favor in preparation for college and of centering their social lives around the activities of the school. The "Burnout" category, on the other hand, intending to leave secondary school for the blue-collar workforce, focuses on the enhancement of social networks and pursuits independent of the school. Students apply these names to members of both sexes and to themselves as well as to others. These particular names arose in many schools around the country during the 1970s, when drugs came to be associated with adolescent rebellion just as sports have long been associated with the clean-cut life style of the school-oriented adolescent. In other times and other places these categories may have different styles and different names – for example, "Collegiates," "Soc's" ("Socialites"), "Preppies," for the Jocks, "Hoods," "Greasers," "Freaks" for the Burnouts – as a reflection of differences in region and era.[4]

Although Jocks and Burnouts take their names from athletics and drugs respectively, these are neither necessary nor sufficient criteria for category membership. While in general usage a Jock may be simply a person who engages regularly in some sport, it is most frequently used for someone whose life style embraces a broader ideal associated with sports in American culture. The high school Jock embodies an attitude: an acceptance of the school and its institutions as an all-encompassing social context and an unflagging enthusiasm and energy for working within those institutions. An individual who never plays sports but who participates in school activities may be

---

[2] The literature on this subject is vast. See, for instance, Cicourel and Kitsuse (1963), Coleman (1966).

[3] This observation dates back to the earliest studies of adolescent society: Hollingshead (1949), Coleman (1961).

[4] Whatever other categories may come and go ("Beatniks," "Punks"), they are structurally subordinate to the hegemonic opposition between Jocks and Burnouts. See Eckert (1989a) for a discussion of this structural differentiation.

unquestioningly referred to by all in the school as a Jock. And just as there are Jocks who are not athletes, there are Burnouts who do not do drugs. Drugs are this generation's most frightening form of rebellion, and as such they are taken as a symbol by and for the school's alienated category. The complexity of the connotations of the category names is reflected in their use. Although the terms *Jock* and *Burnout* are used in certain unambiguous contexts to refer to an athlete or a *druggie*, such specific reference is frequently disambiguated through compounding: *Jock-Jock*, *Sports-Jock*, and *Burned-out Burnout*. The names and the stereotypes of the Jock and Burnout categories belie a broader distinction and a profound cultural split, which reflects in turn the split between the adult middle and working classes.

Representing the extremes of school orientation, Jocks and Burnouts form separate cultures, which lead to different exposures, attitudes, and reactions to the linguistic changes that are in progress at any given time. A good deal of the facts of the spread of sound change can be better understood in the context of differences in the structure and content of Jock and Burnout networks. Basic to the spread of linguistic change, as to adolescent socialization, is the drive of the average adolescent for independence from parents and for identification within a peer-defined world. The ways in which Jocks and Burnouts seek independence from adults lead to very different kinds of social norms and networks and to different kinds of linguistic influence.

Industrial societies remove adolescents from a heterogeneous society and isolate them into age-segregated institutions that by and large focus on the training of the future middle class and marginalize those headed for the blue-collar workforce.[5] This marginalization is effected not only through the devaluation of vocational education in the schools but also through the schools' investment in a corporate life style and stigmatization of alternative styles. The opposition between Jocks and Burnouts is primarily the result of predictably different reactions to this context on the part of students from different backgrounds and with different plans for adulthood. And while the cohort perceives the opposition between the Jock and Burnout categories in terms of differences in interests, attitude toward authority and schoolwork, and a variety of symbolic behavior such as dress, demeanor, and substance use, there are deeper differences in social network structure and norms that reflect the spheres in which the two categories function. As the following discussion will show, the Jocks' assimilation to the corporate norms of the school involves regular negotiation with adults and the development of highly localized networks, within which relationships are largely hierarchical, instrumental, and competitive. On the other hand, the Burnouts' pursuit of personal networks

---

[5] See Stinchcombe (1964) for a discussion of this marginalization.

independent of the school community, and of direct experience with the metropolitan environment, involves oppositional relations with parental-aged adults, close, egalitarian, and cooperative peer networks, and loose extra-local ties. These differences, along with the major differences in contact and influence that they bring, create significantly different orientations to local dialects and to sound changes in progress.

The Jocks and the Corporate Structure of the School

By providing a comprehensive social sphere away from home, the high school offers the opportunity to play adult-like roles away from parental, if not adult, supervision. In return, the student must endorse the corporate norms of the school and the overriding authority of the adults who run it. As a substitute for participation in the larger community, the school offers mobility within an elaborated corporate structure, which is clearly intended as preparation for later participation in an analogous adult structure. The school thus strikes a limited bargain with its student population that mitigates, for some, the loss of freedom that attendance imposes. By and large, this bargain is accepted willingly by those students, particularly the college-bound, whose plans for adulthood require the continued sponsorship of adults and adult institutions, and for whom the kinds of corporate roles offered within the school provide preparation for those they anticipate playing as adults. On the other hand, those who plan to leave high school directly for the blue-collar workplace can see little benefit in participation in this system. While the school has a direct role in procuring college entrance for its academic students, it does not play an analogous role for its vocational students in the blue-collar job market. And while the extracurricular institutions of the school provide training in corporate skills that its future middle class will find valuable, these skills are maladaptive in the blue-collar workplace. The opposition between Jocks and Burnouts therefore is not simply – as many of them believe – a matter of docility versus rebelliousness, but of deep and adaptive differences in norms. The high school extracurricular sphere has the essential features of the adult corporate organization:[6] strict delimitation from other communities, a hierarchical internal structure, action-set determination of personal relationships, and role-determined identification of individuals. The mechanisms of the Jock–Burnout split are directly related to proposed reactions to this structure, and these reactions, in turn, are related to class background and to individual aspirations. The corporate structure of the school embodies norms that are likely to be more familiar and more acceptable to the adolescent from a middle-class background than to the one

---

[6] The structure of the high school closely follows the features of corporate organization as described in Kanter (1977).

from a working-class background. The Jock and Burnout categories embody norms that coincide and conflict, respectively, with the corporate norms of the school, and that can be seen as adaptive to entrance and participation into the corporate and the blue-collar workplaces, respectively. In this sense, these categories constitute class cultures within the adolescent context, and indeed class of origin is related to category affiliation. Sociological studies in the past have shown that those who participate in and dominate school activities tend to come from the upper end of the local socioeconomic continuum, while those from the lower end of the local continuum tend to be alienated from the school and its activities (Coleman 1961; Hollingshead 1949; Larkin 1979). There is a similar tendency in the population to be discussed below, with a correlation between class origins and category membership. However, as there is significant crossover, it would be a serious error to claim that class determines category affiliation; rather, category affiliation constitutes something more like a pivot between childhood class and future adult class. The fact that it is difficult to leave one's childhood networks for a very different network with different norms is clearly an important limiting factor in social mobility.

Effective participation in the high school corporate structure requires that the individual develop a corporate identity, merging personal interests and motivations with those of the organization. This identity is not entirely acquired in school but builds on norms and values characteristic of the middle-class home. The middle-class student brings to school social norms and skills that are adaptive to the corporate structure set out by the school and that conflict in many areas with the norms and skills acquired in working-class homes. Perhaps the most fundamental of these norms is the middle-class career orientation. The Jocks see their high school life as a limited career within the school organization, as a rehearsal for career-making in later life, and as a means of qualifying for entrance into the institutions that create careers. This career is built through upward mobility within the extracurricular institutions of the high school, particularly student government and activities centering around sports.

The Jock career aims at prominence in a hierarchy based on control of crucial school resources. These resources – space, information, freedoms, visibility, the right and the materials to organize a variety of social events – are ultimately controlled by school personnel and are distributed to the student body through student brokers. These brokers are Jocks who are sufficiently successful at dealing with adults to gain the confidence and cooperation of school personnel and who at the same time command a significant student network within which to trade these resources. The integrity of the Jock hierarchy depends on the consuming involvement of its members and on the careful delimitation of its membership. Thus students' commitment to the school involves not only effective participation within the community but also renunciation of involvement without. Jock social networks, therefore, include virtually only people attending the same school. This limitation plays an overt role in Jock social norms, as demonstrated by one student as he explained why he was giving up his friendships with a group from another school:[7]

I don't know, I think if I spend too much time with those guys, the guys at Belten will think I'm a loser.
WHY A LOSER?
Well, maybe not a loser exactly, but like they'll wonder about me always being with guys from Cabot, like I don't care about Belten, and they won't accept me.

Since the school is the locus of Jock activities, Jocks spend relatively little time beyond the school district or even beyond the area served by their specific school. Since their social activities are by and large limited by the school population, taking place either in the school itself or in their own homes, they do not explore the urban area for distractions. The mass exodus of whites from Detroit over the past forty years has brought about the establishment of an almost exclusively white suburban area. Some whites have left Detroit primarily to flee the rapid racial integration of their neighborhoods, while others have left Detroit also as part of an upward socioeconomic move. The latter group, in particular, have left Detroit behind – suburban adults rarely go there and discourage their children from going. To them, Detroit represents danger and trouble, and Jocks, like their parents, have overwhelmingly turned their backs on Detroit, going there only for an occasional sports event:

DO YOU EVER DRIVE AROUND?
We don't go, as a group, to Detroit... You know, it's- it's like you're inviting trouble. You go down there, and you got to- you know, it's- it's something that we don't have to do. It- you know, it just doesn't appeal to us, going out of the city and doing something.

The school population is delimited not only geographically, but by strict age grading. For the Jock, the high school years represent a discrete life stage organized internally by the progression through clear stages represented by each successive year in school and delimited externally by graduation. For Jocks, leaving high school represents a break as they enter the next discrete life stage, which, for most of them, will be college. After graduation, many Jocks will take up residence in college for most of the year, leaving behind not only their school and homes but the social networks they have built in high school. Jocks will return to the high school and reunite with their high school friends only on ritual occasions – occasions that will serve above all to measure the growing differences within the cohort as they pursue their adult careers.

---

[7] The quotations that follow are taken from tape-recorded interviews with adolescents in Detroit suburban high schools. My own speech is in small caps.

The internal organization of the school is also compartmentalized by age. Seniority in the school brings increasingly broad responsibilities and access to more visible and statusful roles within the schoolwide organizations. Thus within this age-graded frame, the Jock relates to an increasingly large population and gains increasingly broad responsibilities each year. But with this increase in domain, the Jock's ultimate power depends on his or her position within the hierarchy defined by the age set, because the school organizes much of its competition within and between age sets. Each graduating class has its own hierarchy which organizes class activities and competitions between classes. Access to roles in schoolwide organizations depends on the visibility and status gained through work within the strict age set of the graduating class and through the accumulation of schoolwide visibility and status as the age cohort matures within the organization. This age-set orientation results in age-homogeneous social networks; just as Jock networks are limited to one school, their primary friendship networks are limited to their own graduating class. While relations with members of other classes are necessary for the success of the individual and of the class, these relations are dominated by upward deference and downward paternalism. Jock norms stigmatize the age integration of friendship networks because such integration violates the hierarchical organization of power. Cultivation of close relationships with members of higher age groups is seen as the cultivation of unfair influence. One Jock described his friends' attitude toward a member of their group who had hung out in junior high with his older brother's friends:

A lot of people didn't like it, I mean that I know, because they'd all say, "well, he's," you know, "just tagging along with his brother," you know, "and using his brother's name and stuff"...

Although Jocks center their lives around an adult-dominated institution, autonomy is nonetheless a principal goal. By accepting the hegemony of the school, Jocks enter a contract among their parents, the school, and the Jock student body. Jocks' parents relinquish a certain amount of control over their children to the school, endorsing virtually any activity that is sponsored by the school (including all-night work sessions, trips, late weeknight activities, etc.). Thus, the Jock is ensured the goodwill of the adult community and is relieved of a certain amount of direct parental control. And because the school itself depends on the goodwill of its Jocks for the success of its programs, it must in turn be cautious in its exercise of power over them. The school, therefore, gives liberties fairly generously as rewards for cooperation in school institutions. Enhanced personal freedom in the school, such as the freedom to walk around in the halls and to miss classes, partially fulfills the adolescent need for autonomy and serves as visible proof of individual status.

The Burnouts and the Metropolitan Environment

For those who plan to leave high school directly for the blue-collar job market, secondary school represents a very different set of opportunities. Some of the instruction, particularly the vocational instruction, provides clear job-related training. However, much of the school's corporate norms and organization stands in the way of, rather than enhancing, the future blue-collar worker's chances in the job market. While the closely bounded age-graded community of the school suits the Jock, for whom adolescence comprises a discrete and institutionally defined life stage, it conflicts with needs arising from the Burnouts' more fluid transition from adolescence to adulthood. While the Jocks' next life stage will be in an isolated and specialized institution like the high school, the Burnout will leave school directly to compete with adults in the workplace. While the high school negotiates the next life stage for its Jocks, it is of little use to the Burnout in finding a place in the job market. Although participation in school activities is an important qualification for college admission, it does little to enhance an individual's qualification for a blue-collar job, and while the school plays an active role in advising for college admission, it does little in comparison towards placing students in blue-collar jobs. Most Burnouts expect to rely on contacts outside of school to find employment, particularly on relatives and friends already in the workforce. Therefore, it is not in the Burnouts' interest to pursue social activities in school but rather to pursue activities and contacts that provide access to the local workforce.

This workforce is centered, not in the affluent suburbs, but in the urban center and the closer, more urban suburbs. A workforce orientation, therefore, is in many ways an urban orientation. Where the Jock finds personal autonomy in the acquisition of institutional roles, the Burnout finds it in integration into the urban working environment. Where Jock networks, therefore, are homogeneous with respect to both age and geography, Burnout networks extend to other age groups and across local boundaries into the urban area. Virtually all Burnouts have close friends outside of their graduating class, and well over half of them have close friends who do not attend their school. In contrast to the Jock norm, discussed above, of confining close relationships to age peers, Burnouts value having older friends. Burnout networks are to a great extent a continuation of neighborhood networks that go back to preschool days: networks that originate in a dense child population that is integrated into cooperative neighborhood-based adult networks. While many Jocks remember their childhood friendships as separate sets of dyads, most Burnouts look back upon a social life dominated by ascriptive membership in a mass of neighborhood kids. This mass, in addition, is based not on age but on residence, and involves interconnecting sets of siblings. Since many within any cohort are put in the care of older siblings, who must take them along to their activities, working-class networks boast an overwhelming age heterogeneity. Children from these neighborhoods, therefore, enter elementary school with a ready-made social network not only within their own grade but extending into the higher grades.

The age heterogeneity of Burnout networks affords both far-reaching ties and a relatively early exposure to, and demand for, the adult prerogatives enjoyed by immediately preceding age groups. The attraction of adult prerogatives is enhanced by the fluidity between adolescence and adulthood. Jocks anticipate that their prolonged dependence on adults in segregated institutions will bring ultimate rewards and greater economic power. The Burnouts, on the other hand, feeling that they have nothing to gain from such dependence and segregation and recognizing that entry into the workforce brings the full range of adult responsibilities, see no advantage in sacrificing personal freedom during the years when they have the greatest leisure to enjoy it. They place considerable emphasis, therefore, on freedom and adventure, both because it provides entertainment in a world that provides virtually none for them, and because it provides experience in the "real world." The Burnouts, in their eagerness to "have it all" while they have the leisure, lead their peers from junior high school in their demand on adult prerogatives. Earlier use of cigarettes, drugs, sexual and romantic involvement, and above all mobility, set Burnouts clearly apart from their Jock peers. Just as older siblings and friends provide an example of experience and maturity, so do peers from Detroit and the more urban suburbs. Continuing migration outward from the urban center guarantees that suburban children and adolescents are constantly reminded of the greater savvy of their urban peers. New arrivals enjoy considerable status among Burnouts for their greater independence and ability to cope with the challenging urban environment, and for their potential for providing contact with their urban knowledge and networks. The denser population and public transportation of the urban area provides greater mobility and contact than the suburban environment – a factor which alone makes suburban children appear more sheltered. One student who moved from Detroit while in elementary school said that her urban experience gave her immediate ascendancy over her new friends:

I thought they were pretty sheltered and stuff, you know, because I'd – you know, like I used to tell them that I used to go out, you know, and walk, you know, across Seven Mile and everything. And they couldn't even cross the street and stuff, and like I'm crossing these big main streets, and, you know –

While mobility alone gives urban children greater autonomy, other kinds of early experience accumulate as they grow older. One Detroiter describe her shock upon arriving in the suburbs:

well, it was like we were years ahead of these people, it seemed... we were much more sophisticated because we, you know, we were all into all this stuff – like we, we had the weirdest ideas. Now this is when we were like little kids, like ten years old. We would sit around and talk about sex and everything, you know, and – it seems kind of ludicrous now, because ten years old, that's like – that seems so little. But then –
DID YOU KNOW PRETTY MUCH EVERYTHING?
Well, you know, we would find out, you know, if we wanted to know. And we had this big group that we all hung around, and we had this club, you know, and it was a real big deal, and I think what was – to get in, you had to wear a bra...
AND HERE THEY WERE ALL LIKE UH –
Yeah, they were – they seemed like, I mean, they were playing on – with dolls, you know, and everything, and I'm going, "oh, my God, what did I move into?" That's – that's why my parents wanted to move there, because things were starting to move like a little bit too fast, you know.

As aging brings progressive mobility, Burnouts move from neighborhood hangouts to city parks and ultimately to metropolitan parks and public facilities (pool halls, bowling alleys, arcades) and urban cruising strips, which afford casual contact with young people from the more urban communities. As Burnouts progress in high school, their networks also provide contact with people from the urban area. Older friends and siblings graduate or drop out of school and get jobs, and friends made in the workplace provide urban contacts for members of their local networks. Peers moving into the school from Detroit share their networks from the old neighborhood and school. Burnout networks thus come to lead toward Detroit. Many have friends in Detroit, some hang out and go to parties in Detroit, all consider Detroit a highly desirable place to visit and cruise.

The corporate skills that prepare Jocks for their future careers are not simply useless but maladaptive within the blue-collar context. It is not competition with peers but cooperation and solidarity that ensures blue-collar economic security. Marginalized in the school, as they will be in the adult economy, Burnouts emphasize close supportive networks based on a clear understanding that those in authority over them are serving separate and conflicting interests. Like their parents in the workplace, Burnouts recognize that they can only protect their interests through solidarity among peers in opposition to their hierarchical superiors. This solidarity dictates a clear separation from the interests of the middle-aged adults who seek to control them in school and out, and the maintenance of close stable friendship networks that compensate for the loss of adult emotional and material support that accompanies this separation. For the Burnouts, therefore, the social network is perceived from the start as a lasting one. Whereas Jocks change friends as their interests and activities change, Burnouts' friendships determine their activities. For most Burnouts, life after high school will be a continuation of high school life. They will stay and seek employment in the area, many of them will continue to live in their parents' homes, a few of them continuing at jobs they hold in high school. Leaving school, particularly after graduation, therefore, does not represent the break in social networks that it does for Jocks.

Polarization of the Categories

The fact that many students in the school do not consider themselves Jocks or Burnouts does not detract from the hegemony of this opposition; rather, the way in which these people perceive their own identities confirms it. Except for the few loners who are not integrated into the peer community, virtually all of the unaffiliated refer to themselves as 'In-betweens' and describe themselves in terms of traits shared with either category, sometimes in terms of linear distance between opposite poles. A few of the In-betweens associate with both Jocks and Burnouts, while others, whose network distance from either category is relatively great, do not associate directly with either. The In-between individuals and groups enjoy greater freedom of choice than those who are tied into the clear Jock and Burnout styles, but they sacrifice the ascriptive status associated with clear membership. Category affiliation during the extremely polarized years of junior high school is prerequisite for social status in the cohort. Jock and Burnout affiliation at this time, constituting a statement of alternative adolescent identity during the initial years when identity is particularly problematic, is tantamount to status within the cohort, and the social networks that form the core of each category constitute competing "popular" groups. The prototype member of each of these categories represents, to its members, the "typical teenager," claiming autonomy and age-group identity through a clearly defined teenage style.

Both the Jocks and the Burnouts seek autonomy in their involvement with youth society, but their definition of, and means of achieving, this autonomy conflict. Jocks seek autonomy in intensive involvement in a complex age-specific social structure and in the development of roles and identities within this structure. To the Jock, independence from adults is pursued in the management of adults and in controlling the closed community of the high school. Burnouts, on the other hand, seek autonomy in separation and independence from middle-aged adults and in dealing directly with the adult world beyond the family, school, and community. This difference cannot be neutral, since the behavior associated with each mode of separation threatens the basis of the other. Within this context, the Jocks and the Burnouts become intensely involved in their mutual differences, emphasizing them through whatever means for symbolic differentiation are at their disposal. The progressive polarization of the Jock and Burnout categories is accompanied by the elaboration of a variety of symbolic oppositions that make Jocks and Burnouts readily distinguishable even to the most casual observer. They have distinct and opposed styles of dress, hair style, makeup, and other adornment; separate territories in school and hangouts outside; different tastes in music; and different patterns of substance use and display.[8] As the following section will show, this symbolic differentiation extends to the use of local phonological variables.

Social Categories and Orientation to Sound Changes in Progress

The relatively high degree of phonological innovation in the adolescent age group with relation to other age groups is an indication that the development of adolescent social structure provides a major impetus for phonological change. Given the intensity of adolescent social life and of the emerging symbolic forms in nonlinguistic areas during this period, it stands to reason that phonological variation should participate in the social development of this age group. A variety of factors arising from the dynamics of the adolescent life stage could lead all adolescents to the use of innovative phonology. The need for autonomy experienced by most of the age cohort, and certainly for the Jocks and the Burnouts, provides a widespread motive to accelerate changes already present in the community. Comparison of speech patterns between parent-aged adults and immediately older peers establishes for each cohort of emerging adolescents the age-salience of innovative phonology and the established direction of change. The simple continuation in this direction, or exaggeration of changes already in progress, thus has the potential to symbolize age-group identity and autonomy from the parental age group.

Another factor in the adolescent use of innovative phonology is the importance of local identity to this age group. Simple limitation of mobility among adolescents dictates that their lives will by and large revolve around the immediate geographic area: their hometown and the surrounding communities. Given this limitation, the development of social identity will be based in the local area, and the intensity of this development will create a particularly strong sense of local identity. Furthermore, this limitation will dictate that local phonology will be sufficiently familiar and thus identifiable to serve as a symbol of identity for the cohort. Thus, local innovations can simultaneously represent for the adolescent the expansion of mobility beyond the family and affiliation with the local area. Adolescent separation from the family involves

---

[8] See Eckert (1982, 1983, 1989a) for discussions of the symbolic differentiation of Jocks and Burnouts.

a gradual expansion of networks and of orientation, and this expansion itself is inseparable from the issue of autonomy. Involvement in local groups and activities, whatever they may be, emphasizes the adolescent's autonomy, and however limited this local context may appear to an adult, it represents a considerable expansion to the adolescent. Sound changes associated with the local area, therefore, can represent expansion and autonomy to the adolescent, as it represents the cohort's involvement in the world outside the home.

Finally, the pressure of adolescent group norms can be expected to exert pressure for conformity to differentiated linguistic norms. Adolescents' anxiety over the loss of ascriptive family status leads them to cleave particularly tightly to their social groups and to monitor each other's behavior closely for signs of disaffection. The rigid group conformity that arises in adolescence as a function of identity development makes adolescent norms tighter than adult norms, and can be expected to exert greater linguistic pressure on their members.[9]

While sound change has a similar function for the entire cohort in symbolizing autonomy from the adult age group, one might also expect it to function to signal distinctions within the cohort. Insofar as the cohort is involved in an emerging and intense social structure, in which differences within the cohort are becoming institutionalized, one might expect the cohort to use the same phonological innovations to emphasize differences among themselves. One might expect, for one thing, the adoption of innovative phonology to be more intense among those for whom the symbolization of independence from adults is the most crucial.

The data to be presented below were collected during two years of participant observation in and around one Detroit suburban school, during which time I followed one graduating class through its last two years of high school. The linguistic sample of 52 speakers to be discussed here was selected from tape-recorded interviews with 200 people from a broad range of social groups in the same graduating class.[10] The interviews were free-flowing discussions of adolescent life and social structure.

The change used to illustrate the role of social categories in the spread of phonological change is the backing and lowering of (uh), a recent step in a series of vowel changes known as the Northern Cities Chain Shift. This shift, characteristic of the northern U.S. cities of Buffalo, Cleveland, Detroit, and Chicago, is discussed in detail in Labov, Yaeger and Steiner (1972). Their

---

[9] Milroy (1982) has pointed out this linguistic potential stemming from the tightness of adolescent groups.

[10] The phonetic transcription of (uh) was done by Susan Blum. Orthographic transcription of the interviews was done by Lynne Robins, Marcia Salomon, and Mary Steedley. Michael Jody joined me in the fieldwork in Redford. I am indebted to all of them for their long and meticulous work on this project.

discussion focuses on the earlier stages of the shift: the tensing and raising of (aeh) and the fronting of (a) and (oh). These shifts are followed by the more recent backing and lowering of (e) and (uh), which are currently spreading out to the suburbs from the urban center. Variants of (uh) in the Detroit area range from the conservative [ʌ] to extremely backed [ɔ], and rounded [ʊ], and to an extreme lowered variant [ɑ]. The [ɔ] and [ʊ] variants are favored by labial environments, particularly when they precede the vowel. In addition, there are small numbers of occurrences of the fronted variants [ɛ] and [ɪ]. Values for each speaker are based on 50 tokens of the variable in free-flowing interview speech. Occurrences represented are all stressed, and occurrences in a few environments have been excluded because of their near categorical backing effect on the variant: occurrences following [w] and occurrences in *just* and *but* have been excluded. In Figures 4.1 and 4.2, variables are assigned weighted values: 0 for non-backed or lowered variants, 2 for the extreme variants [ʊ], [ɔ] and [ɑ], and 1 for intermediate variants (backed and lowered [ʌ]). Each dot represents the average value for the variable (uh) for one speaker.

If the individual's use of innovative variables were a function of socioeconomic class per se, or even neighborhood, one would expect a correlation between adolescent patterns of variation and their parents' socioeconomic membership. Figure 4.1 shows the values for (uh) grouped according to socioeconomic class: working, lower middle, and upper middle. These class assignments are based on combined educational and occupational levels, choosing the highest level attained by either parent. (The resulting figures show no noticeable difference from grouping according to mother's rank, father's rank, or combined values for the two.) It is clear from this figure that parents' socioeconomic class has no significant effect on the individual's participation in this sound change.

Figure 4.2 shows the values of (uh) according to social category affiliation. Those classified in the figure as Jocks or Burnouts are members of Jock and Burnout networks *and* refer to themselves and their friends as members of those categories. Since the In-betweens constitute a residual category, they can best be classified as individuals failing either of the criteria of inclusion as Jocks and Burnouts. As it happens, all of those classified here as In-betweens also refer to themselves as In-betweens. The Jocks represented are all involved in school activities, belong to the same extended cluster within the school social network, and work together on a regular basis in school. Because many of the Burnouts in the school moved there late in elementary school or during high school, the availability of "native" local speakers is far smaller for that category than for the Jocks, hence the smaller representation of Burnouts in the sample. As Figure 4.2 shows, the correspondence between the (uh) variable and social category affiliation is far closer than with traditional parameters. Specifically,

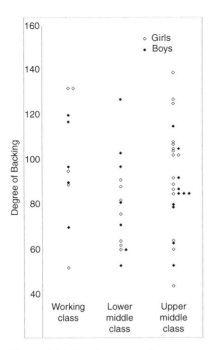

Figure 4.1 (uh) values according to parents' socioeconomic status.

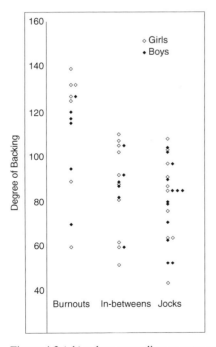

Figure 4.2 (uh) values according to category affiliation.

Table 4.2 *Probability of use of extreme backed and lowered variants of (uh) by social category*

Jocks	In-Betweens	Burnouts	p
.43	.48	.59	.000

the Jock and Burnout values cluster toward the lower and upper ends of the schoolwide continuum, while the In-betweens fall into an intermediate range.

Table 4.2 shows clearly that individual adolescent social identity, rather than ascriptive class, is a powerful determiner of phonological variation. This observation is statistically confirmed by the results of the variable rule program (VARBRUL), which shows socioeconomic class to be insignificant and social category membership to be highly significant in predicting the backing and lowering of (uh).[11]

These statistics are based on the same data as shown in Figures 4.1 and 4.2. However, while the individual values in Figures 4.1 and 4.2 are based on 3 degrees of change, the data subjected to VARBRUL are binomial, with only the extreme values ([ʊ], [ɔ] and [ɑ]) being counted as change (note that figures like 4.1 and 4.2, based on percentages of extreme values, are only negligibly different from those based on weighted values). In addition, phonological constraints are included in the regression, giving better control of accidents of lexical occurrence in the data than can be accomplished with the averaged values.

The urban status of the backing and lowering of (uh), as this change spreads outward to the suburban area, is reflected in differences in vocalic values between Livonia and Redford, the suburb lying directly between Livonia and Detroit. The Redford data were gathered during five weeks of participant observation in the high school serving the southern half of Redford. While the socioeconomic characteristics of the two schools are similar, the Redford school is the wealthier of Redford's high schools, while the Livonia school is in the middle range of Livonia's four high schools. Redford adolescents consider Livonia to be "super-suburban," while Livonia adolescents look upon Redford as almost part of Detroit. Many of the Livonia Burnouts have friends in Redford, and Burnouts from both cities meet frequently on Detroit cruising strips and particularly in Hines Park, a long park that runs east and west through the western urban–suburban continuum. As shown in Figure 4.3, the range of variation in Redford is considerably greater than that in Livonia,

---

[11] I would like to thank David Sankoff for his coaching in the use of this program, and Susan Pintzuk for providing her adaptation of the program to the IBM PC.

Jocks, Burnouts and Sound Change

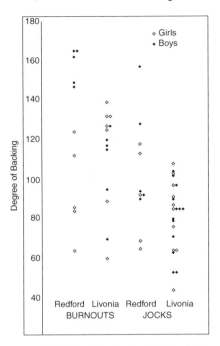

Figure 4.3 (uh) values in Redford and Livonia.

with some very low values but with noticeably higher values at the upper end. Most noticeable is the higher values for boys in both categories, and the particularly high values for the Burnout boys. While the Burnout boys clearly lead the Jock boys in the change, the girls' categories show little difference. The Redford Burnout girls' low values in relation to both the Redford Burnout boys' and the Livonia Burnout girls' are striking and defy explanation at this point, particularly since the ethnographic background in Redford is far less detailed than that in Livonia.

The Burnouts' overwhelming lead in the backing and lowering of (uh) is entirely predicted by the ethnographic facts, inasmuch as the Burnouts have both greater exposure to urban speech and greater motivation than Jocks to adopt variants associated with urban speech. The Burnouts' contact with peers from closer to the city brings them into greater contact with urban changes, while the Jocks' limitation to peers from their own community provides a more localized exposure. Jock and Burnout differences in attitudes toward the urban area, furthermore, provide the Burnouts with greater motivation than the Jocks to emulate the urban patterns they encounter. Burnouts undoubtedly respond to urban speech as symbolic of the urban knowledge and autonomy that they associate with their urban peers and that they themselves value. The

62   My Participation in the Second Wave

more conservative speech of their school community, on the other hand, is associated with those forces aimed at depriving them of this knowledge and autonomy.

The two categories' difference in relation to the age spectrum also provides very different linguistic contacts and motivations. The Burnouts' emphasis on rejection of adult domination might in itself lead to more innovative patterns, while the Jocks' cultivation of cooperative relations with adults might lead to more conservative, adult-like patterns. Furthermore, the Burnout friendship networks, including – from childhood – members of immediately preceding age groups, brings them into contact with the extreme patterns of adolescent speech at a fairly early age, and their general wish to emulate these age groups, like urban groups, no doubt extends to speech patterns. This early contact could thus bring about an acceleration of change as each age cohort of Burnouts is exposed earlier to adolescent patterns and to the social structure that accompanies these patterns.

Finally, one might expect the simple opposition between the Jocks and Burnouts, and their continual efforts at mutual differentiation, to extend to their use of patterns of variation. As long as a variant is unambiguously associated with the urban center and with Burnouts, one might expect Jocks to avoid it. This oppositional model, however, implies a simple linguistic polarization between Jocks and Burnouts, leaving no room for change to spread through the community. It is obvious, however, that the Jocks are using urban variants of (uh), and repeated observation of the social stratification of sound changes in progress suggests that they will use more of them as time goes on.

The question is what mechanism, given the oppositional nature of the categories, can account for the spread of change between them? The intermediate position of the In-betweens in the linguistic continuum cannot be simplistically interpreted as representing a transitional network or the gradual spread of sound change. Some In-betweens are transitional in the sense that they have friends in both the Jock and the Burnout categories; some in the sense that they fall between the two categories in the social network in such a way that they never associate directly with either, but with other In-betweens who themselves fall more toward one or the other pole. The former represent a close network connection between the two categories, while the latter represent a point in a more gradual continuum. But while the In-betweens may not represent a simple continuum of exposure between the two poles, they do represent a vehicle for the reinterpretation of the symbolic value of sound change. A variant that might be unacceptable to a Jock by virtue of its exclusive association with Burnouts becomes more acceptable as it comes to be associated with less extreme individuals who share aspects of the Burnouts' autonomy. A certain amount of independence is required for any adolescent to be socially successful, whether in the Jock or the Burnout category, and the Jocks are, indeed, sensitive to the appearance of adult domination. As variants move beyond Burnout groups, they become somewhat disassociated from that category and associated, within the school context, with broader values that certain In-betweens share with Burnouts. At that point, they may become attractive and acceptable symbols for Jocks to use to express their own autonomy and, at the same time, lose their value to Burnouts as symbols of urban identity. This development has been confirmed in Eckert (1986), which shows that Jock–Burnout differentiation decreases with the age of the sound change.

The clear sex differentiation commonly found in patterns of phonological variation is noticeably missing in these data: indeed, VARBRUL shows sex to be insignificant in predicting the backing and lowering of (uh). Older changes in the Northern Cities Chain Shift show the American pattern of change found in Labov (1966), whereby females lead males in the use of innovative variants in more casual styles. A hint of this pattern shows up in the (uh) data among the Burnouts. Figure 4.2 shows a group of female Burnouts leading the entire community in this change, while among the Jocks and the In-betweens there is no clear pattern of sex differentiation. The issue of sex differentiation in phonological variation is as complex as the social salience of sex, as shown most notably by Eckert, Edwards, and Robbins (1985) and Milroy (1980). The small but observable difference in sex constraints between Burnouts and others could be explained by differences in constraints on the sexes in the social categories. As Trudgill (1972) has pointed out, the relative lack of opportunity for social mobility through economic roles leads women to rely more on symbolic manifestations to assert their identities.

An analogous situation exists in the high school, where girls' status still depends to a great extent on physical appearance and contacts. Girls, therefore, are constrained to exert considerable effort in the symbolic sphere and to pay particular attention to their place in the social system. Thus Jock girls are constrained to maintain a "pure" image, and Burnout girls are eager to express their "toughness" and urban ties. The bind is greater for the Burnout girls, because although the Jock girls can act out their purity, it is riskier for Burnout girls to act out their toughness. With adolescents, girls lose the physical parity that once enabled them to deal on an equal basis with boys. One Jock girl told me, with some nostalgia, of the time in elementary school when she and her best friend had beaten up a (future) Burnout boy who was known as a bully. She expressed a certain loss of satisfaction when, as they got older, they had to resort to more "ladylike" and less direct means of social control. While Burnout girls as a whole continue to fight further into preadolescence and adolescence than Jock girls, they cannot fend for themselves in the urban setting the way boys can. To a great extent, therefore, they must rely on other devices, among them the symbolic, to express their urban identities.

It is perhaps worth pointing out that the two Burnout girls at either extreme of the linguistic spectrum (shown in Figure 4.2) also represent the two extremes of the Burnout social spectrum. The girl with the lowest value for (uh) comes from a Burnout neighborhood and has remained in her Burnout network. However, in junior high school, she wanted to participate in school activities and tried unsuccessfully to convince her friends to do so with her. After a considerable struggle, she abandoned her efforts and dropped out of school activities in order to remain with her friendship group. While she considers herself a Burnout and is thoroughly integrated into the Burnout network and their activities, she expresses little hostility towards Jocks and continues to regret her lack of participation in school activities. The Burnout with the most extreme high values for (uh), on the other hand, is the school's widely acclaimed prototype ("burned-out Burnout"). She sports the most extreme Burnout style of dress, is heavily involved in drugs and marijuana, spends much of her time in the urban area, dates primarily older Detroit boys, and contemptuously regards many Burnouts as "Jocks."

Adolescence and Sound Change

The degree to which a given individual modifies his or her patterns of linguistic usage throughout life remains an empirical issue. However, there is little question that the emotional involvement in social identity during adolescence far surpasses that at any other life stage. It is reasonable to postulate, therefore, that in our society the very uncertainty of the adolescent life stage, and the need to capture a clear identity in the face of uncertainty, provides greater motivation than at any other time in life to adapt linguistic patterns to community structure. This age group, therefore, provides an important key to the study of the mechanisms of such adaptation.

While class differentiation in speech begins in the early years of language learning, to be molded and modified throughout the school years and beyond, it is in the secondary school that the age cohort develops and manages its own class structure, which gives concrete meaning and utility to the adoption of speech varieties. The Jock and Burnout categories articulate socioeconomic class for the adolescent age group, as specific class-based cultural differences between the categories provide contrasting orientation to the local environment and to the adolescent life stage. Burnouts, seeking direct connection and immediate integration into the metropolitan community and orienting themselves to its public facilities and those functioning in it, embrace changes that are identified with that community. Their identity, based on membership in networks that extend into the urban area, provides them with greater exposure to, and motivation to adopt, urban vernacular features. The Jocks, seeking to transcend the community and the urban area through participation in networks and institutions that are abstracted from the local context, are removed from some of the motivations to adopt urban changes in progress. The hostility between these two polarized groups, furthermore, lends motivation for mutual differentiation. The complexity of the relation among adolescent social category affiliation, class, and the metropolitan environment ultimately yields a clear and simple explanation for patterns of the spread of sound change that have been observed on a demographic scale. The explanatory power of these categories clearly illustrates the need for sociolinguists to explore more deeply the rich texture of ethnography, to find the intervening variables between broad demographic categories and the daily realities of social and linguistic life.

5 The Local and the Extra-Local

The speech community was, and to some extent remains, a foundational concept in sociolinguistics. It has always been a problematic concept for me, perhaps because I've been floating around in linguistic atlases and the linguistic continua they represent. I have always believed that the speech community is a convenient, even necessary, fiction – a population that analysts carve out to encompass the social distinctions that they're studying. But there is no such thing in the wild. If there were, Saint Pierre de Soulan would be a classic example – nice and bounded and geographically separate from surrounding communities. But was each village a speech community or were the six villages of the commune one speech community? Some of the villages were less than a kilometer apart, and as people moved and intermarried among them, one person might have houses, barns, meadows and fields in more than one village. People from all the villages attended the same school and the same church, the men hung out at the same café and people bought groceries at the same two stores. But Buleix, at the foot of the mountain, butts right up against Castet d'Aleu, a village in the next commune, which extends up the next mountain over. There were little rivalries among communes and villages, and each village had its own character, and the longer I stayed, the clearer it became that it was differences among villages within and beyond the commune that yielded the orderly heterogeneity that was supposed to define a single speech community. This is not that different from the suburban context.

In my own suburban adolescence in Leonia, New Jersey, I developed a strong local identity, neatly disciplined by my Jocky participation in Leonia High School. But an important part of the local was Leonia's place in the broader suburban area, and particularly the suburb immediately to the south, Palisades Park, whose kids attended Leonia High School. When the kids from less affluent and largely Italian-American Palisades Park joined us in high school, class, ethnicity and geography came together, and Jersey phonology took on more meaning. I liked the fast Italian boys from Palisades Park, and I associated Jersey phonology with the things that made them preferable to the more vanilla Leonia boys – and with girls who snapped their gum and were less goody-goody than me. I associated Jersey phonology not just with social qualities but with the bodily styles that went with them – adornment, movement, posture, facial expressions, actions. Although Leonia and Palisades Park are contiguous in a vast suburban sprawl, we were all acutely aware of the boundary between the two towns. But for the purposes of indexicality, Leonia was meaningless in isolation from the social continuum it was part of. So if any aspect of my dialect had anything to do with identity as a Leonian, it was the less "vernacular" end of my stylistic repertoire. Like Bergen County, New Jersey, the Detroit suburbs constitute a socioeconomic if not an ethnic continuum, and many of the dynamics I encountered in the spread of change there were certainly at work in my own high school.

Lesley Milroy (e.g. 1980) viewed strong local networks as maintaining a stable vernacular, and further argued with Jim Milroy (Milroy & Milroy 1985), that change moves into these networks through extra-local weak ties. Importantly, they emphasized that those weak ties needed to be numerous. Burnouts did not go individually to Detroit, and Jocks did not go individually to interscholastic events. These activities were part of their group practice, and their interpretation of what they encountered in those places, and of the things they heard there, took place jointly. A single individual going to the city and picking up an urban feature will not be able to bring the feature "home" unless it can be made sense of collectively. It is unlikely to spread from individual to individual, but one individual with sufficient meaning-making rights could bring it into his or her group. The one In-between girl at Belten who bought the new fashions the minute they appeared in *Seventeen* magazine was an object of ridicule, as were the small group of people who were into punk. The issue is not simply that they didn't have the status to innovate, but that as a result of their lack of status, their innovative acts could not become community practice. When the *Seventeen* fashions and punk did eventually make it into the mainstream, it was via some larger collective contact and if anything despite these early adopters. I put these thoughts together in a paper I wrote years later for a retirement conference in honor of the very inspiring, wonderful and kind Ronald Macaulay.

VARIATION AND A SENSE OF PLACE

I began my research career in linguistic geography, asking myself how change spread from person to person and village to village across Gascony. But the "across Gascony" part lived in maps and atlases – in isoglosses and areas – while the "person to person" part lived in the worldly relations among the inhabitants of the village of Soulan, sitting on the south side of a lovely Pyrenee. Linguistic geography and sociolinguistic variation have remained surprisingly distant, even though in the eyes of most, they are inextricably connected. In this chapter, I will argue for the embedding of the study of variation within its sociogeographic context, most particularly, for the examination of the borders of communities in search of the articulation of social meaning between the local and the extra-local. At the same time, I will reflect on another aspect of method and personal trajectory – what did I learn from this work that would lead (has led) me to do the next study differently?

At the heart of the study of sociolinguistic variation is the social and geographic placement of the speaker. Different analysts (or the same analysts at different times) approach social location in different ways, sometimes focusing on broad categorizations such as the class system (Labov 1966; Macaulay 1977; Trudgill 1974b) and/or ethnicity (Labov 1972b; Wolfram 1969), and/or gender (Eckert 1989c; Labov 1990), sometimes focusing on smaller social configurations such as networks (Milroy 1980) or peer groups (Cheshire 1982; Eckert 1989a; Labov 1973). These social locations are in turn located within a geographic unit – a speech community – which serves to define the dialect and circumscribe the population under study. The local community, in other words, is treated as a microcosm of the wider society – a kind of free-floating microcosm at that. While the speech community is viewed as being located within dialect space, it is rarely treated as socially connected to anything beyond its boundaries.

Class, ethnicity, race and gender are seen as global categories that function to create distinctions in orientation to local practice. These distinctions are defined in abstraction from the community, but seen as applying similarly across communities. Perhaps because they are conceived of as global categories, they are treated as disconnected, with little attention paid to the connections that facilitate the flow of influence among them. Networks and groups, on the other hand, are seen as kinds of configurations that are defined locally, but that are common to all speech communities. The potential that such configurations offer for the study of connections is explored in Milroy and Milroy (1985), which considers the role of weak ties in the spread of linguistic change through local areas. But weak ties and strong ties are, once again, disembodied – and apparently distinct – abstractions, and as we take up the Milroys' suggestions, one of the first questions we need to ask is: What is the relation between weak and strong ties? Our focus on the social life of variation on categories and communities amounts to a focus on centers, and on the "typical" inhabitants of those centers – of local networks, of neighborhoods, of socioeconomic strata, and of peer groups. We recognize the influence of other communities, but the communities are disconnected entities, and the influence is hence disembodied. Yet people move about, and linguistic influence flows in and out of communities, as well as through them. And to understand the social function of variation and the spread of linguistic change, we need to know more about the connections – to know what happens at the boundaries of places and categories.

What I have to say is not new – only the application of old insights to data on variation. Mary Louise Pratt (1988) observed some time ago that the focus on speech communities indicates a preoccupation with linguistic utopias – that in constructing such entities, linguists are putting into action a theoretical ideology in which normative speakers are monolingual, monodialectal, and core members of communities. Subcommunities are treated separately, but rarely in virtue of their relations. I take my inspiration from Pratt, who argued that linguists should be focusing not on centers, but on borders – that we should move from a linguistics of community to a linguistics of contact. John Rickford (1986a) has argued that norms within speech communities cannot be conceived of as consensual – that conflict may be central to the organization of linguistic behavior within a community. I will take Rickford's argument one step further, and argue that the speech community itself cannot be consensual – that there is no consensual sense of place. In doing so, I embrace Barbara Johnstone's argument in this volume that place is as much ideological as it is physical – or more accurately, that place is an idealization of the physical.

Our focus on speech communities has led us to view the borders of communities as boundaries – as a cutoff between two places where different things are happening, rather than a transitional place where still more things are happening that are inseparable from what happens on either side. Rather than constituting some kind of envelope for the linguistic behavior of its inhabitants, the community is a contested entity that is differentially constructed in the practices and in the speech of different factions, as well as different individuals. When we focus on bounded categories, networks, and groups, and when we analyze linguistic variability within the community in these terms, we tacitly assume a homogeneity of orientation – a kind of consensuality about the boundaries of the community itself. Crucially, although members of a population defined as living in the same community may all agree that they live in a particular area or political unit, they do not orient in a homogeneous way to that area or unit, or its surroundings. Different people in a given community will view the boundaries differently, use different parts of the community, and participate in the surroundings differently. These differences will result in different patterns of contact, which have implications for linguistic influence. They will also relate to different interpretations and ideologies, and will enter into the patterns of diversity within the community. Categories, groups and networks may, as a result, embody differences in spatial orientations and practices, with important consequences for patterns of linguistic variation.

The Detroit Suburbs

A variety of studies (e.g. Blom & Gumperz 1972; Gal 1979; Holmquist 1985; Labov 1963) have shown the importance of orientation to the outside in explaining patterns of variation within speech communities. William Labov's (1963) study of Martha's Vineyard focused on speakers' orientation to the mainland in such a way that the local reversal of a sound change moving from the mainland signals an orientation away from the mainland tourist economy. In his study of the Spanish village of Ucieda, Jonathan Holmquist (1985) argued that the lowering of word-final /u/ to [o] under the influence of Castilian is an expression of movement away from the mountain-farming way of life, to more modern farming and ultimately to work in the factories in town. In both of these cases, the connection between the geographic outside and social issues inside the community brings a synergy between the local and the extra-local.

My ethnographic and sociolinguistic work with adolescents in the Detroit suburbs (Eckert 1989a, 2000) has demonstrated that exploring how these connections are actually made can bridge the space between communities, between the local and the extra-local, and eventually between the local and the global. In the following pages, I will use data from this study to show how the "outsides" are articulated with the "insides" of communities and how language, along with other semiotic resources, brings the "outside" in and the "inside" out. I hasten to point out that I did not begin the study with this insight. My focus was on the internal mechanisms of variation in a variety of communities, possible similarities and differences among them, and their relation to the flow of linguistic change in the Detroit conurbation. What I did not anticipate was the particular way in which local and extra-local practice would explain the spread of linguistic innovation.

For the purposes of this study, I selected five public high schools as discrete and representative speech communities. It is the terms *discrete, representative*, and *speech community* that I wish to problematize here. I chose to work in public high schools because these institutions normally bring together the entire social range of the towns they serve, constituting an adolescent microcosm of the town. I looked, therefore, to the adolescent age group, the town, the school catchment area, and the school building itself to constitute the boundaries around my speech community. And indeed, within the school, I looked to the school's age-grading system for an even closer age boundary, focusing on one graduating class. In constructing these boundaries, I did not necessarily assume that there were important linguistic differences on the other side of any of them, but I did assume that there was greater cohesion within than across the boundaries. And I made the implicit claim that the meaning of variation was constructed within those boundaries – possibly in response to the boundaries themselves and whatever was on the other side, but constructed within nonetheless. What I discovered is that what I was thinking of as boundaries – as some kind of social or geographic space around the community – were in fact borders that link the community in heterogeneous ways to the area around it. Relations to the "outside" were built into relations on the "inside" as local factions aligned themselves with respect to each other and the larger world, orienting to, interpreting, and appropriating the world around them.

The Local Social Order and the Conurbation

In this discussion, I will focus on the issue of borders and boundaries not between groups or categories, but between schools/towns in the Detroit conurbation. It will be apparent, though, that the borders between groups and categories within these schools interact with the borders between schools. The Detroit conurbation consists of Detroit City – a largely poor and African American, urban center – and an array of suburbs that become increasingly affluent and increasingly white as one moves away in any direction from the urban center. Each community, and each high school that serves it, is self-consciously located within the social geography of the conurbation, constructing a local identity in relation to it. The social order that forms within each high school articulates individual identities with local identities. And it is in this articulation that the social meaning of variables is constructed as they spread across the conurbation.

Because societal norms define legitimate adolescence by participation in secondary school, adolescents' identities are closely linked to orientation to school – even those who do not attend at all. The U.S. public high school strives to dominate the lives of students both when they are in school and when they are out. It encourages students to stay after school to participate in extracurricular activities – clubs, athletics, student government – and to devote much of their time outside of school to homework. It also expects students to develop friendships in school, particularly within the age-graded social system of the school. From grade one, students are expected to confine their friendships to others in their own graduating class and to time their social development according to prevailing institutional norms. Hanging out with older or younger kids is taken as a willful rejection of adult expectations for development.

Those who participate enthusiastically in what the school sets down for them as legitimate activities and practices are in a position to gain access to resources and a certain kind of control over the institutional environment. Those who reject such participation are marginalized from the institutional perspective. Such marginalization can be inconvenient and at times unpleasant, but it is not always unwelcome because school participation is a highly ideological arena and there are positive reasons for both participation and non-participation.

In U.S. high schools, an opposition commonly develops between kids who enthusiastically embrace the institution as the center of their social lives, and those who adamantly reject it. The adverbs point to the fact that there are plenty of kids who are neither enthusiastic nor adamant and who emerge as "In-between" in this opposition. In the high schools of the largely white Detroit suburbs, the opposition constitutes two social categories – the *Jocks*, who embrace the school as the center of their social lives and the *Burnouts*, who reject it as such. The Burnouts do not reject the school as a curricular center, but their mistrust of the institution extends to their often feeling that the school is not fulfilling their curricular needs.[1] The categories are class-based, and are a major vehicle for the reproduction of class. The Burnouts come by and large from the lower portion of the local socioeconomic range, whereas the Jocks come by and large from the upper portion. Although the parents' class does not determine category participation, the status of the Jock and Burnout categories do constitute middle- and working-class cultures respectively, and these categories and their class significance take center stage in the school.

The differences in orientations of the Jocks and the Burnouts, while aimed at the school, are played out among the students themselves. The Jocks and the Burnouts construct themselves in mutual opposition, and with considerable separation and even hostility. The hostility emerges from differences in values – in norms that govern friendship and peer relations more generally, as well as relations with adults. And as the Jocks embrace the school's authority, they submit to school adults and at the same time benefit from the power that those adults accord them within the institution. The Burnouts view the Jocks' acceptance of this arrangement as undermining adolescent autonomy and solidarity, while the Jocks view the Burnouts' non-acceptance as compromising what they see as a profitable arrangement with the school.

Regardless of its general socioeconomic makeup, each school in the Detroit suburban area has its Jocks and its Burnouts, who by and large represent the lower and the upper ends of the local socioeconomic hierarchy. This local socioeconomic scene is in turn located within the larger socioeconomic continuum of the Detroit conurbation. Residents locate themselves within this sociogeographic continuum – as residents of particular suburban areas, towns, and neighborhoods. They attribute a particular character to the area, the town, and the neighborhood (or subdivision), and orient themselves as groups and individuals to this character. Each community is a piece of this socioeconomic continuum, with the neighborhoods becoming wealthier as one moves away from the city. The schools that serve the different catchment areas of any town have clear socioeconomic characteristics, and these differences are manifested

---

[1] The Burnouts are overwhelmingly vocational students, and feel that the school neglects its vocational sector, and that they are not receiving training that will maximally help them in the job market.

in attitudes within and among the schools. This pattern is repeated across the suburban area. Schools are an important resource for adolescents to locate themselves within the larger area, as they develop a sense of local sociogeography by comparing the dominant social characteristics of the schools and the towns the schools serve.

Economic geography is built into Jock and Burnout practice as well. The Burnouts, headed for working-class workplaces in the Detroit area after high school, look beyond the school and into the larger urban-suburban area for access to work. They value, therefore, social networks that take them beyond their school and neighborhood and that give them access to the wider conurbation – particularly the "business" end of the conurbation, the places where things are happening. The Jocks, on the other hand, are on an institutional track, intending to leave high school for college, and to base their lives in the institution there just as they have in high school. Indeed, although they express prospective nostalgia for their high school friends, they expect to develop a new social network in college and to move away from the suburban area, at least temporarily. The Jocks, therefore, abstract themselves somewhat from the local area. They limit their main friendships to their own graduation cohort and to their own school, and they avoid the urban area except to participate in institutional activities such as attending professional sports games or visiting museums.

I wish in particular to emphasize the difference between a local and an institutional orientation. If one thinks of Belten High as the speech community in question, then it is the Jocks who are locally oriented. If one thinks of Westtown as the speech community, then the Burnouts are more locally oriented than the Jocks. But the Burnouts' local orientation is not to Westtown itself but beyond Westtown. In fact, many Burnouts express hostility to Westtown – there are no jobs there, there is nothing to do, and they don't feel that the local community is particularly hospitable to them. Rather, they look to the broader conurbation for a sense of place. They frequent parks either outside of or on the borders of Westtown. They strive to expand their networks to include people from other communities – people with access to other spaces, people, and opportunities – and they cruise the streets that lead towards Detroit. This does not go on just in Westtown, but in all the high schools around the suburban area. And the result is a network of arteries and meeting places where kids from all around the area explore the conurbation and seek each other out. It is not everyone who does this, only those who are looking for something outside of institutional life. Thus, although the Jocks and the Burnouts are salient and opposed social categories in each high school, they are also oppositionally inserted into the sociogeography of the conurbation.

If Burnouts meet people from other towns through friends, in parks, and on the street, Jocks meet them at interscholastic functions – athletic events, student government workshops, and cheerleading camp. The Burnouts meet people as individuals, whereas the Jocks meet people in their institutional roles. And in these situations, respect and admiration tend to orient in opposite directions. Burnouts tend to admire people with street smarts, something that is generally attributed to urban dwellers; Jocks tend to admire people with institutional smarts, something that suburban students tend to have more access to.

In this way, social practice within each school merges with geography itself. One might simply say that each school has the same social categories – that the Jocks and the Burnouts constitute a microcosm of the larger socioeconomic system. This is certainly true. However, the Jocks and Burnouts are somewhat distinct from school to school, and this distinctiveness is a function of the sociogeographic location of each school. Jocks in less affluent schools somewhat resemble Burnouts from more affluent schools and may even consider Burnouts in very affluent schools to be Jocks. A Jock in a high school next to the boundary of Detroit told me that she was concerned that, when she reached college, she would not be able to compete in extracurricular activities with the Jocks from more affluent schools. Attending multischool events of various sorts, she had had plenty of evidence that her school's Jock culture was different from that of more affluent schools and that she was not gaining the same exposure to such things as parliamentary procedure and large projects. Students moving from the urban periphery to more distant and affluent suburban schools report having to upgrade their wardrobes. One such student told me that although he had been a Jock in his original school, he did not fit in with the Jocks in his new school, and he eventually became a Burnout. This is not simply because he didn't look and act like a local Jock, but also because the Burnouts are more inclined than Jocks to value "urban immigrants" for their knowledge and contacts. The issue of looking like a Jock or looking like a Burnout leads us to the role of semiotics in the articulation of the local with the extra-local.

Semiotics, the Local, and the Extra-Local

Sue Gal and Judith Irvine (1995) have argued that our speech communities and the languages associated with them are ideological constructs – ideological with respect to linguistic theory and, more generally, with respect to language and society. They outline three semiotic processes by which we construct languages and speech communities out of unconstructed social and linguistic material. These processes are useful in understanding how the social order of each school produces and reproduces the wider sociogeography within which each school is located. According to Gal and Irvine, we create boundaries around dialects, languages, places, and categories through a process of *erasure* by which we make certain differences salient by downplaying, or erasing, certain others. So, for example, a new racial category in the U.S. – Asian American – has been constructed by erasing the enormous differences among Koreans, Chinese, Laotians, Japanese and so on and focusing on differences between all of these and other racialized groups such as European Americans and African Americans. We reinforce the oppositions by nesting them inside the categories they create, a process that Gal and Irvine refer to as *recursivity*. Thus, for example, the construction of a "black" and a "white" race is reinforced by evaluating people assigned to each group according to such things as relative darkness of skin color and hair texture, with the hierarchical relations between the two categories being mirrored in the cline of color within each category. And finally, we assign meaning to our categories through a process of *iconization* – attributing social stereotypes to linguistic practices themselves as a way of constructing a "natural" bond between a linguistic variety and the people who speak it. The common evaluation over the past century of peasant dialects in Europe as illogical and irregular – the products of ignorant and lazy minds – is a famous case in point.

The Jock–Burnout opposition is played out not only in activities within and attitudes towards the school, but in a wide array of interacting semiotic practices that range from territory to eating habits to hair styles. The issue of boundaries and borders is central to these practices, as Jocks continually symbolize their institutional affiliation and the Burnouts continually symbolize their urban orientation. Perhaps the most obvious is their use of territories – gathering places during down time in school. In schools across the United States, the equivalents of Jocks regularly occupy central areas of the school – gyms, offices, front hallways, and activities spaces. The equivalents of Burnouts, on the other hand, demonstrate their "just visiting" status in school by occupying peripheral areas – areas that touch on the outside such as courtyards, front steps and loading docks. In cold weather, Burnouts wear their outdoor jackets in school, whereas Jocks lock their outerwear in their lockers. The lockers and the outerwear, meanwhile, have similar significance. The Jocks signal their residence in the school and their institutional status with the use of lockers as a home away from home, the use of the cafeteria, and the territorial appropriation of extracurricular activity areas. Burnouts' mistrust of the school is itself part of the ideology of rejection, and they signal their rejection of the school's *in loco parentis* role by, say, not eating cafeteria food ("it's unsafe") and not leaving their coats in their lockers ("they aren't secure"). And the jackets with which Burnouts signal their "visitor" status frequently signal urban status as well; popular among Burnouts are jackets with Detroit or auto factory logos. These jackets simultaneously invoke class and geography, and Burnouts who do not wear jackets with insignia often wear the popular working-class jeans jackets over hooded sweatshirt jackets. The Jocks, meanwhile, commonly wear school jackets – varsity jackets, cheerleader jackets, or just jackets with the name of the school. In general, the Jocks' institutional orientation is manifested in a clean-cut collegiate style[2] – designer clothes in bright and pastel colors, school team jackets and sweaters, straight-leg jeans, short hair for boys and short or feathered hair for girls, candy-colored makeup for girls. The Burnouts' anti-institutional orientation, on the other hand, is manifested in an urban working-class style – dark colors, dark eye makeup for girls, long hair for both boys and girls, bell-bottom jeans, rock concert tee shirts, wallet chains, and studs. Students talk about schools in terms of their general character – most particularly, characterizing schools as "Jock" schools, "Punk" schools, "Burnout" schools. These also fit into a larger semiotic whole with such things as clothing. A Belten student, commenting on a local school with a predominantly working-class student body, characterized the school as having "bell-bottoms this wide."

In this way, the sociogeographic setup has a recursivity that builds social geography into each town and into each school. The Jock and Burnout social categories are reified by virtue of their insertion into social geography. This opposition reflects not just local but also regional character. In some schools outside of Baltimore, for instance, the opposition between *Jocks* and *grits* in the high schools echoes the larger opposition between urban and rural, northern and southern. In the southwest, the opposition between *Jocks* and (shit-)*stompers* echoes the larger opposition between townie and rancher.

These material symbols blend with linguistic variation to yield a similar recursivity, as the disposition of linguistic variables within the school map onto the same variables in urban–suburban geography. The current stages of the Northern Cities Shift (Labov 1994; Labov et al. 1972) appear to be spreading outward into the suburbs from the urban periphery. With few exceptions, the backing of (ɛ) to [ʌ], the backing of (ʌ) to [ɔ], and the lowering and fronting of (ɔ) to [a] are more advanced in the schools closer to the urban periphery than in the more distant, suburban schools. Further, the backing and raising of the nucleus of (ay) to [ɔy] is more advanced in the urban schools as well. (See Eckert 2000 for a more thorough discussion of these variables.) Within each school, the Burnouts generally lead the Jocks in the use of the innovative variants of these variables. Figures 5.1 and 5.2 show the percentage of innovative forms of the most salient urban variables, (ay) and (uh), comparing urban and suburban schools to the north and to the west of Detroit. As these figures show, the correlations with social category generally conform to the geographic correlations.

---

[2] These styles are the ones that were current in the early eighties, when the fieldwork for this study was carried out.

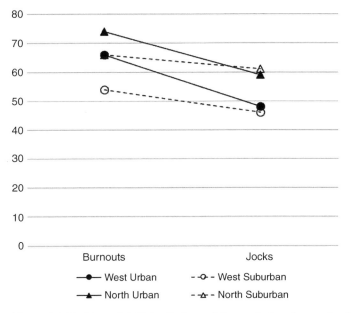

Figure 5.1 Backing of (uh) by Jocks and Burnouts in urban and suburban communities.

If we seek the key to social meaning in variation, the answer is not to be found in oppositions within the community (e.g. Jocks–Burnouts) or in oppositions among communities (e.g. urban–suburban) but in the merger of the two. It is in this way that the geographic and the social spread of linguistic change are one. Although one could say that an urban pronunciation of a vowel is associated with "those people out there," the implication is that local speakers are imitating, or aspiring to, extra-local people or characters. This is where the difference between the study of boundaries and the study of communities is theoretically meaningful. Qing Zhang (2001) has made this point in her study of Beijing yuppies' use of the nonmainland full tone feature. While critics see this use as a kind of "aping" of Hong Kong speech, Zhang argues that the nature of the contact between the mainland and nonmainland dialects of Mandarin has made this tone feature a common resource. Its use does not simply refer outward to nonmainland communities, but also effectively creates a category of Beijingers who span communities and, in the process, expand the relation between Beijing itself and those communities. In other words, the use of linguistic variables does not take place over a static social landscape but effects change in that landscape.

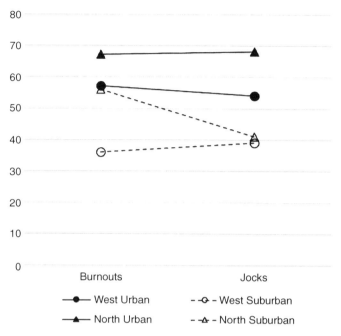

Figure 5.2 Raising of the nucleus of (ay) by Jocks and Burnouts in urban and suburban communities.

A Question of Method

During the two-plus years I spent in these schools, and as it became apparent that social categories in each school were simultaneously based in class and in urban-geography, I was able to shift strategies somewhat. But ultimately, my research design was category-based. I went into the schools looking for the adolescent version of the social class that had been our primary metaphor for explaining sociolinguistic variation. And, indeed, I found conflicting working- and middle-class categories based not on adult class, but on an adolescent social order; and based, not on birth, but on speakers' own construction of their places in that social order. But I was so focused on these categories that they took over in many ways. Thinking categorically, I did not give enough thought to the ways in which these categories served as foci for ideologies and practices across and beyond the community. The correlations shown in Figures 5.1 and 5.2 between urban variants and the Jock–Burnout categories spring not from the status of these variants as markers of category affiliation but from their indexical value (Ochs 1991) based on their urban associations. This value holds across the school population, and the same correlations that

I found between Jocks and Burnouts can also be found across the school population – In-betweens, as well as Jocks and Burnouts – as a function of urban orientation. Urban cruising, for example, is a key Burnout activity; it is also an activity engaged in by many In-betweens, as is smoking dope and cutting school. Also, cruising correlates with the use of urban variables across the In-between population, as well as between the Jocks and the Burnouts. Although my ethnographic work made this clear, my discovery of the categories led me to focus on category members at the expense of deepening my understanding of the structuring of diversity among the In-betweens. Moreover, it kept my gaze on the school rather than on the borderlands inhabited by the Burnouts and other people who do not base their lives in school. The methodological argument that I have made here – that studies of variation should examine the relation between the local and the extra-local – originated in view of both as given rather than as emerging in practice.

This chapter is intended as a contribution to method, which leads me to think not only about how we do our research but also about how we deal with the holes and shortcomings once it's done. I believe that it would benefit us all if we savored and discussed our shortcomings as much (or almost as much) as we savor and trumpet our successes. It is in this spirit that I say that the most important part of the research I've reported on here is not what I did but what I learned to do next time.

6   On the Outs

The Belten project was a turning point in my career, first because I hadn't realized as I embarked on this ethnographic study that it would lead me so far from the received wisdom in the field. Agency and social meaning had been part of the discourse of variation from the start, but not part of the theory. Ethnographic work held the promise of developing this discourse, but the focus in variation circles on macro-social categories and the development of statistical models was putting the "big picture" increasingly at the center. Martha's Vineyard was fading into the discursive distance. Not that my colleagues didn't think what I was doing was interesting, but it seemed that many considered it valuable only to the extent that it answered to the big-picture view. And the more I delved into the social and engaged with social theory, the more difficulty I had accepting the big picture as primary. This was also unfolding in the context of a broader hegemony of big numbers across the social sciences, as explanation seemed to give way to correlation.

Macro-social correlations are essential to the understanding of variation. The macro-social categories are well established, easily replicable, and essential to tracing the broad societal patterns of variation and the path of linguistic change. But in themselves, they only point to the lives and language use of the people who make up the categories. Social exchange tends to be about more nuanced things than being or not being working class, female or African American. This is not to say that First Wave theorizing about class and variation was wrong. On the contrary, it benefited from a deep tradition of social science research on social class. But we owe our understanding of class not so much to survey researchers as to ethnographers such as those in the Chicago School of Sociology. Nonetheless, survey researchers across disciplines commonly claim the scientific high ground on the basis of the replicability of their methods, viewing ethnographic results as hopelessly particularistic. And if the analysis of class variation was based on a strong tradition of social theory, this could not be said of gender. Feminist theory was not only new but apparently out of bounds for my male colleagues, and common ideology – women's supposed properness, status consciousness, and upward mobility – stood in for a theory of gender. I found that the more I talked about gender, the more I was ignored, so my search for explanation put me fairly early on in a somewhat countercultural position within the field of variation. And of course, given my predilection to feminist anger, I imagine I got abrasive.

The Belten project was a turning point in another way, as it pretty much precluded tenure. I threw myself into fieldwork when I should have been cutting up my dissertation into a series of articles. I could make up a bunch of stories about why I couldn't do both, but the bottom line is that I was too scared to publish. The first article I sent off was from my dissertation chapter on intervocalic *n deletion, and I received a very courteous and potentially helpful rejection letter from the journal editor. But I put it in a drawer and never looked at it again. The only paper I published from my dissertation was on the back vowel chain shift (Eckert 1980b), which Bill wanted for his volume on sound change.

Skip Rappaport, Conrad Kottak and Rob Burling, my mentors in the Anthropology department, warned me that I was following a dangerous path by diving into a new study, but they also supported me and the project. In the end, although the Anthropology department put me up for tenure, I was shot down at the dean's level. This is never a good experience, but my department fought for me for two years, so I didn't feel rejected by anyone whose opinion I valued.

Tenure was a kick in the stomach. But while I felt alone and scared, I never thought this was the end, and above all, I felt for the first time that nobody owned me – that I was doing my work purely for myself. I also felt tremendous support from my field. Paul Chapin at NSF picked up my salary so that I could finish the Belten project, my department continued to support me in every way they could, and I got lots of support at NWAV. None of my colleagues could help me out with the practicalities of unemployment once the NSF money ran out – that kind of support I got from the janitor, a great guy with an Olympic bronze medal in rowing. The academic job market doesn't correspond to the unemployment agency's sense of timing, but although I had to stand on line for my check every week, there was some leeway in reporting job applications in the early months. I applied for some academic jobs, and I half-heartedly explored setting up a consulting business with a woman I'd met in the schools. But that felt totally wrong.

Another opportunity came up when NICHD[1] approached me about applying for a grant to study adolescent smoking. This came from that agency's emerging interest in funding ethnography, and from a short paper I'd published on adolescent smoking in the *American Journal of Public Health* (Eckert 1983). While doing my fieldwork at Belten, I had been inspired to write this paper

---

[1] National Institute of Child Health and Human Development.

because it was clear to me that the schools' anti-smoking campaigns were counter-productive, since they failed to recognize the indexical significance of smoking in social polarization. The journal published the paper as a commentary rather than a scientific article since it was based on qualitative research. (I was insulted at the time but I'm over it.) NICHD invited me to Washington, where they sent me to talk to the National Cancer Institute's expert on adolescent smoking. A big numbers guy, he mansplained to me that my ethnography had stumbled upon the important fact – that kids who smoke have friends who smoke. Duh. I submitted my proposal, but since I didn't know that I had to specify that it should go to NICHD, it went to NIDA[2] instead. NIDA apparently thought the proposal was interesting enough to warrant a site visit, at which a bunch of numbers guys grilled me about my dependent and independent variables. They shut me down when I pointed out that those would be determined on the basis of ethnography. This was apparently NOT SCIENCE. So much for that grant.

Meanwhile, I was invited to replace John Rickford at Stanford for the spring quarter while he was on sabbatical. I arrived at Stanford on New Year's Day 1985, found a place to live, and settled in to teach the introduction to sociolinguistics and a seminar on ethnography and variation. Within a week, Ivan Sag and I began to hang out, and we got married less than a year later. This was pretty reckless, but neither of us had ever been in the habit of being otherwise. While at Stanford, I snagged a tenure track job at the University of Illinois at Chicago, so moved back into regular employment and into a commuter marriage.

Needless to say, I found it difficult to settle in to my job in Chicago, and my first year there I applied for a job in the UC Berkeley School of Education. I didn't get that job, but it turned out that psychologist Jim Greeno was among the people who attended my job talk, and he invited me to come speak at the new Institute for Research on Learning (IRL) in Palo Alto. IRL was a nonprofit research institute that was just getting under way at Xerox Palo Alto Research Center. It was a small interdisciplinary community of anthropologists, psychologists, computer scientists and linguists dedicated to developing a socially viable theory of learning. Among this group were anthropologist Jean Lave and computer scientist Etienne Wenger, and we bonded from the very first moment. My talk led to an offer, and for a couple of years I spent the fall and spring quarters in Chicago, and the winter and summer quarters at IRL. In 1989, I gave up tenure and moved to California and to full time at IRL.

Giving up tenure was another of my reckless decisions, but like the previous, it was a great one. Between the collaborative and truly interdisciplinary

---

[2] National Institute on Drug Abuse.

atmosphere of IRL, and Ivan's and my IRL colleagues' unflagging enthusiasm for my ideas, I began for the first time to feel as if I had the right to take up space. It helped to be in an interdisciplinary environment, where I didn't feel as if I should already know everything, and for the first time I understood that my ignorance was an opportunity rather than a death sentence. IRL was an exciting round of reading groups, seminars, and interaction labs, with a lot of space for thought and engagement with social theory. Jean's theoretical intensity and energy had a particularly profound influence on me. She and Etienne were working on their book (Lave and Wenger 1991) on situated learning, and Jocks and Burnouts became part of the discussions. It was in these interactions that I began to think about variation, and language more generally, as practice, and about the implications of thinking of Jocks and Burnouts as communities of practice rather than as social categories.

Communities of Practice

The macro-social approach offers no systematic connection between macro-social categories and practice on the ground, other than resorting to generalizations about the people who make up those categories. Lesley Milroy's (1980) focus on the class-based nature of social networks was a big step in the direction of explanation, connecting the density and multiplexity of networks to class on the one hand, and to linguistic focusing on the other. The community of practice zooms in on the network clusters and the practice that brings those clusters together. All the macro-social parameters that dominate variation studies – class, gender, ethnicity, age – structure the conditions under which each of us lives. And communities of practice emerge in response to the needs, interests and desires that arise under those conditions: car pools, bowling leagues, crack houses, bridge clubs, extended families, sororities, research groups. Every individual participates in a variety of such communities, which are not equally central to the individual's life, nor do they have equally distinctive linguistic practices. What is important is that practices, including linguistic practices, emerge in the course of the community's engagement in their joint practice, which includes not only establishing relations within the community but establishing a joint sense of the community's relation to the wider social context.

The community of practice gains meaning in a larger theory of social reproduction. Anthony Giddens (1979:2) sums up social reproduction simply in his theory of structuration: "In and through their activities agents reproduce the conditions that make these activities possible." In other words, structure conditions, but does not determine, social agency. Pierre Bourdieu (1977) posited the *habitus* as the means by which this takes place on an individual basis, and below the level of awareness. The habitus is the individual's internalization of the social, a set of beliefs and dispositions molded through early and long-term experience in a particular place in society. The habitus is "society written into the body" (Bourdieu 1990:63), shaping the individual's understandings, beliefs, and actions. The Jock and Burnout communities of practice emerged in response to differing places in the class system, and can be traced to children's life in the neighborhood.

My interviews at Belten generally began with the question "Do you remember your first friend?" and then traced the interviewee's friendships and activities up to the present. The Jocks, coming primarily from middle-class families, had parents who managed their pre-school social lives by arranging play dates. Many of them came from neighborhoods with few children, and while some played with a neighbor or two, their social lives were dominated by play dates with children of their parents' friends outside the neighborhood. The Burnouts grew up primarily in a couple of neighborhoods where there were a lot of kids, and they were expected to play with others in the neighborhood, usually in the care of older siblings. The ready-made network in the neighborhood provided autonomy, and the age heterogeneity provided the support, resources and information for which the Jocks had to rely on their parents. The age heterogeneity also exposed kids earlier to the prerogatives that come with age, which became a source of friction with adults, particularly in school.

These different social backgrounds brought kids into different relations with the school from the very start. School provided Jocks with their first opportunity to make their own friends, while it isolated the Burnouts from their neighborhood network. The Jocks' new freedom to make friends was shaped by their classes in school, so that their friendships supported the institutional age-graded structure. The age-heterogeneity of the Burnouts' friendships, meanwhile, put them at odds with the school's norms from the outset. Based as they were in the institution, the Jocks' relationships were potentially temporary and competitive, while Burnouts' friendships were long-lasting and supportive. These early differences, among others, led to different world views, ideologies and emotional makeups – habitus – which supported the differences in Jocks' and Burnouts' functioning in school and later in life. The communities of practice that structured these experiences – families, neighborhood friendship groups, school classes, Jocks, Burnouts – disposed Jocks and Burnouts to act differently, to see the world differently, to react differently to situations. Normal human agency, then, is not the same as free will. Our capacity to act, to make choices, is shaped by the habitus. And these acts are not necessarily conscious or intentional; many of them are quite automatic, part of the give and take of everyday life. But dominant ideology, particularly that of the school, overwhelmingly attributes them to the choices of individual parents, kids, and families.

There was some pushback on the community of practice construct, and I have heard the critique that while there is a procedure for discovering social networks, and for assigning speakers to macro-social categories, there is no procedure for identifying the boundaries of communities of practice. This seems to suggest that the construct is inadequate in some way, but I would begin by referring to Chomsky's (1957) critique that American structuralists confused theory with discovery procedures. It takes ethnography to identify a community of practice and to ascertain individuals' forms of participation in it. And while there is no cookbook for doing ethnography, a good ethnography yields empirical facts supported by principled accounts of analytic practice. Not everyone has the time or the inclination to do ethnographic work, but not everyone has to study communities of practice. They have only to recognize their role in a theory that links local practice to macro-social structures. Of course, if you can assign people to places in social networks, you can assign them to communities of practice. Every network is based on some thing people do together – work, friends, leisure activities, church, etc. – and communities of practice are clusters that form among these ties. The important part, though, is understanding the practice that makes the cluster a community, because it is in that practice that variation and style take on meaning.

Liberated by Gender

Although I'd been involved with feminist activism since the sixties, the burgeoning field of language and gender hadn't interested me much, since it was all about interaction and I was quite narrowly focused on sound change. However, I wasn't wild about the way variationists were talking about gender. Graduate students Alison Edwards and Lynne Robins and I gave a talk at NWAV in 1985 on the problems with using biological categories in variation. I wish I could remember what we said (Lynne can't remember either), but it got me thinking about the issue. And as the data emerged in my high school study, it became clear that there was a fundamental problem in looking for gender explanations in a male–female binary, and expecting that binary to have a single effect on variation across society. Emboldened by my new IRL sense of entitlement, I began saying stuff out loud, and David Sankoff, as editor of the brand new journal *Language Variation and Change*, asked me to write about gender for the journal's second issue. I suspect it was his intention to stir something up.

THE WHOLE WOMAN: SEX AND GENDER DIFFERENCES IN VARIATION

The tradition of large-scale survey methodology in the study of variation has left a gap between the linguistic data and the social practice that yields these data.[3] Since sociolinguistic surveys bring away little information about the communities that produce their linguistic data, correlations of linguistic variants with survey categories have been interpreted on the basis of general knowledge of the social dynamics associated with those categories. The success of this approach has depended on the quality of this general knowledge. The examination of variation and socioeconomic class has benefited from sociolinguists' attention to a vast literature on class and to critical analyses of the indices by which class membership is commonly determined. The study of gender and variation, on the other hand, has suffered from the fact that the amount of scientific attention given to gender over the years cannot begin to be compared with that given to class. Many current beliefs about the role of gender in variation, therefore, are a result of substituting popular (and unpopular) belief for social theory in the interpretation of patterns of sex correlations with variation.

Sociolinguists are acutely aware of the complex relation between the categories used in the socioeconomic classification of speakers and the social practice that underlies these categories. Thus, we do not focus on the objectivized indices used to measure class (such as salary, occupation, and education) in analyzing correlations between linguistic and class differences, even when class identification is based on these indices. Rather, we focus more and more on the relation of language use to the everyday practice that constitutes speakers' class-based social participation and identity in the community. Thus, explanations take into consideration interacting dynamics such as social group and network membership (Labov 1973; Milroy 1980), symbolic capital and the linguistic marketplace (Bourdieu & Boltanski 1975; Sankoff & Laberge 1978; Thibault 1983), and local identity (Labov 1973, 1980). The same can be said to some extent of work on ethnicity and variation, where researchers have interpreted data on ethnic differences in variation in terms of complex interactions between ethnicity, group history, and social identity (Horvath & Sankoff 1987; Labov 1972b; Laferriere 1979). The study of the sociolinguistic construction of the biological categories of age and sex, on the other hand, has so far received less sophisticated attention (Eckert, Edwards & Robins 1985).

---

[3] This work was supported by the Spencer Foundation and the National Science Foundation (BNS 8023291). I owe a great debt of thanks to David Sankoff for his very generous and important help with this article. The value of his suggestions for strengthening both the conception and the presentation of these arguments is immeasurable.

The age continuum is commonly divided into equal chunks with no particular attention to the relation between these chunks and the life stages that make age socially significant. Rather, when the full age span is considered in community studies, the age continuum is generally interpreted as representing continuous apparent time. At some point, the individual's progress through normative life stages (e.g. school, work, marriage, childrearing, retirement) might be considered rather than, or in addition to, chronological age. Some work has explored the notion of life stage. The very apparent lead of preadolescents and adolescents in sound change has led some researchers to separate those groups in community studies (Macaulay 1977; Wolfram 1969), and some attention has been focused on the significance of these life stages in variation (Eckert 1988; Labov 1972b). There has also been some speculation about changes of speakers' relation to the linguistic marketplace in aging (Eckert 1984; Labov 1972a; Thibault 1983). Most interestingly, there have been examinations of the relation of age groups to historical periods of social change in the community (Clermont & Cedergren 1978; Laferriere 1979). But taken together, these studies are bare beginnings and do not constitute a reasoned and coherent approach to the sociolinguistic significance of biological age.

Like age, sex is a biological category that serves as a fundamental basis for the differentiation of roles, norms, and expectations in all societies. It is these roles, norms, and expectations that constitute gender, the social construction of sex. Although differences in patterns of variation between men and women are a function of gender and only indirectly a function of sex (and, indeed, such gender-based variation occurs within, as well as between, sex groups), we have been examining the interaction between gender and variation by correlating variables with sex rather than gender differences. This has been done because although an individual's gender-related place in society is a multidimensional complex that can only be characterized through careful analysis, his or her sex is generally a readily observable binary variable, and inasmuch as sex can be said to be a rough statistical indication of gender, it has been reasonable to substitute the biological category for the social in sampling. However, because information about the individual's sex is easily accessible, data can be gathered without any inquiry into the construction of gender in that community. As a result, since researchers have not had to struggle to find the categories in question, they tend to fall back on unanalyzed notions about gender to interpret whatever sex correlations emerge in the data and not to consider gender where there are no sex correlations.

Gender differences are exceedingly complex, particularly in a society and era where women have been moving self-consciously into the marketplace and calling traditional gender roles into question. Gender roles and ideologies create different ways for men and women to experience life, culture, and society. Taking this as a basic approach to the data on sex differences in variation, there are a few assumptions one might start with. First, and perhaps most important, there is no apparent reason to believe that there is a simple, constant relation between gender and variation. Despite increasingly complex data on sex differences in variation, there remains a tendency to seek a single social construction of sex that will explain all of its correlations with variation. This is reflected in the use of a single coefficient for sex effects in variable rule or regression analyses of variation. This perspective limits the kind of results that can be obtained, since it is restricted to confirming the implicit hypothesis of a single type of sex effect or, worse, to indicating that there is no effect at all. Second, we must carefully separate our interpretation of sex differences in variation from artifacts of survey categories. I would argue that sociolinguists tend to think of age and class as continua and gender as an opposition, primarily because of the ways in which they are determined in survey research. But just as the class effect on variation may be thought of in terms of the binary bourgeois–working-class opposition (Rickford 1986b), and just as there is reason to believe that the age continuum is interrupted by discontinuities in the effects of different life stages on people's relation to society and, hence, on language, variation based on gender may not always be adequately accounted for in terms of a binary opposition.

Interpretations of Sex Differences in Variation

There is a general misconception among writers who do not deal directly with variation that women's speech is more conservative than men's. Indeed, women do tend to be more conservative than men in their use of those vernacular forms that represent stable social variables. On the other hand, the very earliest evidence on variation (Gauchat 1905) showed women leading in sound change, a finding that has been repeated in Labov's work in New York City (1966) and Philadelphia (1984), in Cedergren's work in Panama (1973), and in my own work in the Detroit suburbs. If these trends were universal, the coefficient of the sex variable (1 = female, 0 = male) in a variable rule or regression analysis of variation would always have positive sign for changes in progress and negative sign for stable variables.

But the picture is not quite as simple as this generalization suggests. First of all, men do lead in some sound changes. Trudgill (1972) found men leading in most changes in Norwich, and Labov found men leading in some changes in Martha's Vineyard (Labov 1963) and Philadelphia (Labov 1984). Thus, there is every reason to assume that sex differences may vary from one variable to another. As Labov argued (1984), one might expect different sex correlations with old or new changes, for instance. This could still all be represented by a single sex effect in a statistical analysis, but the sign of the effect would depend on the particular variable. Second, sex does not have the same effect on language use everywhere in the population. Women's overall lead in the population could hide a variety of complex patterns among other social parameters, the simplest of which would be a sexual crossover along the socioeconomic hierarchy. Labov (1984) found just such a pattern in Philadelphia, for several vowels, with women leading at the lower end of the socioeconomic hierarchy and lagging at the upper end. Statistical analyses in these contexts require more than a single sex effect; either an interaction should be included or separate analyses done for women and men. Not only is it a mistake to claim that women are more or less innovative than men, but at this point in our research it is a mistake to claim any kind of constant constraint associated with gender. It is, above all, this mistake that characterizes much current work on sex differences in variation. It is commonplace for sociolinguists to allow the gender categories that they use to classify speakers (i.e. male vs. female) to guide their thinking about the effects of gender in variation. In particular, men and women are perceived as categorically different, indeed opposite and opposed, in their use of linguistic variables.

Hierarchy

Labov's (1966) original findings in New York City clearly lined up socioeconomic class, style, sound change, prestige, and evaluation on a single axis. The hierarchical socioeconomic continuum is also a continuum of linguistic change, wherein extent of historical change correlates inversely with socioeconomic status. At any place along this continuum, speech style reproduces this continuum, with each speaker's stylistic continuum from more casual to more careful speech reflecting a segment of the socioeconomic continuum. A causal connection between the two is based on the assumption that speakers look upward in the socioeconomic hierarchy for standards of correctness and feel constrained in their formal interactions to "accommodate" upward. Thus, there is a folk connection between old and new, formal and informal, better and worse, correct and incorrect. The notion of conservatism in language, then, takes on a simultaneously historical and social meaning. Finally, responses to matched guise tests confirm that members of the community associate the use of linguistic variables with individuals' worth in the marketplace. With this overwhelming stratificational emphasis in the study of variation, sex differences in behavior placed along this continuum are seen in relation to it; hence, when men and women differ in their use of sound change, this tends to be explained in terms of their different orientation to class.

Labov and Trudgill have both emphasized a greater orientation to community prestige norms as the main driving force in women's, as opposed to men's, linguistic behavior. Trudgill's findings in Norwich led him to see women as overwhelmingly conservative, as they showed men leading in most change.

Furthermore, women in his sample tended to over-report their use of prestige forms and men tended to under-report theirs. He therefore argued that women and men respond to opposed sets of norms: women to overt, standard-language prestige norms and men to covert, vernacular prestige norms. Overt prestige attaches to refined qualities, as associated with the cosmopolitan marketplace and its standard language, whereas covert prestige attaches to masculine, "rough and tough" qualities. Trudgill (1972:182-3) speculated that women's overt prestige orientation was a result of their powerless position in society. He argued that inasmuch as society does not allow women to advance their power or status through action in the marketplace, they are thrown upon their symbolic resources, including language, to enhance their social position. This is certainly a reasonable hypothesis, particularly since it was arrived at to explain data in which women's speech was overwhelmingly conservative. However, what it assumes more specifically is that women respond to their powerlessness by developing linguistic strategies for upward mobility, that is, that the socioeconomic hierarchy is the focus of social strategies. There are alternative views of exactly what social strategies are reflected in women's conservatism. An analysis that emphasizes the power relations implicit in the stratificational model was put forth by Deuchar (1988), who argued that women's conservative linguistic behavior is a function of basic power relations in society. Equating standard speech with politeness, she built on Brown's (1980) and Brown and Levinson's (1987) analyses of politeness as a face-saving strategy, arguing that the use of standard language is a mechanism for maintaining face in interactions in which the woman is powerless.

I would argue that elements of these hypotheses are correct but that they are limited by the fact that they are designed to account for one aspect of women's linguistic behavior only: those circumstances under which women's language is more conservative than men's. Based on the multiple patterns of sex, class, and age difference that he found in Philadelphia sound changes in progress, Labov (1984) sought to explain why women are more conservative in their use of stable variables but less conservative in their use of changes in progress and why women lead men in some changes and not in others. Although his data do not show women being particularly conservative, he based his analysis on the assumption that women's linguistic choices are driven by prestige. What he sought to explain, therefore, are cases where women's behavior is not conservative. Based on his Philadelphia data, Labov argued that women lag in the use of variants that are stigmatized within the larger community, that is, stable sociolinguistic variables and changes in progress that are sufficiently old and visible as to be stigmatized within the larger community. Women's behavior in these cases, then, is driven by global prestige norms. At the same time, women lead in changes that are still sufficiently limited to the neighborhood and local community to carry local prestige without having attracted a stigma in the larger Philadelphia community. In this case, Labov argued, women's behavior is driven by local prestige norms. If this explanation accounts for the Philadelphia data, it does not cover the New York City cases of (aeh) and (oh) (Labov 1966), where women led in sound changes that had grown old and stigmatized. But more important, I can see no independent reason to seek explanations for women's behavior in prestige.

It is important to note at this point that three kinds of prestige have been put forth so far: (a) global prestige, based on norms imposed in the standard language marketplace; (b) covert prestige, based on opposition to those norms; and (c) local prestige, based on membership in the local community. Although the notion of covert prestige has come under attack, and conflated by some with local prestige, I have argued that all three of these forces play a role in variation (Eckert 1989b). Later in this article, I suggest that not prestige but power is the most appropriate underlying sociological concept for the analysis of gender-based linguistic variation.

Sex Differences as Opposition

If the focus on class as a continuum has led to the interpretation of sex differences in speech as differences in orientation to the class hierarchy, the focus on sex as a two-way opposition has led also to interpreting sex differences as sex markers. Brown and Levinson (1979) argued against the treatment of sociolinguistic variables as markers, pointing out that the correlations may well be masking intervening variables. Although much work on phonological variation does not explicitly refer to variables as markers, the view of variables as markers is implicit when linguists attribute individuals' use or non-use of a variable to a desire to stress or deny membership in the category with which it is being correlated at the moment. Related to the view of sex differences as markers is the oppositional view of gender differences in variation – a reification of a particular view of gender deriving from the ease of identifying individuals' sex category membership and reflecting the common expression "the opposite sex." Two instances can serve as examples in relation to gender.

Don Hindle (1979) examined one female speaker's use of variables in three situations: at work, at the dinner table with her husband and a friend (Arvilla Payne, the fieldworker), and in a weekly all-women's card game. Based on an assumption that speakers will implement vernacular sound changes more in egalitarian situations than in hierarchical ones, Hindle's initial hypothesis was that the speaker would show more extreme (vernacular) forms at the dinner table with her husband and a friend, because he believed social relations in that setting to be less hierarchical than in the other settings. As it turned out, she showed more advanced change in the card game. One might argue that this does not disprove Hindle's underlying assumption, that speakers show more vernacular variants in more egalitarian situations, since there is reason to believe that relations among a group of women playing cards on a weekly basis are less hierarchical than those between a husband and wife – perhaps particularly in the presence of a third person. However, he chose to attribute the use of extreme variants in a change, in which women lead community-wide, to accommodation to the group of women.

The theory of accommodation depends on the notion of marker, and this explanation essentially asserts that the speaker's use of the change among women was an attempt to mark herself as a fellow woman. One might consider, however, that her enhanced use of this phonological change at the card game is related to an affirmation of – indeed, perhaps a competition among equals for – some aspect of social identity that has nothing at all to do with gender. In other words, that these women are together in a particular set of social relationships that happen among women encourages them to emphasize some aspect of their social identities.

Whereas Hindle has attributed this woman's extreme use of a sound change to accommodation to women, others have attributed similar behavior to differentiation from men. Tony Kroch has argued that the curvilinear pattern frequently found in the socioeconomic stratification of linguistic variables is due to male speech only. Specifically, he speculated that if the sexes are examined separately, women's speech will show a linear pattern, reflecting the regular spread of sound change upward from the lowest socioeconomic group. The curvilinear pattern, then, is the result of a sudden drop in the use of extreme variables by men in the lowest socioeconomic group in relation to the adjacent higher group. This drop, according to Kroch (personal communication. And see Guy, Horvath, Vonwiller, Daisley and Rogers 1986:38), is the result of an avoidance on the part of men in this socioeconomic group of what they perceive as a female speech pattern. Labov (1984) found the pattern that Kroch predicted for the raising of the nucleus in Philadelphia (aw) (Figure 6.1), and Guy et al. (1986) found it for the Australian Question Intonation (Figure 6.2).

If one were prepared to accept this argument, Guy et al.'s data are more convincing than Labov's. However, in both cases, one could argue that it is only the lower working-class men's divergence from a linear pattern that creates enough of a woman's lead for it to acquire significance. In the case of Philadelphia (aw), aside from the working-class men's sudden downturn in use, the men lead the women in change in all socioeconomic groups. In the case of Australian Question Intonation, although the women lead in the middle class, there is virtually no sex difference in the upper working class. The lower working-class men's perception of the pattern, then, would have to be based on the speech of women at a considerable social remove – a remove that itself could be as salient as the sex difference. I venture to believe that if the pattern

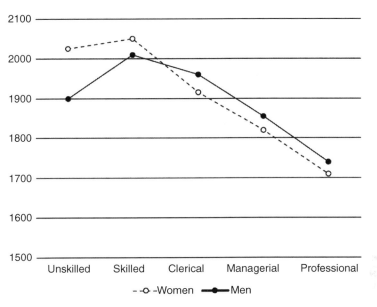

Figure 6.1 Occupation coefficients for F2 of (aw) for men and women in Philadelphia neighborhoods (from Labov 1984).

had been the other way around, with the lower working-class women showing the downturn, the typical explanation would have attributed their conservatism to prestige factors and upward mobility. I seriously doubt that these men's motivation for conservatism is upward mobility, just as I doubt upward mobility as an explanation for women's conservatism. But above all, it is problematic to seek the explanation of their behavior in simple differentiation from the "opposite" sex group.

I do not mean to argue that speakers never associate specific variables with gender, nor would I argue that there are no cases in which men or women avoid variables that they perceive as inappropriately gender marked. I would not even argue against the claim that men are more likely to avoid such variables than women, since there are greater constraints on men to be gender appropriate in certain symbolic realms. However, I believe that variables that function as something like gender markers must have some iconic value. The Arabic palatalization discussed by Haeri (1989) is a candidate for such a variable, although that case also points to intervening variables (Haeri, personal communication). But, as Brown and Levinson (1979) pointed out, a correlation with a particular social category may mask some other attribute that is also associated with that category. One that comes easily to mind in relation to gender is power. This

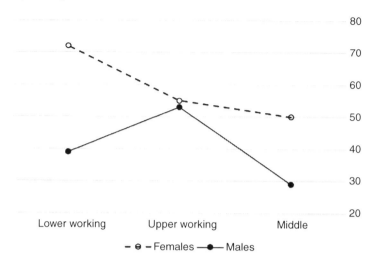

Figure 6.2 Probability of Australian Question Intonation use by class and sex (from Guy et al. 1986:37).

could clearly apply in the case of Australian Question Intonation. Guy et al. (1986) described this intonation pattern as a confirmation-seeking strategy, which one can assume is associated with subordination regardless of sex (Baroni & d'Urso 1984).

What I will argue is that gender does not have a uniform effect on linguistic behavior for the community as a whole, across variables, or for that matter for any individual. Gender, like ethnicity and class and indeed age, is a social construction and may enter into any of a variety of interactions with other social phenomena. And although sociolinguists have had some success in perceiving the social practice that constitutes class, they have yet to think of gender in terms of social practice.

There is one important way in which gender is not equivalent to categories like class or ethnicity. Gender and gender roles are normatively reciprocal, and although men and women are supposed to be different from each other, this difference is expected to be a source of attraction. Whereas the power relations between men and women are similar to those between dominant and subordinate classes and ethnic groups, the day-to-day context in which these power relations are played out is quite different. It is not a cultural norm for each working-class individual to be paired up for life with a member of the middle class or for every black person to be so paired up with a white person. However, our traditional gender ideology dictates just this kind of relationship between men and women. If one were to think of variables as social markers, then, one might expect gender markers to behave quite differently from markers of class or ethnicity. Whereas the aggressive use of ethnic markers (i.e. frequent use of the most extreme variants) is generally seen as maintaining boundaries – as preventing closeness – between ethnic groups, the aggressive use of gender markers is not. By the same token, the aggressive use of gender markers is not generally seen as a device for creating or maintaining solidarity within the category. To the extent that masculine or feminine behavior marks gender, its use by males and females respectively is more a device for competing with others in the same category and creating solidarity with those in the other category, and aggressive cross-sex behavior is seen as designed to compete with members of the other sex for the attention of members of the same sex.

Two other things follow from the specialization of gender roles, which may apply also to other kinds of differences such as ethnicity.

1. To the extent that male and female roles are not only different but reciprocal, members of either sex category are unlikely to compete with (i.e. evaluate their status in relation to) members of the other. Rather, by and large, men perceive their social status in relation to other men, whereas women largely perceive their social status in relation to other women.[4] Thus, differentiation on the basis of gender might well be sought within, rather than between, sex groups.
2. Men and women compete to establish their social status in different ways, as dictated by the constraints placed on their sex for achieving status. This is particularly clear where gender roles are separate, and in fact when people do compete in the role domain of the other sex, it is specifically their gender identity that gets called into question.

Power, Status, and Other Things

All of the currently leading hypotheses about the effects of gender on variation recognize, however implicitly, that linguistic differences are a result of men's and women's place in society at a particular time and place. What differs in

---

[4] This is an oversimplification. Gender inequality imposes a canonical comparison, whereby higher and lower status accrue automatically to men and women, respectively. It is this inequality itself that leads to the tendency for intra-sex comparisons and for the different terms on which men and women engage in these comparisons. Men tend to compare themselves with other men because women don't count, whereas women tend to compare themselves with other women with an eye to how that affects their relation to male-defined status. (My thanks to Jean Lave for helping me work out this tangle.)

these hypotheses is the specificity and the depth of the causes in society and, hence, their changeability over time and from community to community.

Milroy (1980) traced sex differences in the use of vernacular variables to differences in the nature of men's and women's social networks – differences that are themselves a result of material factors. Based on the understanding that dense, multiplex, locally based social networks enforce the use of vernacular variables, Milroy argued that where economic circumstances allow women to form such networks, their speech takes on the characteristics of men's speech under the same conditions. In this case, then, the explanation for sex differences in variation does not lie in differences between men's and women's fundamental relations or orientation to society per se, but in the differences in the circumstances in which they normally find themselves. Closely related to the dynamics invoked by Milroy, particularly to the importance of work patterns on the nature of social networks and to social forces behind the use of vernacular or standard language, is the notion of marketplace. Nichols (1983) showed that differences between women as well as between women and men can be a function of their access to jobs that determine their participation in the standard language marketplace (Sankoff & Laberge 1978). Both Milroy's and Nichols' examples suggest that it is the configuration of contact and interaction created by economic conditions that ultimately determines individuals' linguistic patterns, and in both cases the linguistic patterns may be as changeable as the economic conditions that underlie them.

The purpose of these analyses is to show that gender differences in variation are attributable to social forces that attach to women by virtue of their place in the economy. And whereas common sense supports this view, it is also evident that although employment conditions may change, the underlying relations of power and status between men and women can remain quite unchanging. So whereas economic explanations focus on the marketplace, they attribute gender differences in language to social forces that could presumably continue to operate on the individual speaker regardless of his or her personal relation to the economy. Since actual power relations between men and women can be expected to lag behind (indeed perhaps be orthogonal to) changes in relative positions in the marketplace, one can expect such a dynamic in language to outlive any number of economic changes. One might argue that the socioeconomic hierarchy, in this case, is the least of women's problems, since their powerless position is brought home to them, in a very real sense, in every interaction. Women's inequality is built into the family, and it continues in the workplace, where women are constantly confronted with a double bind, since neither stereotypic female nor stereotypic male behavior is acceptable. Thus, one might expect that some gender differences in language are more resistant to small-scale economic differences. In particular, the common claim that women are more expressive with language (Sattel 1983) resides in deeper differences than the vagaries of the local economy.

The domestication of female labor – according to Marx, one of the earliest manifestations of the division of labor – involves a strict division of roles, with men engaged in the public marketplace and women's activities restricted to the private, domestic sphere (Elshtain 1981; Sacks 1974). The man competes for goods and power in the marketplace in the name of the family and controls these within the family. Thus, although the woman is solely responsible for maintaining the domestic unit, she has no direct control over that unit's capital. Although a man's personal worth is based on the accumulation of goods, status, and power in the marketplace, a woman's worth is based on her ability to maintain order in, and control over, her domestic realm. Deprived of power, women can only gain compliance through the indirect use of a man's power or through the development of personal influence.

Since to have personal influence without power requires moral authority, women's influence depends primarily on the painstaking creation and elaboration of an image of the whole self as worthy of authority. Thus, women are thrown into the accumulation of symbolic capital. This is not to say that men are not also dependent on the accumulation of symbolic capital, but that symbolic capital is the only kind that women can accumulate with impunity. And, indeed, it becomes part of their men's symbolic capital and hence part of the household's economic capital. Whereas men can justify and define their status on the basis of their accomplishments, possessions, or institutional status, women must justify and define theirs on the basis of their overall character. This is why, in peasant communities as in working-class neighborhoods, the women who are considered local leaders typically project a strong personality and a strong, frequently humorous, image of knowing what is right and having things under control.

When social scientists say that women are more status conscious than men, and when sociolinguists pick this up in explaining sex differences in speech, they are stumbling on the fact that, deprived of power, women must satisfy themselves with status. It would be more appropriate to say that women are more status bound than men. This emphasis on status consciousness suggests that women only construe status as being hierarchical (be it global or local hierarchy) and that they assert status only to gain upward mobility. But status is not only defined hierarchically; an individual's status is his or her place, however defined, in the group or society. It is this broader status that women must assert by symbolic means, and this assertion will be of hierarchical status when a hierarchy happens to be salient. An important part of the explanation for women's innovative and conservative patterns lies, therefore, in their need to assert their membership in all of the communities in which they participate, since it is their authority, rather than their power in that community, that assures their membership. Prestige, then, is far too limited a concept to use for the dynamics at work in this context.

Above all, gender relations are about power and access to property and services, and whatever symbolic means a society develops to elaborate gender differences (such as romance and femininity) serve as obfuscation rather than explanation. Whenever one sees sex differences in language, there is nothing to suggest that it is not power that is at issue rather than gender per se. The claim that working-class men's speech diverges from working-class women's speech in an effort to avoid sounding like women reflects this ambiguity, for it raises the issue of the interaction between gender and power. Gender differentiation is greatest in those segments of society where power is the scarcest – at the lower end of the socioeconomic hierarchy, where women's access to power is the greatest threat to men. There is every reason to believe that the lower working-class men's sudden downturn in the use of Australian Question Intonation shown in Guy et al. (1986) is an avoidance of the linguistic expression of subordination by men in the socioeconomic group that can least afford to sound subordinate.

For similar reasons of power, it is common to confuse femininity and masculinity with gender, and perhaps nowhere is the link between gender and power clearer. Femininity is a culturally defined form of mitigation or denial of power, whereas masculinity is the affirmation of power. In Western society, this is perhaps most clearly illustrated in the greater emphasis on femininity in the south, where regional economic history has domesticized women and denied them economic power to a greater degree than it has in the industrial north (Fox-Genovese 1988). The commonest forms of femininity and masculinity are related to actual physical power. Femininity is associated with small size, clothing and adornment that inhibit and/or do not stand up to rough activity, delicacy of movement, quiet and high-pitched voice, friendly demeanor, politeness. The relation between politeness and powerlessness has already been emphasized (Brown 1980) and surfaces in a good deal of the literature on gender differences in language. Although all of these kinds of behavior are eschewed by men at the lower end of the socioeconomic hierarchy, they appear increasingly in male style as one moves up the socioeconomic hierarchy until, in the upper class, what is called effeminacy may be seen as the conscientious rejection of physical power by those who exercise real global power (Veblen 1931) by appropriating the physical power of others.

The methodological consequence of these considerations is that we should expect to see larger differences in indications of social category membership among women than among men. If women are more constrained to display their personal and social qualities and memberships, we would expect these expressions to show up in their use of phonological variables. This necessitates either a careful analysis of statistical interaction, or separate analysis of the data from each gender group, before any comparison.

Gender and Adolescent Social Categories

In this section, I discuss some evidence from adolescent phonological variation to illustrate the complexity of gender in the social scheme of things. Adolescents are quite aware of the gender differences I have discussed, particularly since they are at a life stage in which the issue of gender roles becomes crucial. By the time they arrive in high school, adolescent girls (particularly those who have been tomboys) are getting over the early shock of realizing that they do not have equal access to power. One girl told me of the satisfaction it still gives her to think back to the time in elementary school when she and her best friend beat up the biggest male bully in their class and of the difficult adjustment it had been to finding less direct means of controlling boys. In fact, she was very attractive and was aware but not particularly pleased that her power in adolescence to snub troublesome males was as great as her past power to beat them up.

Whether or not they wielded any direct power in their childhoods, adolescent girls know full well that their only hope is through personal authority. In secondary school, this authority is closely tied up with popularity (Eckert 1989a, 1990), and as a result, girls worry about and seek popularity more than boys. And although boys are far from unconcerned about popularity, they need it less to exert influence. For a boy can indeed gain power and status through direct action, particularly through physical prowess. Thus, when they reach high school, most girls and boys have already accepted to some extent that they will have different routes to social status. In many important ways, boys can acquire power and status through the simple performance of tasks or display of skills. A star varsity athlete, for instance, regardless of his character or appearance, can enjoy considerable status. There is virtually nothing, however, that a girl lacking in social or physical gifts can do that will accord her social status. In other words, whereas it is enough for a boy to have accomplishments of the right sort, a girl must be a certain sort of person. And just as the boy must show off his accomplishments, the girl must display her persona. One result of this is that girls in high school are more socially constrained than boys. Not only do they monitor their own behavior and that of others more closely, but they maintain more rigid social boundaries, since the threat of being associated with the wrong kind of person is far greater to the individual whose status depends on who she appears to be rather than what she does. This difference plays itself out linguistically in the context of class-based social categories.

Two hegemonic social categories dominate adolescent social life in American public high schools (Eckert 1989a). These categories represent opposed class cultures and arise through a conflict of norms and aspirations within the institution of the school. Those who participate in school activities and embrace the school as the locus of their social activities and identities constitute, in the high school, a middle-class culture. In the Detroit area, where the research I report on was done, members of this category are called "Jocks" whether or not they are athletes, and they identify themselves largely in opposition to the "Burnouts." Burnouts, a working-class culture oriented to the blue-collar marketplace, do not accept the school as the locus of their operations; rather, they rebel to some extent against school activities and the authority they represent and orient themselves to the local, and the neighboring urban, area. The Burnouts' hangouts are local parks, neighborhoods, bowling alleys, and strips. They value adult experience and prerogatives and pursue a direct relation with the adult community that surrounds them. The school mediates this relation for the Jocks, on the other hand, who center their social networks and activities in the school. The Jocks and the Burnouts have very different means of acquiring and defining the autonomy that is so central to adolescents. Whereas the Jocks seek autonomy in adult-like roles in the corporate context provided by the school institution, the Burnouts seek it in direct relations with the adult resources of the local area.

Within each category, girls and boys follow very different routes to achieve power and status. The notion of resorting to the manipulation of status when power is unavailable is in fact consciously expressed in the adolescent community. Girls complain that boys can do real things, whereas boys complain that girls talk and scheme rather than doing real things. By "real" things, they mean those things that reflect skills other than the purely social and that reflect personal, and specifically physical, prowess. Boys are freer in general. For example, Burnout boys can go to Detroit alone, whereas girls must go under their protection; this seriously curtails a Burnout girl's ability to demonstrate urban autonomy. The Jock boys can also assert their personal autonomy through physical prowess. Although it is not "cool" for a Jock boy to fight frequently, the public recognition that he could is an essential part of his Jock image. In addition, Jock boys can gain public recognition through varsity sports on a level that girls cannot. Thus, the girls in each social category must devote a good deal of their activity to developing and projecting a "whole person" image designed to gain them influence within their own social category. The female Jocks must aggressively develop a Jock image, which is essentially friendly, outgoing, active, clean-cut, all-American. The female Burnouts must aggressively develop a Burnout image, which is essentially tough, urban, "experienced." As a result, the symbolic differences between Jocks and Burnouts are clearly more important for girls than for boys. In fact, there is less contact between the two categories among girls, and there is far greater attention to maintaining symbolic differences on all levels – in clothing and other adornment, in demeanor, in publicly acknowledged substance use and sexual activity. There is, therefore, every reason to predict that girls also show greater differences than boys in their use of any linguistic variable that is associated with social category membership or its attributes.

I have shown elsewhere that the most extreme users of phonological variables in my adolescent data are those who have to do the greatest amount of symbolic work to affirm their membership in groups or communities (Eckert 1989b). Those whose status is clearly based on "objective" criteria can afford to eschew symbolization. It does not require much of a leap of reasoning to see that women's and men's ways of establishing their status would lead to differences in the use of symbols. The constant competition over externals, as discussed in Maltz and Borker (1982), would free males from the use of symbols. Women, on the other hand, are constrained to exhibit constantly who they are rather than what they can do, and who they are is defined with respect primarily to other women.

Phonological Variation

The following data on phonological variation among Detroit suburban adolescents provide some support for the discussion of the complexity of gender constraints in variation. The data were gathered in individual sociolinguistic interviews during two years of participant observation in one high school in a suburb of Detroit. During this time, I followed one graduating class through its last two years of high school, tracing social networks and examining the nature of social identity in this adolescent community. The school serves a community that is almost entirely white, and although the population includes a variety of eastern and western European groups, ethnicity is downplayed in the community and in the school and does not determine social groups. The community covers a socioeconomic span from lower working class through upper middle class, with the greatest representation in the lower middle class.

The speakers in the Detroit area are involved in the Northern Cities Chain Shift (Labov, Yaeger & Steiner 1972), a pattern of vowel shifting involving the fronting of low vowels and the backing and lowering of mid vowels (Figure 6.3). The older changes in this shift are the fronting of (ae) and (a), and the lowering and fronting of (oh). The newer ones are the backing of (e) and (uh).

The following analysis is based on impressionistic phonetic transcription of the vocalic variables from taped free-flowing interviews.[5] A number of variants were distinguished for each vowel in the shift. Both (e) and (uh) have raised, backed, and lowered variants. Backing is the main direction of movement of both (e) and (uh). In each case, two degrees of backing were distinguished:

$[\varepsilon] > [\varepsilon^>] > [\Lambda]$

$[\Lambda] > [\Lambda^>] > [\mathrm{ɔ}]$

---

[5] The transcription of these data was done by Alison Edwards, Rebecca Knack, and Larry Diemer.

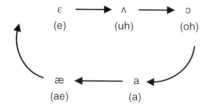

Figure 6.3 The Northern Cities Chain Shift.

Both variables also show lowering: [ae] for (e) and [a] for (uh). There are also some raised variants [ɛ^] and [ɪ] for (e) (the latter occurs particularly in *get*) and [ə] and [ʊ] for (uh). The lowest value for (ae) is [æ^]. The movement of the nucleus of (ae) has clearly been toward peripherality (Labov et al. 1972), as the higher variants show fronting:

[æ^] > [ɛ] > [e]

Two degrees of fronting were distinguished for (a):

[ɑ] > [a] > [æ>]

(a) also showed some raising to [a^] and [ʌ]. Finally, three degrees of fronting were distinguished for (oh):

[ɔ] > [ɔ<] > [ɑ] > [a]

(oh) also fronted occasionally to [ʌ]. Extreme variants in the main direction of change were chosen for each of the variables to represent rule application. These extreme variants are:

(ae) nucleus = [e] or [ɛ], with or without offglide

(a) = [æ] or [a<]

(oh) = [a<] or [a<]

(uh) = [ɑ] or [ɔ]

(e) = [ʌ] or [ʊ]

The two common social correlations for phonological variables in these data are with social category membership and sex. Sex and category affiliation are not simply additive but manifest themselves in a variety of ways among these changes. They interact in ways that are particularly revealing when seen in the context of the overall pattern of linguistic change. Table 6.1 contains a

On the Outs

Table 6.1 *Percentage of advanced tokens of the five vowels for each combination of social category and sex*

	Boys		Girls	
	Jocks	Burnouts	Jocks	Burnouts
(ae)	39.7 (n=531)	35.3 (n=286)	62.2 (n=392)	62 (n=287)
(a)	21.4 (n=548)	22 (n=350)	33.8 (n=450)	38.2 (n=350)
(oh)	7.4 (n=598)	10.2 (n=333)	29.8 (n=450)	38.7 (n=338)
(e)	26.2 (n=557)	33.2 (n=340)	23.8 (n=433)	30.9 (n=333)
(uh)	24.6 (n=496)	35.3 (n=184)	25.8 (n=364)	43 (n=249)

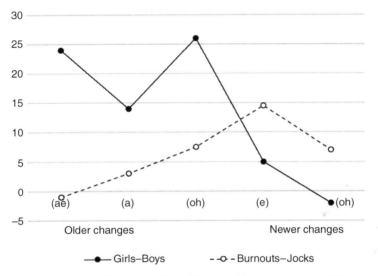

Figure 6.4 Contrast between girls and boys and between Jocks and Burnouts as differences in percentages when calculated for the combined data in Table 6.1.

cross-tabulation by social category and sex of the percentage of advanced tokens for each vowel. Differences in the percentages shown in Table 6.1 between boys and girls and between Jocks and Burnouts for each of the changes are displayed in Figure 6.4: one line shows the lead of the girls over boys, whereas the other shows the lead of the Burnouts over the Jocks, for each of the changes in the Northern Cities Shift. As Figure 6.4 shows, the girls have the clearest lead in the oldest changes in the Northern Cities Chain Shift whereas social category

Table 6.2 *Significance (yes or no) of social constraints on the vowel changes that constitute the Northern Cities Chain Shift (pl-values of log-likelihood test calculated for each constraint separately using variable rule program on data of Table 6.1)*

	Sex	Social Category
(ae)	yes ($p < .001$)	no ($p < .77$)
(a)	yes ($p < .001$)	no ($p < .16$)
(oh)[a]	yes ($p < .0001$)	yes ($p < .001$)
(uh)	no[b] ($p < .04$)	yes ($p < .001$)
(e)	no ($p < .38$)	yes ($p < .004$)

[a] Both constraints remain significant for (oh) when the effects of the other are taken into account.

[b] The sex effect loses significance ($p < .19$) for (uh) when social category is taken into account.

differences take over in the later changes. Note that each line dips into negative figures once – at each end of the shift. The boys have a slight lead in the backing of (e) and the Jocks have a slight lead in the raising of (ae). The statistical significance of each of the differences is given in Table 6.2. A treatment of variation that views variables as markers would call the fronting of (ae) and (a) "sex markers," the backing of (uh) and (e) "social category markers," and the fronting of (oh) both.

In an earlier article, I expressed some puzzlement about the lack of sex differences in the backing of (uh), having expected a simple relation between sex and any sound change (Eckert 1988). More careful examination of the backing of (uh), however, shows that a simplistic view of the relation between gender and sound change prevented me from exploring other ways in which gender might be manifested in variation. In fact, gender plays a role in four out of the five changes in the Northern Cities Chain Shift, although it correlates only with three out of five of the changes, and the role it plays is not the same for all changes.

As can be seen in Table 6.2 and Figure 6.4, the oldest change in the Northern Cities Chain Shift, the raising of (ae), shows no significant association with category membership in the sample as a whole. The same is true within each sex group taken separately (girls: $p < .96$; boys: $p < .22$). However, the girls lead by far in this change. The second change in the Northern Cities Shift, the fronting of (a), also shows only a sex difference, once again with the girls leading. The lack of category effect holds true within each sex group considered separately (girls: $p < .19$; boys: $p < .76$).

On the Outs

The lowering and fronting of (oh) shows a significant difference by both sex and social category, and these effects appear to operate additively in a variable rule analysis:

> Overall tendency: 0.182
> boys: 0.300 girls: 0.700
> Jocks: 0.452 Burnouts: 0.548

When the sexes are separated, however, it turns out that the category difference is only significant among the girls ($p < .009$) and not the boys ($p < .14$).

In the backing of (uh), category membership correlates significantly with backing for the population as a whole, with Burnouts leading, but sex does not. When each sex is considered separately, however, it is clear that the category difference is much greater among the girls. The backing of (e) shows a significant category difference, with the Burnouts leading, but no significant sex difference. In this case, when the two sexes are considered separately, the category difference is the same among the girls and among the boys.

Figure 6.5 compares the differences in the percentages in Table 6.1 between the Jocks and Burnouts, within the girls' and boys' samples separately. None of these differences is significant for (a) and for (ae). For (e) they are significant and identical for the two sexes. For (oh) and (uh), however, there is a clear tendency for there to be greater social category differentiation among the girls than among the boys.

These results throw into question general statements that women lead in sound change or that sex differences are indicative of sound change. In fact, in my data, the greatest sex differences occur with the older – and probably less vital – changes, involving (ae), (a), and (oh). I would venture the following hypotheses about the relation of gender to the older and the newer changes in these data. It appears that in both sets of changes, the girls are using variation more than the boys. In the case of the newer ones, the girls' patterns of variation show a greater difference between Jocks and Burnouts than do the boys'. In the case of the older ones, all girls are making far greater use than the boys of variables that are not associated with social category affiliation. I have speculated elsewhere (Eckert 1987) that the newer changes, which are more advanced closer to the urban center, are ripe for association with counter-adult norms. The older changes, on the other hand, which have been around for some time and are quite advanced in the adult community, are probably not very effective as carriers of counter-adult adolescent meaning, but they have a more generalized function associated with expressiveness and perhaps general membership. In both cases – the girls' greater differentiation of the newer changes and their greater use of older changes – the girls' phonological behavior is consonant with their greater need to use social symbols for self-presentation.

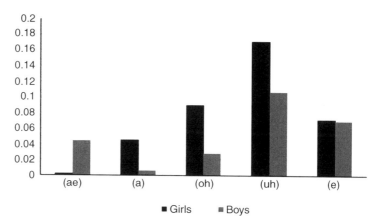

Figure 6.5 Absolute differences of percentages for Burnouts and Jocks, calculated separately for girls and boys (note that for (ae), Burnouts actually trail Jocks).

Conclusions

I would not, at this point, claim that the relation shown in these data between new and old changes is necessary, particularly in view of the fact that Labov (1984) found that women in Philadelphia led in new sound changes, whereas sex differences tended to disappear in older changes. It is apparent, then, that generalizations about the relation between sound change and gender are best deferred until more communities have been examined.

The first clear conclusion from these data is that sex and social category are not necessarily independent variables but that they can interact in a very significant way. It is the nature of that interaction, which occurs here with (oh) and (uh), that is of interest in this article. It is not the case with these phonological variables that there are large sex differences in one category and not in the other. In other words, sex is rarely more "salient" in one category than the other. One certainly cannot say that the boys and/or girls are asserting their gender identities through language more in one category than in the other. Rather, there are greater category differences in one sex group than the other. In other words, category membership is more salient to members of one sex than the other; girls are asserting their category identities through language more than are the boys. This is consonant with the fact that girls are more concerned with category membership than boys, as well as with the fact that girls must rely more on symbolic manifestations of social membership than boys. And this is, in turn, the adolescent manifestation of the broader generalization that women, deprived of access to real power, must claim status through the use of symbols of social membership.

These data make it clear that the search for explanations of sex differences in phonological variation should be redirected. All of the demographic categories that we correlate with phonological variation are more complex than their labels would indicate. Indeed, they are more complex than many sociolinguistic analyses give them credit for. Some analyses of sex differences have suffered from lack of information about women. But it is more important to consider that where most analyses have fallen short has been in the confusion of social meaning with the analyst's demographic abstractions.

* * * * *

I guess this paper marks the beginning of my public difficulties with the variation mainstream. Sankoff had Bill Labov write a response (Labov 1990) for the next volume. The response felt dismissive. I felt bludgeoned by numbers – numbers that I had no argument with, but that could point to more than one story. Around the same time, I gave a plenary at the 1990 NWAV, entitled "Where the Rubber Hits the Road." The talk called into question the reliance on macro-social categories to explain variation, and while I don't remember well what I said in the talk, I do remember blowback on my discussion of gender. I processed it as a bunch of guys refusing to listen. It wasn't until nine years later, at a conference that Carmen Fought organized in Ronald Macaulay's honor, that Bill (at his initiation) and I actually sat down and talked about what I meant by "gender."

It's become pretty clear to me recently that a lot of these feelings of conflict were unnecessary. My impostor syndrome made it impossible for me to engage with my critics. Fear shut me down in face-to-face interactions, as I felt my entire worth as a human being depended on my not being wrong. Because being wrong would mean I was stupid. This got in the way of dealing with – even enjoying – disagreements, and shut me out from what could have been the most productive (sometimes even fun) part of academics. Instead, I crawled into a corner and tried to figure out things all by myself, wasting my own time and not contributing to the wider discourse. Those nine years were scary, as I was in and out of academics, and felt conflict where there could have been lively engagement.

But my new focus on gender led me to new people and ideas. I had met Sally McConnell-Ginet in 1982, when my college classmate Joel Sherzer organized a series of talks at Oberlin, featuring Oberlin graduates who had become linguists. Sally was a pioneer in the study of language and gender, and when I began to take gender seriously, she was the person I went to. Serendipitously, she was invited to write an article on Language and Gender for the 1992 *Annual Review of Anthropology*, and I was invited to teach a course on Language and Gender at the 1991 Linguistic Institute at Santa Cruz. We teamed up on both projects, beginning a decades-long collaboration and a lifelong friendship. These events coincided with the heyday of the Berkeley Women and Language Group (BWLG). Mary Bucholtz and Kira Hall, both graduate students at Berkeley, were the primary movers and shakers in this group, which organized a biennial Language and Gender conference and published elegant proceedings for each in record time.[6] The BWLG conferences were not just the best conferences I'd ever attended, but the most fun and the most inspiring. They offered a diverse and challenging intellectual atmosphere, robust support for new ways of thinking about language and society, and a more critical theoretical discourse. As I focused increasingly on gender as structuring possibilities among women and among men, and on the central binary fact that women show a greater range of variation than men, my interest in style intensified.

---

[6] The Berkeley Women and Language Group held its last conference in 1998, and the following year a bunch of us founded the International Gender and Language Association (IGALA). I have been less active in recent years as my work no longer focuses on gender.

7 Foregrounding Style

The focus on style in variation had always been on style shifting, but the Jocks and Burnouts work had gotten me interested in style as structured co-occurrences of features. It also got me to see the significance of variation as tied up with that style. During my Stanford stint in 1985, students Sharon Inkelas, Melissa Moyer, Sue Uhland and I had gone to interview kids during their lunch break at Palo Alto High School, to find out what the social categories were. Knowing that people are reluctant to admit to categorizing others, we approached small groups of kids and asked them about their style. Most kids were intrigued by the idea and we began with each one describing what they were wearing. When we asked what other styles there were in the school, of course, we began to hear about the social categories. But in the course of this little project, social categories receded into the background, as style itself came into focus, and as I thought more and more about the relation between material and linguistic style.

Several years later, when I was at IRL, I started working on style with an amazing bunch of graduate students, along with Tom Veatch and Livia Polanyi. I pulled out the Paly High tapes from 1985, and we fell on an interview that Sue Uhland had done with two girls. We did an analysis of the style of the dominant speaker of the two, whom we came to call "Trendy." Calling ourselves the "California Style Collective," we presented our analysis at the 1993 NWAV. We never published it, though, both because we scattered at the end of that year, and because we found that the statistics were not as robust as we had originally thought. And as I look back, the fact that we didn't yet have a good handle on the California variables limited our effectiveness. While we still have the paper, the figure is lost forever as are some of the measurements. But the introduction to this paper was the first laying out of the perspective on style that gave rise to the Third Wave. Since people still refer to it, and since it is a good statement of the perspective, I include the introduction to the paper here.

VARIATION AND PERSONAL/GROUP STYLE

The following discussion presents a preliminary exploration of an aspect of style that has not yet made its systematic way into the study of sociolinguistic variation: that is, what one might call "personal" or "group" style. Group style is the basis upon which people identify others as members of such groups as "Valley Girl" or "New York Jew" or, at a more local level, "Burnout" or "Hard Rock." Such public naming of styles is a process of stereotyping – a reification of the named group as sufficiently constituting community to develop a joint style, and as sufficiently salient to public life to name and learn to recognize. These reifications then turn around and serve as resources for other styles – for those who may want to incorporate in their own style a bit of what they see as attractive, interesting or striking about New York Jews or Valley Girls. In this way, group style stands at a level of sociolinguistic practice that allows us to examine the production and reproduction of social meaning in variation.

In 1985, Penny Eckert, Sharon Inkelas, Melissa Moyer, and Sue Uhland did a series of interviews with kids on the campus of Palo Alto High School in Northern California, and in the nearby shopping center where many hung out at lunch and after school. Although the original purpose of these interviews was to explore social categories in the high school, the interviews were phrased in terms of style. People were approached with the following request: "We're doing a study of style. You guys clearly have a distinctive style – would you be willing to talk to us about it?"

Style is eminently public, and people are far more willing to embark on a discussion of style with a stranger than a discussion of social categories in their high school – a potentially political and sensitive topic. They are more willing to explore their relation to others in terms of style, since style allows them to get around the questions of status, stigma and judgment that are so highlighted in discussions of high school social categories. Nonetheless, once embarked on this topic, people are likely to move quickly and with abandon into discussions of the social categories in the school.

We discuss here the style of one girl whom we refer to as "Trendy." Trendy was a sophomore at Palo Alto High School when Sue Uhland interviewed her and her friend in the spring of 1985. The name "Trendy" did not originate with this girl. Rather, it was used by her schoolmates in other groups, who referred to her group, and to their style, as trendy because they saw them as responding to mainstream consumerism and building their style in terms of expensive brand names. This is reflected in Trendy's own description of what she's wearing, the request for which serves as the opening of the interview:

Foregrounding Style

Okay, I'm wearing, um, blue ACA Joe pants, Nike socks, um, a Ton Sur Ton jacket, and a Maui Tee Shirt.

In this interview, Trendy is placing herself within a social landscape peopled with social categories – with styles. In describing, commenting on, and joking about these categories, she is both positioning herself within this landscape and coloring the landscape in with attitude. This positioning is part of the mutual, community-wide process that won Trendy her name. Here, for example, are pieces of her descriptions of stoner girls, nerds, and cheerleaders:

TRENDY: The stoner girls wear like – some of them wear like kind of like cocktail dresses and high heeled shoes.
FRIEND: Oh yeah.
TRENDY: You know what I'm talking about? Like, just like bright colored cocktail dresses and stuff – and it's just kind of like – more like the San Francisco slut style.

* * *

TRENDY: Just – they [nerds] wear things like – I don't know, I know this one girl who wears like dresses and skirts and stuff that looks like she's like from sixth grade, you know – like wearing things that look like tablecloths and stuff, you know – just like with little prints on them and stuff. Just ugly ...

* * *

SUE: What kind of people are cheerleaders at Paly?
FRIEND: like the –
TRENDY: A lot of sluts – a lot of fat people.

The attitude that permeates Trendy's talk is not random "teenage" local color, but part of the process of the local construction of class, gender, and even age. Eckert's work (1989a) on high school social categories argues that these categories are a major locus of the reproduction of social class. The link between this very local style and broader patterns of variation is part of this process of reproduction. The guts of class, age, ethnicity, gender – the beliefs, activities, attitudes and power relations that constitute them – live in the everyday practice of local communities.

As Trendy talks about style, she *does* style. Her presentation of herself to Sue relies precisely on her ability to convey herself as the embodiment of a style that goes with a particular attitude and place. But the perspective we are taking is not simply that Trendy is "doing" Trendy. Such a view would suggest that she is simply performing a style and in the process presenting herself as a member of a group characterized by that style. This view would require that we accept three things as static: the group's existence, the style, and the relation between the group and the style. This static view would allow us to view the use of the style as simply constituting a statement on Trendy's part about her relation to the pre-existing group – for example, as laying claim to membership in the group. This view, which is the common one taken in studies of variation, is a useful abstraction from practice for the study of the place of the community and of the style in the social world. But we have chosen to focus on the practice from which this abstraction is made. Groups and their styles do not exist independently of their members' construction of them, and while that process of construction can be ignored for many purposes, it is still a key fact.

We see the performance and the construction of a style as simultaneous, and we see the construction of a style as part of the construction of the community. For precisely in the nexus between the group, the individual, and the style, lies the possibility for change. As Trendy uses her style, she is acting in and on the social world. And in this process, the meaning of both the style and the action develops and changes. And to the extent that her actions carry weight in her group and in the larger community, these meanings will change for the group and the community as well.

The construction of a style is a process of bricolage. Resources from a broad social landscape can be appropriated and recombined to make a distinctive style that will be identifiable not only by which resources it uses, but how it uses each resource and how it combines all its resources. Key to the issue of social reproduction is the fact that the choice of stylistic resources is neither neutral nor random. Any particular element that gets incorporated into a style may be local, regional, national or international. It may come from repeated face-to-face encounters, from encounters through loose ties, from observation in public, or from the media. But what all these resources have in common is that they have some kind of social meaning for the speaker who takes them up – the bricoleur. The meaning of an element of style for a bricoleur is the product of his or her interpretation of the social significance of the style that serves as its source. And this interpretation is based in a textured understanding of the relation between style and social address.

In this interview, Trendy, her friend, and Sue Uhland are involved in a co-production of meaning. This interaction is not only a presentation of Paly High styles to Sue, but part of Trendy and her friend's ongoing construction of their view of their social world, of their place and places in it, and of their style.

* * * * *

One of my Paly High interviews was with two girls who belonged to the Preppy crowd, and it turned out to be particularly provocative. These girls said that they had always admired the "New Wavers" (precursors of Goth) in their school, whom they saw as more independent. While Preppies wore designer jeans and pastel designer shirts, the New Wavers dressed primarily in black and wore pegged pants. In a move to show their partial orientation to the New Wavers, these two Preppies pegged their blue jeans. They were quite explicit that black would have been too much of a statement, so they had selected the cut of the jeans as indexing the aspect of New Wave identity that they wanted to appropriate. This was the ultimate example of style as bricolage (Hebdige 1984), and would stick with me for good. These girls had parsed the New Wave and Preppy styles, assigning meaning to visual elements, to be extracted and imported into another style. In this case, it was pants leg cut that was imported, but this selection also called up the de-selection of other elements of the New Wave style, such as color. And it was imported specifically into jeans, not other kinds of pants the Preppies might wear. I will return to this example later, but even at this point I want to emphasize that there's nothing random about bricolage. This is a particularly clear example of the link between stylistic elements and ideology, and the status of stylistic moves as ideological moves.

Back to Elementary School

The Trendy project unfolded somewhere between Stanford and IRL, and it reminded me of what I was missing being outside of academics. IRL was a rich social-theoretical experience, but it was distancing me from Linguistics. So in 1994 when Stanford came up with a half-time position in Linguistics, I jumped on it.

That same year, filling the IRL half of my time, I began a new field project that brought together my interests in style and gender. Suzanne Romaine (1984b) had placed the beginning of systematic phonological gender differences in pre-adolescence. It occurred to me that this coincides with the emergence of the heterosexual market in late elementary school (Thorne 1993), which brings a transformation of the age cohort's gender order. I thought that the emergence of gender differences in language must be part of stylistic practice involved in this transformation, and I decided to trace this process ethnographically. With the support of an IRL partnership with a school district in San Jose and funding from the Spencer Foundation, I began an ethnography in two elementary schools.

I followed an age cohort from fifth grade into eighth grade, working in two schools that were close enough to each other to go back and forth in a few minutes, but far enough that they served completely different neighborhoods. The school I call "Steps" served a poor and ethnically diverse neighborhood, while the one I call "Fields" served a predominantly white Anglo middle-class neighborhood. Christi Cervantes, a graduate student in psychology at UC Santa Cruz, worked with me throughout at Fields, but the principal at Steps preferred that I work alone. Christi was a great ethnographer, and far more meticulous than me. And having two ethnographers added amazing value to the work, expanding coverage, depth and perspective. As a result, the ethnography at Fields is in some ways more complete than that at Steps – something I regret deeply. We followed the age cohort intensively through the spring of fifth grade and all of sixth grade. In seventh grade, we followed our cohorts to two different middle schools. This was a challenge since our elementary school cohort constituted only about a fifth of their middle school class. I would have loved to follow them to high school, but by then I was pretty burned out and Christi needed to write her dissertation.

Doing ethnography in an elementary school was unbelievable fun – way more fun than working in a high school. Elementary schools are kid-centered, and teachers don't feel threatened by their students. And nobody seemed to feel threatened by me, so I always felt welcome. Every day of fieldwork was a giant dose of anti-depressant. I had stayed out of classrooms at Belten so as not to be associated with authoritarian practices – I learned early on that teachers would try to recruit me into those practices. The elementary schools were completely different in that respect. The teachers and the principal had no trouble treating me like another student. My entire lunch table at Steps had to pick up trash on the playground one day because I had failed to stop talking when the principal flashed the lunchroom lights. (This was the signal for silence towards the end of the lunch hour to make sure that kids actually ate something.) I had the advantage of a reasonable lack of protective instincts, so I almost never felt an urge to intervene. And the kids as well as the teachers understood that. Somehow what has made ethnography in schools come naturally is that I've never really felt older than the kids I work with. On the contrary, I felt like a traitor in the elementary school when I got in my car at the end of the day and went wherever I wanted. This is not to say that the kids didn't see me as an adult, but they saw me as an anomalous one – one who was interested in whatever they did, who wanted to understand them, and who didn't judge. And I saw them as people.

What Christi and I were following was the emergence of a peer-based social order, with a "popular crowd" at its center. The crowd was a community of practice whose shared enterprise was to lead the cohort into adolescence, appropriating adult social control into the age cohort, and setting norms for a status system based in heterosexual social practice. The following is the first thing I wrote about this work.

VOWELS AND NAILPOLISH: THE EMERGENCE OF
LINGUISTIC STYLE IN THE PREADOLESCENT
HETEROSEXUAL MARKETPLACE

The challenge of a theory of linguistic practice is to locate the speaking subject within a social unit in which meaning is being actively constructed, and to investigate the relation between the construction of meaning in that unit and the larger social structure with which it engages. It is for this reason that Sally McConnell-Ginet and I (Eckert and McConnell-Ginet 1992) have called

Foregrounding Style 115

for using the community of practice as the site for the study of language and gender. A community of practice, as defined by its originators, Jean Lave and Etienne Wenger (1991), is an aggregate of people who, through engagement in a common enterprise, come to develop and share ways of doing things, ways of talking, beliefs, values – in short, practices. For the sociolinguist, the value of the construct *community of practice* resides in the focus it affords on the mutually constitutive nature of individual, community, activity, and linguistic practice. For the student of language and gender, it offers the possibility to focus on the local construction of gender – to see how gender is co-constructed with other aspects of identity, and to identify what one might abstract from this as gender.

In the following pages, I will briefly sketch a series of events and developments as a community of practice within a cohort of preadolescents moves through fifth and sixth grades. Originating in a loosely assembled collection of childhood playmates and classmates, this community of practice develops in the form of a heterosexual crowd. The crowd's membership and practices are in continual and rapid flux as its members jointly move towards adult social heterosexuality. I will focus on the emergence of a local style among the female participants in this crowd – a style that they see as "teen" style but that others, depending on their point of view, might see as reflecting gender, ethnicity, class, attitude. Through an account of some day-to-day events, I hope to describe the nature of stylistic development, the interconnection of language with style in action and appearance, and its role in the co-construction of gender, class, age, ethnicity, and a number of interrelated terms of identity. These events take place at Steps Elementary, a school in Northern California serving a low-income, ethnically heterogeneous student population composed primarily of Mexican Americans, Asian Americans, particularly Vietnamese, and smaller numbers of African Americans, Pacific Islanders, white Anglo Americans and other groups.

The passage from childhood to adolescence brings the emergence of a peer-dominated social order. In the process, the very meaning of gender is transformed since it brings, most saliently, a transition from a normatively asexual social order to a normatively heterosexual one, transforming relations among and between boys and girls. While heterosexuality is quite commonly viewed as an individual development, observing preadolescence makes it quite clear that heterosexuality is above all a social imperative (Rich 1980), and changes in individual relations between boys and girls are mediated by a cohort-based heterosexual market. In *Gender Play* (1993), Barrie Thorne documents the beginnings of the heterosexual market in elementary school. She notes the frenetic engagement in pairing up, fixing up, and breaking up; and girls' engagement with the technology of femininity – coloring nails and lips, frequently with age-appropriate semi-pretend cosmetics such as lip gloss and felt-tip pens; and the rejection of childish games.

The transition into a heterosexual social order brings girls and boys into mutual and conscious engagement in gender differentiation, in the course of which boys appropriate arenas for the production of accomplishment, and girls move into the elaboration of stylized selves. Both boys and girls come to view themselves as commodities on the heterosexual market, but while boys' value on the market is tied to the kinds of accomplishment that they have been cultivating throughout childhood, the girls' value is tied to the abandonment of boys' accomplishment and the production of style and interpersonal drama. Girls become engaged in the technology of beauty and personality, learning to use a range of resources in which language use is elaborated along with the adoption of other resources such as nail polish, lip gloss, hair style, clothing, and new walks. It is not uncommon in fifth grade to see girls and boys running around, making sudden movements, rolling on the floor or throwing themselves to the ground, using their bodies in much the same way. Increasingly in sixth grade, girls stop running and start monitoring their facial expressions, striking feminine and dramatic poses, adorning and inspecting their hands in a disembodied manner, arranging their breasts. And boys begin to subdue their facial expressions, control their hair, spread out their shoulders, develop deliberate tough or athletic walks and flamboyant moves on the athletic field or court, consciously deepen their voices. The process of objectification affects both boys and girls, as they work to produce value as complementary commodities on the market. But the nature of this complementarity is not neutral but involves qualitative changes in girls' place in the world. As boys take over casual playground sports, girls replace vigorous physical playground activity with observing, heckling, and occasionally disrupting boys' games, and with sitting or walking around in small and large groups. The practice of walking around has in itself symbolic significance. Moving away from the crowd and walking around slowly, intensely engaged in conversation draws attention to those who do it, by contrasting with the fast movements of their peers, with play, with the larger groups engaged in games, and with the louder tone of children's talk. This walking, furthermore, is a visible occasion on which girls engage in intense social affiliation activities, negotiating heterosexual pairings and realigning friendships.

Not everyone is engaged in the heterosexual market. Indeed, the market is located locally within particular communities of practice – heterosexual "crowds." While any dyad or triad of girls can walk around and talk, only certain girls' walking and talking will carry status. The crucial ingredient is the public knowledge that they have something important to talk about – that the social relations they are exercising in their talk are important social relations – those of the emerging heterosexual crowd. The boundaries of the crowd are quite fluid, and part of community practice is the management of participation, marginality, and multiple membership. In particular, since among the girls much of the activity has to do with realignments, the management of fluidity is central to community practice. Thus it is not simple engagement in heterosexual social practice that signals the entrance into adolescence, but the cohort-wide co-construction of social status and heterosexual practice. Furthermore, the development of a "popular crowd" that is by definition heterosexual brings the cohort, simultaneously, into engagement with the world beyond the age cohort. Participation in the heterosexual market offers new possibilities for the construction of a public persona. The crowd dominates the public sphere, partially by inserting the private sphere into it. Heightened activity and style draw attention to those who are engaged in it, and make their private affairs public events. In this way, they take on status as public people. This "going public" is a crucial component of the process of maturation taking place in this age group. Such things as girls' trips to the mall, and gang-oriented territoriality, are primarily about inserting and viewing the self as an independent agent in the public domain.

Both the negotiation of heterosexuality and relationships in general, and the technology of beauty and personality, become professional areas, in which girls are recognized as more knowledgeable than boys. Since it is still new and mysterious, this knowledge is respected and a source of status and admiration from both boys and girls. Heterosexuality is, in some important sense, a girls' pastime, engaging girls more among themselves than with boys. Boys play a more passive role in the process, leaving the girls to do much of the initiating, and frequently passively participating in girls' strategies. One boy, for example, broke up with his girlfriend of six months at the request of her friends, who wanted to punish her for being "a bitch." There is an excitement about all this realignment, about venturing into the unknown. Seeking legitimate agency, girls opt for power and excitement in the heterosexual market. Seeing that they won't gain recognition for the pursuits that boys are taking over, girls choose to call the shots, and to become experts in a whole new arena. Girls become heighteners of the social, breathing excitement into heretofore normal everyday people and situations, producing desire where none was before. The direction of all this energy to the sphere of social relations throws girls into a conscious process of stylistic production as they jointly construct group and individual styles, and in the process propel themselves into the public arena. This stylistic production brings together resources from a broad marketplace of identities, merging aspects of gender, ethnicity, age-appropriateness, heterosexuality, class, immigration status etc. into one highly meaningful local style.

Linguistic style is a way of speaking that is peculiar to a community of practice – its linguistic identity (California Style Collective 1993). Briefly put, style is a clustering of linguistic resources that has social meaning. The construction of a style is a process of bricolage: a stylistic agent appropriates resources from a broad sociolinguistic landscape, recombining them to make a distinctive style. In this way, the new style has a clear individual identification, but an identification that owes its existence to its life in a broader landscape of meaning. Above all, that style is not simply a product of community practice – it is not just a way of displaying identification – it is the vehicle for the construction of this identification. It is precisely the process of bricolage that allows us to put together meanings to construct new things that are us and that place us in relation to the rest of the world. This process of bricolage takes place within communities of practice, and to a great extent is the joint work of the community and of the tensions between individual and community identities. I relate the following series of vignettes in order to illustrate the emergence of a complex style as the age cohort moves into heterosexual social practice. This emergence of style is accomplished in a complex interplay between group and individual identity and style (see Wenger 2000). In the following account, I focus on the interaction between Trudy, a stylistic icon, and the home girls, the community of practice that is most prominent in her school-based activities.

In February of fifth grade, as I walked out of the lunchroom onto the playground, Trudy and Katya, who normally played Chinese jump rope at recess, rushed over and invited me to come with them. They told me that they no longer always played at lunchtime – sometimes they just talked instead. Katya said "just talk" with a hunch of her shoulders, wide eyes, and a conspiratorial grin. They led me over to some picnic tables, telling me behind their hands that what they talk about is boys, and that Trudy is "with" someone. Once we were seated on the picnic tables, Trudy and Katya hesitated, giggled, and looked around conspiratorially. Trudy then whispered behind her hands, informing me that it was Carlos that she was with, and then told us both that he had kissed her. Katya "ooooo"ed and looked wise. I asked where he'd kissed her and she laughed uproariously and pointed to her cheek. We sat for a few more moments, and then went off to play hopscotch.

A few weeks later, as I was playing Chinese jump rope with Alice and two other girls, Trudy, Katya and Erica came along and tried to join in. Alice, whose rope we were using, said they couldn't join. In a fashion reminiscent of the way in which boys occasionally disrupt girls' games, Trudy and Erica jumped into the circle both at once, taking giant leaps onto the rope, creating chaos and laughter, simultaneously outjumping Alice and dismissing the game. Alice got upset and folded up the rope. This was the last time I ever saw Trudy play a "child's game." This is not to suggest that the transition away from kid stuff is abrupt – Trudy may well have played Chinese jump rope at home some more, as adolescent behavior is slowly incorporated into day-to-day practice.

Foregrounding Style 119

A year later, for example, Trudy reached into her low-slung baggy jeans to show me her new sexy lace underpants, saying, "Yesterday I wore kid pants" (meaning cotton pants).

Trudy moved quickly into the world of teen behavior, of heterosexuality, flamboyance, and toughness. She took to walking around the playground with a group of girls, talking and heckling a group of boys as they played football. Together, this group of girls and of boys came to constitute a highly visible, predominantly Mexican American, heterosexual crowd. Trudy became a key player in this crowd, flamboyant in her style and highly active in pursuing relationships among both girls and boys. As fifth grade drew to a close and sixth grade took off, crowd activity progressed fast and furiously, as male and female pairings were made and broken, as girls' friendships shifted, and as drama built with girls accusing each other – or girls outside the group – of "talking shit," and kissing or trying to steal their boyfriends. Trudy emerged as a stylistic icon: she had more boyfriends (serially) than anyone else, she was more overt in her relations with her boyfriends, she dressed with greater flair, she was sexier, tougher, louder, more outgoing, more innovatively dressed, and generally more outrageous than any of her peers. The highly prominent style that became Trudy's hallmark was simultaneously an individual and a group construction. The heterosexual crowd supported Trudy's activities, providing the social landscape, the visibility, and the participation necessary to make them meaningful. At the same time, Trudy made meaning for the crowd and for its members individually and severally, her actions drawing others into the adolescent world, taking risks in their name.

After school one day, a small group of girls fussed over Trudy, who was crying because her boyfriend had told someone that he wanted her to break up with him. "He won't do it himself, he wants me to do it," she sniffed. The assembled group of admiring and sympathetic girls criticized the boyfriend. "That's what he always does," said Carol. Sherry said "He just uses girls." Trudy sniffled, "I like him so: much." In her heartbreak, Trudy established herself as way ahead in the heterosexual world – as having feelings, knowledge and daring as yet unknown to most of her peers. At the same time, she gave Carol and Sherry the opportunity to comfort her, to talk knowingly about her boyfriend's perfidy – to participate in the culture of heterosexuality. In this way, her flamboyance propelled Trudy and those who engaged with her into a new, older, sphere.

After the breakup, Trudy "got with" Dan. "I love Da:n," she kept saying in my ear, the vowel nice and backed, "I love Da:n." During hands-on science, my tape recorder sat turning in the middle of the table. Every once in a while Trudy leaned forward to the microphone and whispered, "I love Da:n." Her group asked me later if I'd listened to the tape – they asked, with a frisson, if I'd heard what she was whispering. Her pronunciation of the vowel in *Dan* has special significance. In Northern California Anglo speech, /ae/ is splitting into two variants, raising before nasals and backing elsewhere. Latino speech is set apart from other local dialects of English with the lack of such a split – occurrences of /ae/ are pronounced low and back, and this pronunciation is commonly foregrounded as a stylistic device.

One day, a group of girls sat at the edge of the playground complaining that there weren't any cute boys (i.e. the boys in their class hadn't become cute over the summer). As they talked, they kept their collective eye on the boys who were goofing around nearby. One of them pointed out that there was one cute boy, at which point they all called out in unison, "Sa:m!" As they intoned his name, pronouncing the vowel long and low, the girls attracted Sam's attention as well as that of the group of boys. They moved on to make humorous observations about other boys, and about each other's activities with boys, hooting loudly after each observation in a kind of call and response. The boys began to get agitated, and Jorge yelled something at them. Trudy stood up, stuck out her butt at him and called, "Kiss my ass, Jorge, you get on my nerves!" Linguistic devices, such as the pronunciation of /ae/, the meat of studies of variation, take on their social meaning in use – in the occasions on which they are given prominence in connection with social action. Trudy's use of language, like her use of other aspects of style, has a special status. Her flamboyance is a platform for the construction of meaning of all sorts. As other girls report her actions to each other, as they take on bits of her style, they are propagating sound change (the backing of /ae/) along with the meaning that Trudy and her community of practice have imbued it with. This meaning, though, is constructed not for the vowel in isolation, but for the larger style.

As sixth grade got under way, the girls' crowd expanded, and dubbed itself the "home girls." They took to greeting each other with a hug in the morning as they arrived at school, and as they emerged from their different classrooms at recess, as they split up at the end of recess, and before they went home at the end of the day. At first awkward and self-conscious gestures among Trudy and a small handful of friends, the hugs spread and became stylized – a brief one-armed hug became the favorite. This greeting clearly indicated who was part of the crowd and who was not, at the same time that it endowed the crowd with an air of maturity. Fortuitously, in an attempt to regulate unwanted physical contact among students, teachers and administrators "outlawed" hugging when it began to spread, conveniently imbuing the hug with mild defiance as well. Hugging, thereafter, had additional value as an act of defiance, particularly as the girls, on the way to the playground at recess, took to stopping by one classroom to give a quick hug to other home girls who were being kept in from recess because of unfinished work or misbehavior.

Girls' open defiance towards teachers was incorporated into home girl style in the course of sixth grade. But most girls found it difficult to display defiance

Foregrounding Style

in the classroom, and once again Trudy stepped in for them. Her defiance, however, only verged on being openly rude, and aimed to be an entertaining stylistic display. One day, for example, the teacher went around the class asking students how they rated a report they had just heard. Trudy was inspecting her long red fingernails, and clicking them loudly on her desk to the admiration of many in the room. The teacher called out, "Trudy?" Trudy answered, "What." The teacher, mishearing, said, "Did you say 'two'?" Trudy said, "No. I'm all 'what.'"

Trudy sprawled across her table, squirming and calling out unwanted answers and comments to the teacher. She told me she had had too much chocolate at lunch and she was feeling "hyperactive." When recess finally arrived, she burst onto the playground, jumping on and off a picnic table shouting "whassup? whassup? whassup?" She climbed on the table, struck a pose with hips out, told me she'd beaten up Sylvia "because she's a bitch," and gave me a blow-by-blow story of the fight that would have put any tough guy to shame.

One day, Alicia entered the classroom, standing unusually tall. She strolled over and rested her fingertips on my table, tilted her head back, hand on hips, and said, "Whassup?" In this way she signaled to me that she was now hanging with the home girls.

All of these – the ritual hugs, the greetings, the songs, the accusations, the fight stories – are part of an emerging style. The transition into a heterosexual social order brings boys and girls into mutual and conscious engagement in gender differentiation, in the course of which girls move into the elaboration of flamboyantly stylized selves. The development of flamboyant linguistic style is a key part of this elaboration, and inseparable from the emerging use of other aspects of gendered style such as nail polish, lip gloss, hair style, clothing, and new walks. These stylistic endeavors are inseparable from the construction of meaning for the community of practice, and from the construction of an identity for the individual as a participant in that community. At the same time, they are what provide the emergence of the adult from the child – and for girls, the transfer of meaning and excitement from the physical to the social. What is particularly important about this entire process is that what will later be adult endeavors with grave consequences are initially engaged in for a kind of childish excitement and then for a sense of power in the heterosexual market, with no clear view of the subordination that lies around the corner. The development of an adolescent persona is a gradual process that begins with playing with small stylistic components – nail polish, a watch, a hair arrangement, a pose, a dance step, a facial expression, a phrase, a pronunciation, a song. It begins with the development of "attitude" toward boys, transforming them into objects, in relation to which one can display new styles of behavior, and play out scenarios. Initially a terrain for the development of new initiative, it gradually transforms into a discourse of female objectification and subordination.

* * * * *

I began to understand Judith Butler's theory of performativity watching these kids' joint transformation from children to teenagers. Building from the notion of the performative speech act, or "that discursive practice that enacts or produces that which it names" (Butler 1993:13), Butler argues that gendered acts are not the consequence, but the cause of gender identity. The social order (in this case the gender order) regulates the legitimacy of such acts, constraining individuals to perform them legibly:

[G]ender is in no way a stable identity or locus of agency from which various acts proceede [sic]; rather, it is an identity tenuously constituted in time – an identity instituted through a stylized repetition of acts. (Butler 1988:519)

While our performances are constrained and automatic, there is always room for small performative innovations, which can accumulate to bring about change in the social order even as it reproduces it. It is also how we progress through life, becoming slightly different people as we go. As Bambi Schieffelin and Don Kulick put it (Schieffelin and Kulick 2003:351), "All interactions performatively materialize different kinds of subjects." Trudy was, interaction by interaction, moving simultaneously through her moments, her days, her life – and the moments, days and lives of the people around her and the world around them. Trudy's affective display when her boyfriend dumped her was an act of interpellation, drawing her friends into participation in heterosexual drama. And their enjoyment of this new status, I might add, made hurt and rejection seem desirable. Trudy and her cohort referred to their friendships as who they "play with" rather than who they "hang out with." But playing was giving way to hanging out, as the girls spent more and more time engaged in social engineering than physical games. Trudy's interruption of the Chinese jump rope game was emblematic of her giving up "playing" for "hanging out." Each of these little moves was an infinitesimal piece in the transformation of the cohort.

Part III

The Third Wave

The dual IRL–Stanford affiliation was wonderful in many ways. I got to be Norma Mendoza-Denton's advisor, and she became part of the IRL community, where she wrote much of her dissertation (which became the basis of Mendoza-Denton 2008). But things were going downhill at IRL, and I mention it here because it suffered the fate of many wonderful intellectual adventures. IRL had been completely funded in the beginning by the Xerox Foundation, with the understanding that it would gradually become self-supporting. This turned out to be more difficult than people had expected. Government funders wanted curriculum development and corporations wanted consulting; few really wanted research, no matter how action-oriented. The need to attract corporate partners for workplace ethnography projects created internal tensions, and Jean, who blessedly refused to play nice, left early on for Berkeley. This was a terrible loss for those of us at IRL who came to refer to ourselves as the "scruffies." Rather than continuing to move forward theoretically, IRL began selling itself on the basis of Communities of Practice. I'm reminded of the quote (which I've never been able to track down) attributed to Wittgenstein, "Resting on your laurels is as dangerous as resting when you are walking in the snow. You doze off and die in your sleep." To my mind this is what happened to IRL. Theory became a commodity, and at that point, as far as I was concerned, IRL lost its soul. This happened to us as a community, and while some of us were more adaptive than others, most of us were in pain. I discovered that I had a talent for writing hype, and in my efforts to contribute to IRL's survival, I became alienated and disgusted with myself grinding out PR material. I still cannot tolerate the words *vibrant* and *foster*. Fortunately for me, an external review of the Linguistics department recommended that I be taken on full time, bless their hearts, so the year Norma graduated I left IRL definitively. IRL ended not long after, and I still mourn it. It helped me find myself, and I couldn't keep it from losing its self.

Those last years at IRL were very stressful, and I desperately wanted to be a full-time linguist, and to be able to pursue my linguistic goals guilt-free. I had taken up the elementary school research both out of interest and out of a need to support IRL. But I hadn't yet done justice to my high school work.

Jocks and Burnouts contained very little linguistic stuff, and aside from the 1988 paper included in this volume, I hadn't published anything very substantive. I had fallen into giving talks and then writing them up for conference proceedings, allowing my work to be guided by invitations rather than taking control. I decided to do a book bringing together all the elements of the Northern Cities Shift into a linguistic ethnography, but also a theoretical argument for viewing variation as social practice. This, of course, was scary, and took a lot of arguing with myself. And since my previous analyses had been done variable by variable over a protracted period, I reanalyzed all my data. The result was slightly cleaner files, but basically the same results. And a lot of time. It was on the basis of that book that I entered into the next stage of my theoretical life.

8 The SLIC Generation

My move to full time at Stanford in 1997 coincided roughly with Miyako Inoue's arrival as Assistant Professor of Anthropology, and with an extraordinary bunch of sociolinguistics graduate students. Eager to engage with social theory and style, many of them inspired by Miyako's course "Language and Political Economy," the students organized a seminar in the academic year 1999–2000, inviting a series of sociolinguists and linguistic anthropologists each to spend a couple of days with us. Thanks to funding provided by Stanley Peters, then chair of the department, we were able to invite inspirational figures – Mary Bucholtz, Nik Coupland, Sue Gal, Kira Hall, and Judy Irvine – to talk to our seminar and to spend a day meeting with students. We came to call this seminar SLIC – the Style, Language and Ideology Cooperative/Collaborative. While John Rickford and I were the instructors on paper, making the seminar an official course, the seminar was a collaborative initiative by an amazing collection of graduate students: Sarah Benor, Kathryn Campbell-Kibler, Andrea Kortenhoven, Rob Podesva, Jacqueline Rahman, Sarah Roberts, Mary Rose, Jen Roth Gordon, Devyani Sharma, Julie Sweetland, Andrew Wong, and Qing Zhang. Most readers of this book will recognize several of these names, because they are the heart of the Third Wave. Indeed, this seminar was the real beginning of the Third Wave – not simply because of the ideas that were coming together, but because of the community that developed around the ideas. Emma Moore from the University of Manchester and Pia Quist from the University of Copenhagen joined this cohort as visiting students while they were working on their dissertations, and while they had both missed SLIC, they have always been central members of the SLIC cohort.

SLIC was the beginning of a cure for my impostor syndrome – from the SLIC moment on, I have not felt alone. The original SLIC group molded the Third Wave, and successive cohorts of students have moved it along at a stunning speed. There's no question that the teaching has gone in all directions – freeing me up to think crazy thoughts and to always have a phenomenal community to think my crazy thoughts with. Some people find this community among their fellow students in graduate school, some with colleagues. I hadn't, and probably not because it wasn't there to be had, but because I wasn't ready for it.

126   The Third Wave

That same SLIC year, Don Kulick caused a stir with a paper on an online symposium, calling for a focus on desire in the study of language and sexuality.[1] At a time when it looked like the study of language and sexuality was going to go down the same binary path as the study of gender had, he argued that linguists should be focusing not on identity categories (e.g. "lesbian," "gay," "straight"), but on the semiotics underlying sexuality and its expression. While Kulick's paper was about sexuality, it was intended to shift the ground more generally to the study of "culturally grounded semiotic practices." I was asked to write a response to this paper for the symposium, a task that I learned a tremendous amount carrying out, since Kulick's paper was above my sophistication level.

The Slicsters organized the first IGALA conference at Stanford, and one of the featured events was a panel on Queer Linguistics. They put together a volume (Campbell-Kibler, Podesva, Roberts & Wong 2002) based on this panel, and included an improved version of my Kulick paper. This paper reads like a kind of Third Wave manifesto.

DEMYSTIFYING SEXUALITY AND DESIRE

Introduction

Don Kulick (2000) has proposed recasting the study of language and sexuality as the study of language and desire. This shift, he says, would move us away from a focus on identity categories (such as *gay* and *lesbian*), and from the enterprise of describing how people talk *as* members of these identity categories. In other words, he is calling for an avoidance of the category-bound pitfalls that haunt sociolinguistics, particularly the reduction of the social meaning of linguistic practice to an expression of membership in, or affiliation with, predetermined and fixed identity categories. He argues that by extending our interest to desire more generally, we will move away from a focus on the groups of people who engage in particular kinds of desire, to a focus on "culturally grounded semiotic practices." I certainly agree that a focus on the language use of identity categories in the study of sexuality (and indeed in the sociolinguistic study of everything) can be problematic. And I believe that viewing the study of language and sexuality as part of a wider study of language and desire

---

[1] This paper is not publicly available as far as I know, but its theoretical content appears in Kulick (2000), which he was working on at the time.

is an interesting idea. My concern is not with Kulick's proposal, nor with any of his arguments for this proposal, but with some pitfalls that surely await its implementation.

As Kulick argues (2000:271), the focus on identity categories distracts the analysis from sexuality itself. But I doubt he is suggesting that we dispense with such categories altogether. Discarding an interest in identity categories presents the risk of discarding the social from the analysis of sexuality. And moving to the study of desire intensifies this risk. As linguists, our interest in sexuality is in its social life – in how we use language to accomplish sexual ends, how we talk about sexuality, how we index sexuality when we talk about other things, how we use language in and around sexual activity, how we use language to organize ourselves socially around sexuality, and how we use language to organize ourselves sexually around sociability. Most readers will have no difficulty with this statement of the endeavor, and I believe that the statement demystifies the subject to some extent. But it is a little more difficult to recast this statement substituting *desire* for *sexuality*, because we can bring ourselves to conceptualize sexuality, but not desire, purely in terms of activity. And it is the activity that makes it easy for us to think of sexuality as social. We tend to view desire, on the other hand, as an individual, private, thing. It is desire, in other words, that brings the mystification into the study of sexuality, and it is in contemplating desire that we are inclined to fall into an asocial and naturalized view of sexuality. The challenge, then, is to adopt an approach that focuses on the social mediation of desire: to construct a view of desire that is simultaneously internal and individual, and external and shared. In the interests of such an approach, I wish here to explore the social nature of desire, and to expose the potential for the kind of mystification and naturalization that can stand in the way of this exploration.

Personae and Identity Categories

While Kulick does not intend it, his paper is apt to be interpreted as a denial that the study of identity categories and the study of culturally grounded semiotic practices can be compatible. I will begin by trying to rescue identity categories from the analytical trash basket, for while an exclusive focus on such categories is problematic, we cannot do sociolinguistics without them. The problem of working with identity categories in sociolinguistics in general lies not in attention to the categories, but in the way in which the categories are selected and the manner in which they are invoked. Problems arise when one limits attention to categories, takes them as given rather than as products of social practice, and focuses on boundaries rather than on what people do with boundaries.

The study of language and sexuality has to a great extent been dominated by a focus on the identity categories *straight*, *gay* and *lesbian*. Putting the sex/gender of people's sex partners at the center of the endeavor in this way folds sexuality into gender, and elevates a cultural preoccupation with choice of partner to a primary analytic scheme. The fact that these categories are actually lying on the ground – that this preoccupation exists – certainly makes them important analytic constructs. But their importance does not lie simply in their potential to yield ready-made categorizations of speakers. When categories are put at the center of analysis, they take on a significance that masks much of their functioning in practice. While indeed highlighted gay speech styles are prominent and interesting, their existence and their interest do not lie in category membership, but in the *idea* of category membership. The life of "gay language" is in the complexity of the social landscape that ties people to each other and to the rest of the world as "gay," "not gay," "maybe gay," "aligned with gay," and as educated, artistic, political, biker, shopper, and any number of activities and characteristics that come somehow to be tied in some circumstances to gayness. People have quite different orientations to their own sexuality and that of others, and to the relation between that sexuality and the other things and people in their lives. There may be linguistic effects that one finds only within communities of practice that are defined by sexuality. And these linguistic effects may spread beyond these communities of practice to the extent that people wish to project affiliation with the practice of these communities, whether they are actually participants in them or not. And the practices that they affiliate with may not be the sexual ones, but something else altogether. And at this point, sexuality bleeds into the rest of the world, as the categories defined by choice of sexual partner simply provide the background against which all kinds of meaning can be made.

In this volume, Katherine Campbell-Kibler, Rob Podesva and Sarah Roberts approach the study of "gay" speech in terms of the use of a range of linguistic resources to position oneself in a variety of ways in a broader social landscape – a landscape that is peopled not by gays and straights, but by gays, straights, lawyers, liberals, conservatives, serious people, flamboyant people, etc. As they say, "the idea of a singular 'gay way of speaking' homogenizes the diversity within the gay community and reifies as gay certain linguistic practices that are shared throughout society." Examining the release of word-final stops in the speech style of a gay activist lawyer, they emphasize that while this feature has been frequently associated with gay speech, this lawyer's status as gay in this situation is inseparable from his status as an activist, a lawyer, a serious and articulate person. And his linguistic style conveys the entire package. But the fact that this feature has been found in the speech of gay people does not make it gay. That is, it does not mean that this feature means 'gay.' It's far more interesting than that.

Sarah Benor (2001) has noted that the release of final stops is characteristic of "Jewish speech" and Mary Bucholtz (1996) has shown its use by teenage girls in constructing a "nerd" style. To say that stop release is "gay" is both incorrect and uninteresting. It is the very fact that this linguistic resource is available to everyone, and used by a variety of people in constructing styles that makes it interesting. And the wide range of its use is what makes it useful for the construction of particular kinds of styles that include "gay" as part of them. The question is, then, is the release of final stops associated with something like articulateness? And if so, what is the role of this meaning in the construction of different gay styles?

Note that as we talk about variation at this level, we move away from categories to something more like personae. The lawyer is presenting himself not as a gay man, or as a lawyer, or as an activist, but as a particular intersection of these – and no doubt other things. But the success of his presentation of a persona depends on his ability to call on categories to make that persona meaningful and recognizable. Personae are built against the background of a social landscape – a landscape that is rendered meaningful by categories in varying stages of reification. One might say that an identity category is a reified locus of iterability. *Gay*, *straight*, and *Jew* are what one might call major identity categories. *Nerd* is an identity category when people – including the nerds – make it one. What about compulsive shoppers? Shoe fetishists? To the extent that people identify themselves as aligned in some way by their habits of accumulation – with, for example, the help of the institutionalizing effect of such things as self-help books and support groups – they come to constitute identity categories. And as they constitute identity categories, they are no doubt more likely to develop common ways of speaking.

Naturalizing Sexuality, Desire and Emotion

As we move into the use of variables across the social landscape, we move the variationist enterprise closer to the semiotic practices that Kulick argues should be at the center of the study of language and desire or sexuality. But things such as stop release are still related to what one might call recognized properties of people, available for study divorced from the interactions they facilitate. But Kulick raises the interest of precisely the kinds of linguistic practices that resist association with categories of people:

the sexual desire of a man for a woman is conveyed through a range of semiotic codes that may or may not be conscious, but that are recognizable as conveying desire because they are iterable signs that continually get recirculated in social life. The iterability of codes is what allows us to recognize desire as desire. This means that all the codes are resources available for anyone – whether straight, gay, bisexual, shoe fetishists, or anything else – to use. (Kulick 2000:273)

A focus on how people talk to their lovers, how they talk about sex, or what kinds of vocalizations they make when they're engaged in sexual acts is sociolinguistically interesting to the extent that it links these in a meaningful way to wider conventions of social and linguistic practice. What are the limits of these conventions? Just as variationists suffer from the tendency to think of identity categories in terms of those that appear in sociology textbooks, we also don't tend to pay attention to variables like voice quality or intonation – most of us are terminally stuck on apparent vowel changes in progress. It may well be that the linguistic units we are quantifying are not the ones that are actually doing social work. For example, the choice of phonological variables is often led by an interest in certain parts of the phonology – as in the case of the Northern Cities Vowel Shift in my own work (Eckert 2000) – rather than by virtue of their possible social meaning. The study of desire presents a particularly interesting challenge, not just because we begin with the social meaning to seek our variables, but because some of the variables that potentially signal affect may originate outside the linguistic system as currently defined. I would argue that when we move into the realm of sexuality and desire, we move into a new set of semiotic practices that will stretch the tolerance of sociolinguistics, particularly of variationist sociolinguistics. And I want to go there.

It is important to recognize the great potential for naturalization in the study of sexuality in its relation to language. And I would argue that this potential increases as our focus shifts to desire and to emotion more generally. The shift is likely to awaken the belief that there is something more real or basic – something more sexy – about desire than about, for instance, identity categories. The naturalizing force of discourses of sexuality lies in the location of desire in the body. The focus on where our libido leads us – whether into identity categories or into expressions of desire – allows us to ignore that the centerpiece of sexual ideology is that sexual desire is *natural*, unfolding unmediated from a physiological and individual need. Cementing this centerpiece into place is the concern with the social allocation of libido: One must not have too much or too little libido for the social location of one's body. Women should have less than men, European Americans fear that African Americans have more than they do, and a classmate in college once told me that Jewish men had too much. In order to get on with it, we need to recognize that sexuality is eminently social, and that our desires and emotions do not form our social lives, but are formed by our social lives as well. But sexuality is not just about desire; it is also about undesire. For many, perhaps particularly victims of assault, abuse, and unwanted attention, sexuality can be as much about revulsion, fear, or lack of desire as it is about desire. It is all framed by desire, of course – and by what one might call the desire imperative – but we cannot study desire and be done with sexuality. So perhaps the study of sexuality is not located within a study

The SLIC Generation 131

of desire, but overlaps with it. Perhaps the study of desire is located within a more general study of affect.

So the study of sexuality will involve the social mediation of the "natural." Of particular interest in this regard is the potential for "natural" sounds to be used as conventionalized expressions of inner states – for example, as what Erving Goffman (1981) refers to as *response cries*. Goffman argues that "eruptions" such as *ouch!, oops!, shit!, brrr!, eek!* make a momentary and limited claim on the attention of others in the situation, displaying the utterer's alignment to immediate events (such as tripping on the sidewalk or walking out into a snowstorm). The response cry thus draws the attention of others to the utterer's inner state (or what the utterer would claim to be his or her inner state).

> Just as most public arrangements oblige and induce us to be silent, and many other arrangements to talk, so a third set allows and obliges us momentarily to open up our thoughts and feelings and ourselves through sound to whosoever is present. Response cries, then, do not mark a flooding of emotion outward, but a flooding of relevance in. (Goffman 1981:121)

In other words, response cries are not just socially mediated inner eruptions. Rather, the inventory of such cries constitutes a culturally sanctioned set of inner feelings – the broader set of "unconscious foreclosures" (Kulick 2000:274–5).

These sounds also can be exploited for more general variables. A moan can occur as a response cry marking sexual pleasure. It can also be built into voice quality, producing a variety of voice qualities that I will loosely refer to as "sexy voice," and that many people adopt to "do" sexually aroused. Producing sexy voice can be auto-erotic, it can arouse others, and it can signal arousal. People can use sexy voice independently of actual arousal to engage others in sexual activity, to harass others sexually, to present themselves as sexually aroused, or to mock someone who does not arouse them, to present themselves as a sexy person. Sexy voice can be used to express cathexis of all sorts – for things that feel good like food, perfumes, soft fabrics; and for more distantly desirable things such as articles of clothing, works of art, pieces of furniture, flowers, cars, buildings, jobs. And the repeated expression of cathexis for particular classes of objects can contribute to the construction of a persona – perhaps as a compulsive shopper, an artistic person, a sensual person. But that persona is derived from a quality shared with others, and that sense of sharing is the beginning of an identity category.

Semiotic practices are available – among other things – for the production and reproduction of identity categories. Sexy voice can be combined with other linguistic resources to construct a variety of styles, and it is a voice quality that one might adopt in making sexiness – or by extension promiscuity – central to one's persona. In this way, what is a strategic resource may become common enough in some people's speech that it can be said to be part of their style, and it may signal to others that they belong to a category of sexy or promiscuous people – whether or not, in practice, they are sexy or promiscuous.

We can identify semiotic resources, but trying to separate them from the people that use them is assuming a homogeneous speech community. Semiotic resources are laden with their social histories, relating what an individual does to things that categories of people do. Those categories may be the classical ones, they may be related to the classical ones, or they may lie somewhere else altogether. Right down to silence, sighs or grunts, we have some idea of how our vocalizations (or lack thereof) fit into common and uncommon practice. But the popular identity categories have a kind of public and ideological status that makes them a particular kind of social, hence linguistic, resource, both because they mirror the current focus of sexual ideology, and because the negotiation of membership and identity has far-reaching effects on language. But we're talking degree, not difference here. Moving from identity category as given to the use of semiotic resources in stylistic production focuses on the use of language to produce the fluid connection between personae and identity categories.

The very mention of the word *desire* invokes the specter of the natural. Society mystifies and romanticizes desire, and in the study of desire, we have to problematize not only its objects but its source. The expansion of focus from language and sexuality to language and desire should not extend naturalistic arguments into the study of desire but should, on the contrary, draw the study of language and sexuality away from such arguments. Perhaps, in fact, the analytic endeavor should be a study of naturalizeable linguistic resources. The identity categories that dominate sociolinguistic work have varying potential for naturalization – gender has greater potential than age or race, which in turn have greater potential than class. The conventionalization of overall voice pitch builds on a statistical difference in post-pubertal fundamental frequency. But the availability of "natural" sounds for conventionalization places sexuality in a privileged position – along with fear, sadness and anger. Indeed, it places sexuality in the complex of emotions, another area in which we have erased history. Emotions, like sexual desire, are commonly treated as unmediated natural responses. We read that as part of their socialization, boys learn not to cry when they're overcome with sadness. But we don't read that equally, girls learn *to* cry when they're not so overcome, and as they learn to cry they may eventually learn to be overcome. The management of emotion is not simply a matter of suppressing the "natural" – but of constructing it. In fact, much of the study of development could well focus on the appropriation and construction of the natural. It is particularly important in this regard to recognize the extent to which the sexual order serves not only the gender order but the social order more generally.

Sex, Desire, Emotion and the Heterosexual Market

At the 1999 Linguistic Institute at the University of Illinois, I asked the students in my class on the ethnographic study of variation to think of an age-related social construct that could be important for the study of variation. One group suggested the loss of virginity. It was not the sexual initiation itself that they were viewing as related to language, but the social salience of sexual activity at a certain life stage. Indeed, during the life stage when people are expected to be moving into sexual activity with others, orientation to this activity becomes an important focus in the structuring of identities and alliances. And as time goes by, the female categories of *slut* and *nice girl* become major sexually defined categories, which in fact correlate locally with sociolinguistic variables.

My own recent work, in which I've followed an age cohort from late childhood (fifth grade) into adolescence[2] tells me that heterosexual practice structures the emergence of the peer-dominated social order that separates adolescence from childhood. And its beginnings – and its middle – are anything but sexual. Rather, the adolescent social order emerges in such a way as to provide a structure in advance for organizing sexual desire.

During childhood, children's social lives in school are to a great extent circumscribed by the classroom unit, and dominated by the classroom teacher. In the transition from childhood to adolescence, the student cohort organizes itself into a peer-based social order through a process in which they jointly transcend the classroom, and appropriate power and authority from school adults. Fundamental to organizing a social order is the need to establish a locus for the negotiation of knowledge and value. This locus emerges in the elementary school in the establishment of a heterosexual market. It is well known that in late elementary school, a subset of kids begin a frantic and highly visible activity around forming boy–girl couples.[3] These couples form and break up at a dizzying rate – most last a few days, maybe a couple of weeks. But an alliance that begins in morning recess can easily be over by lunch.

Most of the alliances are achieved through one or more intermediaries, and have more to do with relations among intermediaries than with relations between the two people who are being paired up. The relationships themselves are almost entirely instrumental, and most of the activity is about getting together or breaking up rather than actually being together. In fact, the activity is engaged in, not by the members of the couples, but as a collaborative endeavor that defines a newly formed heterosocial community of practice – an emerging popular crowd. As the first major girl–boy joint endeavor, this crowd represents to all the new social order, and the co-construction of social status

---

[2] This research has been supported by the Spencer Foundation.
[3] This is discussed in some detail in Thorne (1993) and Eckert (1996).

and heterosexual practice. Adults view this frantic activity as evidence that kids don't know what heterosexuality is about. But in fact, it is very much about heterosexuality, for heterosexuality and the institutions that support it in adult society are also more about alliances and non-sexual matters than they are about sex.

The rapid activity of the early days lays down the foundations of a market, as a system of social value is created. People are elevated to status on the basis of their tradeability (whom they get paired up with) and of their role in effecting trades (their role as brokers). And in spite of all the breaking up, few people's feelings are hurt in the process, for this is a collaborative process for all involved, and the activity is not about relations between individual girls and boys, but about relations and alliances within the cohort more generally. The emotions that come into play in this market are not related to the relationship within the couple, but to the relationships of the people who are engaging in social engineering. Friendships and alliances can be volatile, they can break up with great passion, and friends can spend hours intervening for split-up friendship couples. But when a heterosexual couple breaks up, it is done in a matter of minutes – engineered by go-betweens – and with few regrets. At this early stage, the important social issue is both the creation of the market and the individual's relation to it. Whether a kid chooses to move ahead of the cohort or decides to lag behind, whether one becomes an *innocent*, a *slut* or a *stud*, is more important during this passage than most other aspects of social practice. But what is at stake is not sexual desire so much as social desire as it plays out in the sexual arena.

It is significant that heterosexuality should be the underlying metaphor of the social order well before many of the participants become interested in their own sexual activity. In this way, the co-construction of status and heterosexuality, the sexualization of peer society, and the socialization of sexuality are well in place in time to organize kids' development of sexual desire for each other.

Angela had a long-standing struggle to get recognition from some of her gang-oriented Latina peers, who considered her uncool and white. One Saturday night she lost her virginity, and the following week she told me the long story, beginning with a flirtation with a boy, and the jealousy that his attention evoked from these tough Latina girls. The story moved on to another day and another week, through space as she walked the neighborhoods with a succession of cuter and scarier boys, under the eyes of more jealous enemies and worried friends, and ended up in an empty lot behind the hall where a party was taking place. The actual loss of her virginity was encapsulated in the final event of the narrative: "and then we did it." No carnal pleasure, only some disappointment that it hadn't amounted to much. This story was not about sexual desire or sensation. And it wasn't really about boys. It was about outdoing those girls who called her white. And indeed, as she told me this story, I heard a remarkable transformation of her speech, as she constructed her stance through the authoritative use of Chicano English in a startling contrast to the way she'd sounded in our conversations in the previous weeks and years. (I hasten to add that sexual engagement and Chicana identity do not necessarily go together – this is one particular tough brand of Chicana identity that Angela is after, and this is a strategy that Angela came up with to claim it.) Angela really had no particular desire to stay with this boy – beyond her desire to make the point that she could have him. And she had no particular desire to have sex again, beyond her sense that it accomplished social work for her.

This is not a story about girls having sex to gain social status. It's about the fact that sexuality is not just about sex. And this leads me to my point – that if we focus on sexual desire, we're likely to make the same mistakes in the study of language and sexuality that have all too often been made in the study of language and gender. In this case, every act that indexes masculinity or femininity isn't necessarily about being male or female. And Angela's sexual activity is not about sex. It's about being Chicana, and about being tough. And if sexuality is about desire, the object of Angela's desire is not so much the boy or physical pleasure, but the girls' recognition and legitimation in the Chicano community.

* * * * *

The Issue of Agency

Because of the variationist focus on sound change, regional dialectology and class stratification, the kinds of variables people studied had been limited to sound changes, or to variables known or suspected to correlate robustly with macro-social categories. This led to a treatment of variables as basically homogeneous – as uniformly indexing class and/or ethnicity, tempered by gender – and supported the view of the meaning of variation as resulting from its social distribution rather than vice versa. This seemed to support a view of variation as passively acquired and deployed, and of stylistic practice as limited to the suppression of stigmatized variants. Stylistic practice, then, had to be conscious, hence outside the regular processes that constitute linguistic competence. Lesley Milroy adamantly argued for agency in variation, and work in the Third Wave has followed on by problematizing the relation between agency and consciousness.

Nik Coupland (2000, 2007) introduced *persona* into studies of variation, in its literary and psychological sense, as a self that the individual presents to others. By speaking in a particular way speakers are putting forth a potential self, making a claim about the kind of person they are, and what they're about in the moment. Coupland's work had a profound effect on the Slicsters, because it provided a sound basis for the study of meaning in variation. If the meaning of variation is not pre-determined, then how does it get constructed? What is the nature of stylistic constructions, and to what extent is the meaning of variation compositional? There's no question that stylistic practice in the construction of persona involves agency. This has led many variationists to disregard the study of persona, apparently because they believe that agency entails awareness. The entire issue of awareness lies at the center of the study of variation, in the vernacular construct.

Hosting NWAV in 2002, the Slicsters organized a panel entitled "Elephants in the Room," aimed at raising issues that we felt were left unexamined in linguistic practice. One of these issues was the notion of authenticity and the Authentic Speaker. Mary Bucholtz and Nik Coupland were the speakers on authenticity, and their papers appeared in the *Journal of Sociolinguistics* along with my short introduction. This introduction focused on the role of the vernacular construct in naturalizing variation, hence drawing a strict line between unconscious and conscious processes.

ELEPHANTS IN THE ROOM

Research is a zoo. There are elephants in the room, moose on the table – large presences that we collectively ignore, issues that we set aside in order to get on with our research enterprise. One might say that we can't do research without elephants, for if we didn't take some things as given, we'd never be able to investigate anything. But eventually we have to look at those givens and consider their implications for what we've done, and for what we will do in the future. The two papers that follow, by Mary Bucholtz and Nikolas Coupland, offer timely examinations of one such elephant that has become increasingly visible in recent years: the notion of the "Authentic Speaker."[4] This spontaneous speaker of pure vernacular is the dialectological poster child, providing direct access to language untainted by the interference of social agency. As the following two papers will show, authenticity is a rich ideological construct that is central to the practice of both speakers and analyst-speakers of language. Buried unquestioned in our practice, it calls for us, as analyst-speakers, to turn our analytic gaze to it.

Variability in language is to a great extent the product of speakers' social agency, yet the models of language that dominate sociolinguistics, particularly

---

[4] Earlier versions of these papers were presented in a panel at NWAV31 at Stanford in 2002, a conference whose theme was "Elephants in the Room". Other elephants discussed at this conference were the issues of the critical period for dialect acquisition and the influence of the media on language.

the study of variation, focus on patterns that are thought of as automatic, leaving more intentional variation outside of the paradigm. This does not simply marginalize the study of the intentional, it leaves unexamined the relation between the automatic and the intentional. Authenticity is constructed in relation to particular locations such as the traditional peasant in an isolated community (Holmquist 1985), the street kid in the inner city (Labov 1972b), the burned-out Burnout in a midwestern high school (Eckert 2000). Locally located and oriented, the Authentic Speaker produces linguistic output that emerges naturally in and from that location. The notion of the Authentic Speaker is based in the belief that some speakers have been more tainted by the social than others – tainted in the sense that they have wandered beyond their natural habitat to be subject to conscious, hence unnatural, social influences. Thus the villager who has had contact with people from the city, or the working-class speaker who aspires to be middle class, or even the African American speaker who uses African American Standard English, are all viewed as linguistically less natural than their peers who have not strayed from the local variety. The general view of women's speech as hypercorrect (e.g. Trudgill 1972) adds the gender spin to this picture for, as Mary Bucholtz mentions in her paper, authenticity is normally gendered – indeed it is part of gender ideology. Jane Hill's discussion (1987) of the gendered use of Spanish and Mexicano is a case in point, as women are sanctioned for laying linguistic claim to native authenticity through the use of "pure" Mexicano, or to Spanish authenticity through the use of standard Spanish. Keith Walters (2003) has laid this out nicely in the case of Tunisia, as women's greater use of French – and particularly standard French – is seen as a sign of their inauthenticity in contrast with men's greater use of Arabic and heavily accented French. And sociolinguists have participated in this gendering in, for example, focusing studies of African American Vernacular English on the speech of urban boys. Their authenticity as speakers of AAVE is tied to their participation in urban male street life, and in certain authentically urban male speech events (e.g. playing the dozens). The assumption that African American girls and women are somehow less urban, less authentic AAVE speakers, if not stated, is implied by their absence. So who, as both of the following papers ask, gets to define authenticity?

The fact is that neither social locations and identities, nor language, are static. Is the person who remains centrally located in what is viewed as prototypical practice more authentic than the person who is pushing the envelope? Should our focus be solely on those who reproduce the meanings from which social locations are constructed, or should we also be focusing on those who are at the vanguard of the production of new social meaning? From this perspective studies, for example of speakers who push the gender envelope (Bucholtz 1996; Gaudio 1997; Hall & O'Donovan 1997), take center place in sociolinguistics.

Work on clearly intentional variability, such as Mary Bucholtz's (1999) study of adolescent white boys' use of AAVE features, may strike some as pretty far removed from the kinds of more automatic patterns that we find in our studies of, for example, rotations in vowel systems (e.g. Labov 1994). Can these studies be part of the same enterprise? The obvious answer is that such linguistic behavior constitutes a conscious manipulation and as such is qualitatively different from the unconscious patterning of the vernacular. What I wish to interrogate here is that imagined line between the two kinds of phenomena – a line whose very existence is central to analytic practice. Between the extremes of the most automatic and the most intentional are studies such as Allan Bell's (1984) work on audience design, in which one might say that changes in audience trigger fairly automatic adjustments of dialect. And then there is Nikolas Coupland's work (1985, 2000), which shows the seamlessness of a Cardiff DJ's use of his native dialect features and of features of other dialects, as he negotiates meanings and identities with his audience and his subject matter. Our data are full of these kinds of acts of identity (Le Page & Tabouret-Keller 1985), but they remain at the margins of theoretical practice because they run counter to the central ideology of linguistics – that is, that what is interesting in language is what is beyond the conscious control of speaker agency.

In a discussion of style, Leonard Meyer points out (Meyer 1979:5) that "By far the largest part of behavior is a result of the interaction between innate modes of cognition and patterning, on the one hand, and ingrained, learned habits of discrimination and response, on the other." Beyond that, he argues, are the creative things we do to make what I would call stylistic moves. In linguistics, some might argue that the innate lies in universals, and more generally in cognitive and articulatory limitations on acquisition, processing and production, while the features of particular languages are the ingrained, learned habits. Modern linguistics defines itself in relation to the innate end of this continuum and sociolinguistics, particularly the study of variation, does as well. Thus while the data of variation lie in the continuum between the ingrained and the creative, the tension from the field is to discount all but the ingrained. This exclusion of evidence of social creativity constitutes what Latour (1993) refers to as the process of "purification" that constructs an opposition between the natural and the social – an opposition that underlies modern scientific practice. It is the status of language as a natural and transcendent phenomenon – as an inalienable part of human nature, the product of the human mind, defining of our species, and involving forces beyond our conscious control – that makes it a proper object of scientific investigation.[5]

---

[5] I am grateful for fruitful discussions on the scientific construction of linguistics with Ashwini Deo and Itamar Francez.

With a view of language as "in" the human mind, waiting to be discovered, sociolinguists boast the ability to get at language in its natural state in the form of the vernacular. If the Authentic Speaker is an elephant hovering in the corner, the vernacular is a moose sprawling in the middle of the table. The vernacular is defined (e.g. Labov 1972c) as the individual's most natural speech, learned early in life, and forever "fixed" in the speaker's ingrained patterns thanks to a critical period for language – and dialect – acquisition, that brings us closer to nature through our similarity to baby ducks. These ingrained patterns are produced in spontaneous speech, which is not only the most regular but is also the source of natural linguistic change. And for change to spread from speaker to speaker requires sufficient continuous contact to allow the unconscious absorption of these patterns. Conscious monitoring of speech, on the other hand, interrupts the regularity of the vernacular and slows down the progress of change.

The Authentic Speaker, the vernacular, the critical period, the need for regular contact for spread, are all wildlife supporting the view of language as a natural object. I would certainly not argue with some version of some of these, but I would not take any of them for granted. It is not clear, in fact, how much the age constraints on acquisition, and perhaps particularly of dialect features, are due to nature and how much to nurture.[6] And while there is evidence that speakers lose some ability to adapt their phonology to new dialects as they approach adolescence, there is also some evidence (e.g. Paunonen 1994) that speakers' phonetic output can change – and in the direction of the vernacular – as late as late adulthood. We also fortify our view of the vernacular as natural or at least ingrained in our view of the necessity of regular contact for the spread of change. We have all been told by non-linguist acquaintances that language change comes from the television. The idea that language change could be accomplished in such a trivial fashion is part of the popular "bag o' words" view of language (Pullum & Scholz 2001) that we're all tired of dealing with. However, we shouldn't ignore the possibility that not all changes are equal. We need to ask ourselves what kinds of changes require the kind of repeated exposure that regular social interaction gives, and what kinds can be taken right off the shelf.

I recognize that in my characterization of sociolinguistics as cleaving to the natural, I am creating something of a caricature. In practice, we all recognize the complexity of the relation between social agency and automatic behavior. But inasmuch as the line between the social and the natural is itself a social construction, and poised as we are at that line, the very status of language as natural – the location of that line – is, or should be, a central issue in

---

[6] Eve Clark and Gillian Sankoff presented papers on the issue of the critical period in the same panel as the papers under discussion here. See Clark (2000) for a discussion of this issue.

sociolinguistics. Is there a fluidity between ingrained behavior and conscious speech monitoring? The lengthening of vowels before voiced consonants is not universal, hence natural, but a deeply engrained feature of English.[7] If I really wanted to, could I train myself to consistently produce short vowels in this environment? No doubt not. But could I train myself to consistently lengthen post-tonic syllables? And could this become so automatic that I'd have trouble getting rid of it? Quite possibly.

The issue of the Authentic Speaker is ultimately an issue of where the social resides in sociolinguistics. In 1968, Uriel Weinreich, William Labov and Marvin Herzog argued for the incorporation of social variation in models of grammar. The battle that they began back in the sixties is finally bearing fruit or, I might say, the "core theorists" have finally discovered variation on their own and are rapidly laying claim to it. What for years was "not linguistics" has now been incorporated into the new stochastic models of grammar. But, predictably, it's been asked to leave its social friends at home. If we concern ourselves primarily with how the social deployment of language hooks onto an asocial model of grammar, we may look more like "linguists," but we will most certainly not be exploring the nature of the social in language. It is thanks to elephants such as the Authentic Speaker that the study of variation has moved so far since Weinreich, Labov and Herzog's (1968) groundbreaking paper. What I am arguing here is not that they are improper constructs, but that they have done their work and it is now time to pull them out and examine what they have helped us take for granted. Sociolinguistics should be located not at the edge of social variability, but squarely in the center. This means that we have to view language and the social world – including the social locations that provide our ideological map of that world – as a continuous human production. And it is up to us above all, to explore the nexus between that world and whatever that linguistic system is that resides in our most ingrained behaviors.

* * * * *

Certainly if we're in search of the origins of sound change, we need to delve into the most automatic, uncontrolled, speech. When one assumes a clear consciousness boundary, though, the vernacular becomes a kind of holy grail, as there is no guaranteed method of eliciting it, and no absolute way of identifying it. It's not clear whether the vernacular variants and the accompanying channel cues in the telling of danger of death stories ("increase in volume pitch, tempo, breathing, or laughter" [Labov 1972c:113]) are signs of minimal attention to speech or of dramatic stylizing. And it's not clear to me that it isn't both.

---

[7] I owe this observation to Robert Podesva.

More importantly, though, agency does not require attention or even awareness. Work in cognitive science (e.g. Smith & Kosslyn 2007) reveals attention as a selective mechanism that brings relevant information to awareness, but is not necessary for most action. Conscious attention and conscious action are only the tip of a very large iceberg, as most of what we perceive and do is below the level of awareness. This is as true of social cognition as of language; so much of our stylistic practice can go on quite unconsciously. As far as I know, awareness is an issue only in the study of variation. No linguist to my knowledge has raised the issue of the role of awareness in passivization or dative alternation – both of which are in part stylistic – and these are far more available to conscious manipulation than the pronunciation of a single segment. The issue of awareness, in other words, arises solely from the centrality of the vernacular construct to the study of sound change.

Attention is certainly required when the speaker is out of his or her element and feels called upon to speak someone else's variety. Socially mobile (downward as well as upward) people may feel quite continually out of their comfort zone, and it is possible that occurrences of a lower middle-class crossover (Labov 1972a, 2001) are due to the social distance that many lower middle-class speakers have to travel between home and the workplace. For example, a receptionist living in a working-class neighborhood with primarily working-class friends and family, has to make a significant shift if she goes off every day to work in a corporate office. The greater regularity of this crossover pattern among women may well be related to the fact that it is primarily women whose jobs require this kind of linguistic travel. And just as things requiring attention at first can become automatic (Smith & Kosslyn 2007), I would guess that with time and experience, some of the more careful styles become less and less of a reach for these people.

This does not mean, though, that everything involved in persona construction is accomplished unconsciously, for meaning is constructed in the full range of stylistic moves. And reaching beyond one's usual repertoire can be an important move. When I asked Judy, a burned-out Burnout, what she was going to do after graduation, she first let out a sigh and said, in a breathy voice, "I don't know" [haj dowʔ noːh], followed by a very vernacular-sounding "I- I- I don't know" [ʔʔ aj ʔajɾənʌw]. One might say that the first was double voicing (Bakhtin 1981) the "responsible adult," the kinds of people who had warned her of the dire consequences of her way of life – teachers, counselors, parents – and that the second was voicing the self that didn't know what she was going to do. Each of these versions gave meaning to the other, and indeed, each is located in Judy's stylistic landscape. I have characterized Judy elsewhere (Eckert 2000) as a stylistic icon, and her trademark is stylistic variety, including continual voicings of others and of past versions of herself. Her voicing of the responsible adult is not inauthentic, but a reaching out into the stylistic landscape. This kind of reaching is a central part of Judy's persona, and each such reaching activates social construals of the potential meaning of this particular kind of hyper-articulation. Certainly someone studying the progress of sound change would not want such occurrences in their data. But someone studying the social meaning of sound change cannot do without them.

9 The Nature of Indexicality in Variation

In 2007, Miyako Inoue and I co-taught a course at the Linguistic Institute on variation and social theory. We focused heavily on indexicality in this course, and our many conversations led me to think about the underspecified status of variables, and their vivification in the context of style. (Ivan proposed the term *vivification* because, unlike *specification*, it carries no implication of fixedness or selection among clear alternatives.) Mary Bucholtz and Kira Hall were editing a special issue of the *Journal of Sociolinguistics* on the relation between sociolinguistics and linguistic anthropology, and I put my thoughts about variation and indexical order into the following paper for this issue.

VARIATION AND THE INDEXICAL FIELD

Introduction

The distinction between sociolinguistics and linguistic anthropology became an issue as the quantitative study of variation gained hegemony in sociolinguistics, subordinating the examination of the social to questions of linguistic theory and to the needs of regression analysis (see also Bucholtz and Hall, this volume). By viewing the social as a fixed and external structure that is only reflected in linguistic variability, the study of sociolinguistic variation has remained safely within the bounds of linguistics as a cognitive science. I say this not to deny the interest and importance of the work that has been done in this vein, but to note that ultimately the variation (and the entire linguistic) enterprise must be integrated into a more comprehensive understanding of language as social practice. William Labov's comment (2002:283) that "The great chain shifts sweeping across North America are more like ocean currents than local games" suggests that the local indexical work that speakers do with variation is dwarfed in importance by the power of the internal workings of the great linguistic system. To seek explanations for chain shifts in the day-to-day construction of meaning would certainly be futile and ridiculous. But to ignore what people do with the elements of these chain shifts to construct social meaning is to turn a blind eye to an aspect of human competence that is at least as mind-blowing as the ability to maintain distance between one's vowels.

As Kathryn Woolard (this volume) emphasizes, linguistic anthropology foregrounds the ongoing construction of meaning in human activity. In the study of sociolinguistic variation, on the other hand, meaning has been the stuff of casual speculation, but not part of the enterprise. In the following pages, I propose an approach to the study of social meaning in variation that builds upon linguistic-anthropological theories of indexicality, and most particularly Michael Silverstein's (2003) notion of indexical order. I argue that the meanings of variables are not precise or fixed but rather constitute a field of potential meanings – an *indexical field*, or constellation of ideologically related meanings, any one of which can be activated in the situated use of the variable. The field is fluid, and each new activation has the potential to change the field by building on ideological connections. Thus variation constitutes an indexical system that embeds ideology in language and that is in turn part and parcel of the construction of ideology. This concept leaves us with a new (that is, an additional) enterprise of studying variation as an indexical system, taking meaning as a point of departure rather than the sound changes or structural issues that have generally governed what variables we study and how we study them.[1]

The Fate of Meaning in Variation Studies

The early moments of the quantitative study of variation held promise for the analysis of social meaning. In his study of Martha's Vineyard, Labov (1963) found correlations of centralized /ay/ with a range of social categories – fishermen, people living at the fishing end of the island, teenagers who planned to spend their adulthoods on the island. He interpreted these correlations as evidence of an association of the old island variant with local authenticity based in the English-descent island-based fishing community and its resistance to mainland incursion. This very local construction of meaning in variation, the recruiting of a vowel as part of a local ideological struggle, suggested that variation can be a resource for the construction of meaning and an integral part of social change. But this power of variation was lost in the large-scale survey studies of sound change in progress in the years that followed, as social meaning came to be confused with the demographic correlations that point to

---

[1] The idea of the indexical field emerged in my many discussions with Miyako Inoue, particularly as we prepared and taught a course at the Linguistic Society of America Summer Institute at Stanford University in 2007. I am deeply indebted to Miyako for immense intellectual fun and inspiration. I am grateful also to Michael Silverstein not only for providing the theoretical basis for this paper, but for remarkably painstaking, gracious, and helpful comments on the first draft.

it. Social meaning remained as a subtext in community studies, but with no real place in the theory. Peter Trudgill (1972), for instance, called upon the perceived toughness of working-class men as a motive for middle-class men to adopt local working-class sound changes, accounting for the upward spread of change. But this account was vague about the nature of the connection between toughness, gender, and class, and did not open up an account of how meanings become associated with social categories or with variables. Rather, it was absorbed into a view of the meaning of variables as consequences of the abstract demographic categories that structure survey research – socioeconomic class, gender, and ethnicity.

This view of variables began with the sociolinguistic focus on the spread of sound change. In this view, the socioeconomic hierarchy is a social space through which change spreads, and speakers' place in that space determines when they "receive" the change. Speakers' agency in the use of variables has been viewed as limited to making claims about their place in social space by either emphasizing or downplaying their category membership through the quantitative manipulation of markers. But clearly, women (and men) are not saying "I'm a woman" when they use a "female-led" change, nor are they saying "I'm not a woman" when they do not. The generalization that women lead in a particular sound change is the outcome of a general statistical result by which in the aggregate, women use advanced variants more than men (Eckert 1989c). This generalization says nothing about the kinds of behaviors and ideologies that underlie these patterns, what kinds of meaning people attach to the conservative and innovative variant, who does and does not fit the pattern and why. It says nothing about language use and gender in everyday life, and it says nothing about why the same generalization applies to class stratification – that is, not only women, but working-class people, lead in sound change. Yet variationists continue to use labels such as "female-led changes" as if such changes all had a direct relation to gender. Quantitative generalizations of the sort made in survey studies are important, but exploring the meaning of variation requires that we examine what lies beneath those generalizations. The very fact that the same variables may stratify regularly with multiple categories – e.g. gender, ethnicity, and class – indicates that their meanings are not directly related to these categories but to something that is related to all of them. In other words, variables index demographic categories not directly but indirectly (Silverstein 1985), through their association with qualities and stances that enter into the construction of categories.

Variables, Style, and Social Meaning

Speaking in the social world involves a continual analysis and interpretation of categories, groups, types, and personae and of the differences in the ways they talk – in social cognition terms, a development of *schemata* (Piaget 1954).

These emerge as we come to notice differences, to make distinctions, and to attribute meaning to them. Thus we construct a social landscape through the segmentation of the social terrain, and we construct a linguistic landscape through a segmentation of the linguistic practices in that terrain. The level of social practice that corresponds to distinctions in the terrain in which we study variation is style. In all areas of art, style is what characterizes schools, periods, and individuals. Style has a similar function in everyday language, picking out locations in the social landscape such as Valley Girls, Cholos, Cowboys, Jocks, Burnouts, Italian Hoods. Variables occur only as components of styles, and interpreting variables requires an analysis of these components. The ability that a human being exercises from birth to acquire language no doubt persists through life as we strive to understand the social significance of linguistic form – as we analyze the nuances of the linguistic variability around us.

This kind of style (what one might call *persona style*) is orthogonal to the formality continuum that is associated with style in traditional variation studies (e.g. Labov 1972c). The focus on formality in these studies keeps the study of variation in the cognitive realm (see Eckert 2004) as it determines the amount of attention paid to speech, limiting stylistic agency to the manipulation of status in the socioeconomic hierarchy. Styles associated with types in the social landscape bear an important relation to class, but not a direct one. They are the product of *enregisterment* (Agha 2003) and I might call them *registers* were it not for the common use of the term in sociolinguistics to refer to a static collocation of features associated with a specific setting or fixed social category. Asif Agha's account (2005) of *enregistered voices* is quite precisely what I am talking about here, locating register in a continual process of production and reproduction. Sociolinguists generally think of styles as different ways of saying the same thing. In every field that studies style seriously, however, this is not so – style is not a surface manifestation, but originates in content. The view of style I present here precludes the separation of form from content, for the social is eminently about the content of people's lives. Different ways of saying things are intended to signal different ways of being, which includes different potential things to say. I will return to the issue of content below.

Persona style is the best level for approaching the meaning of variation, for it is at this level that we connect linguistic styles with other stylistic systems such as clothing and other commoditized signs and with the kinds of ideological constructions that speakers share and interpret and that thereby populate the social imagination. Ideology is at the center of stylistic practice: one way or another, every stylistic move is the result of an interpretation of the social world and of the meanings of elements within it, as well as a positioning of the stylizer with respect to that world. Whether the speaker is a teenage girl adapting a Valley Girl feature to position herself as cooler than her interlocutors or a fisherman on Martha's Vineyard (Labov 1963) centralizing the nucleus of /ay/ to position himself as an opponent to the incursion of the mainland economy on the island, stylistic moves are ideological (see also Woolard, this volume). And while these styles and stylistic moves can be quite local, ultimately they connect the linguistic sign systematically to the political economy and more specifically to the demographic categories that both emerge from and constrain local practice (Bourdieu 1977) and that have been the preoccupation of variation studies.

By *stylistic practice*, I mean both the interpretation and the production of styles, for the two take place constantly and iteratively. Stylistic practice is a process of bricolage (Hebdige 1984), in which individual resources (in this case, variables) can be interpreted and combined with other resources to construct a more complex meaningful entity. This process begins when the stylistic agent perceives an individual or group style – perhaps the style will bring his or her attention to those who use it; perhaps the users will call attention to the style. But the noticing of the style and the noticing of the group or individual that uses it are mutually reinforcing, and the meaning of the style and its users are reciprocal. The style itself will be noticed in the form of features that the stylistic agent separates out for notice. Susan Gal and Judith Irvine (Irvine & Gal 2000; Irvine 2001) have provided an account of the semiotic processes by which categories of speakers and their linguistic varieties come to be perceived as distinct, as an ideological link is constructed between the linguistic and the social. These processes apply equally well to the construction of meaning for styles (Irvine 2001) and for individual variables. This process of selection is made against a background of previous experience of styles and features; a stylistic agent may be more attuned to particular kinds of differences as a function of past stylistic experience. (This point appears rather small in the present context, but social differences in stylistic perception and production are structured and fundamental to the role of political economy in stylistic practice.) Once the agent isolates and attributes significance to a feature, that feature becomes a resource that he or she can incorporate or not into his or her own style. The occurrence of that resource in a new style will change the meaning both of the resource and of the original style, hence changing the semiotic landscape.

Material style, particularly clothing and other forms of adornment, provide important clues to the study of linguistic style. One example of bricolage in clothing style comes from a series of interviews that some of my students and I did in Palo Alto, California, in 1985. (This example is described in more detail in Eckert 2000.) We were interviewing students at Palo Alto High School about their styles, introducing ourselves as researchers simply interested in style and asking them to describe their own style. At the time, "new wave" style was big on the Palo Alto adolescent scene, and a group of New Wavers were the local counterculture. The New Wavers dressed almost exclusively in black, with distinctive pegged pants (pants that narrowed at the ankles). In contrast, the mainstream "Preppy" group wore pastel colors and straight-leg designer blue jeans.

Two girls who were members of the popular Preppy group told us with great pride of a stylistic move they had made. These girls characterized themselves as school-oriented and quite conformist. Nonetheless, they admired the New Wavers' independence and sought to distance themselves just a little from the extreme conformity normally expected of Preppies. They chose to adopt some small sign of independence by appropriating something of New Wave style. Dismissing the dark eye makeup (which they took to be scary and slutty) and the wearing of black (which they took to be too rebellious, slutty, and adult), they pegged their blue jeans. In other words, they segmented the New Wave style into meaningful elements, most saliently cut and color, identified the cut of one's jeans as indexing autonomy but not rebellion or sluttiness, and worked it into their otherwise Preppy style, ultimately making a claim to being both Preppy and independent.

While the social categories at work in these girls' stylistic moves are local, they deal with fundamental issues related to gender and adolescence: innocence and independence. And the symbolic material the girls were working with is not local – there is a culture-wide association of pastels with innocence and black with adulthood, sophistication, and the ominous. At the same time, pegged pants had a more fluid association (indeed, the girls knew nothing about the heyday of pegged pants in the prewar era of zoot suits worn by African American and Mexican American working-class males and the more conservatively pegged pants of the postwar beatniks), making pegging available for segmentation and (re)interpretation. It is also to be noted that the ratio of the width of the knee and the bottom of pants legs was already salient, as fashion had moved in the preceding years from bell bottoms to straight legs (Eckert 1982). One could say that in adopting the pegged look they were carrying this process one step further. Thus while these girls were engaging in stylistic moves that they viewed as strictly local to their school and social groups, the resources they were using were available and salient because they had been established at a much more generalized cultural level.

These girls were able to articulate every detail of their interpretive process. And although linguistic style is rarely constructed in as intentional a fashion as clothing style, it is similarly a process of bricolage. The big question for the study of meaning in variation is how linguistic styles are constructed: what kinds of meanings can variables have, and how do they combine to yield the larger meanings of styles? I offer the following discussion, therefore, as a beginning in dealing with this problem.

Belten High Adolescents

In my study of white adolescent speech in Belten High in the Detroit suburbs (Eckert 1989a, 2000), I found that the differential use of variables

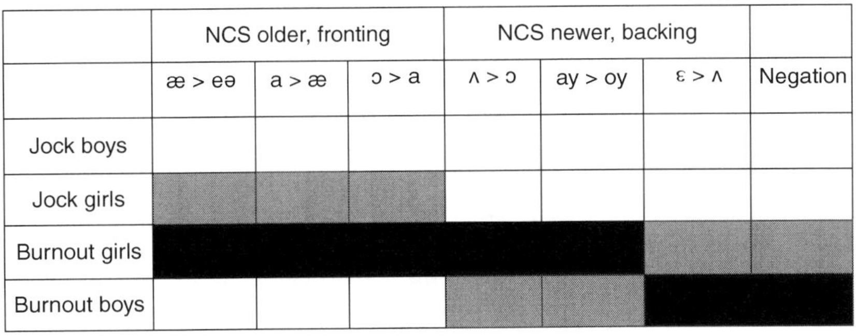

The Nature of Indexicality in Variation

	NCS older, fronting			NCS newer, backing			Negation
	æ > eə	a > æ	ɔ > a	ʌ > ɔ	ay > oy	ɛ > ʌ	
Jock boys							
Jock girls	▓	▓	▓				
Burnout girls	■	■	■	■	■	▓	▓
Burnout boys				▓	▓	■	

Figure 9.1 Use of Detroit variables by gender and social category.
Black = greatest use, gray = second greatest use.

constituted distinct styles associated with different communities of practice: the school-oriented Jocks and the urban-oriented and school-alienated Burnouts. I considered six vocalic variables: the mid and low vowels involved in the Northern Cities Shift, and the raising and backing of the nucleus of /ay/ (so that *fight* sounds more like *foyt*). I also examined one syntactic variable: negative concord. As shown in Figure 9.1, the seven variables pattern quite differently across the categories of gender and style. I have marked only the leaders in the use of the advanced variant (black) and the "runners up" (gray). The older components of this shift, which appeared to have stabilized across the suburban area, were used predominantly by girls while the newer changes, which were more advanced closer to the urban center, were used predominantly by Burnouts. The Burnouts, in other words, were leading in the use of urban variants, embedding a linguistic opposition between city and suburb within a community to support a local opposition between urban- and school-oriented kids.

But just as women are not making direct gender claims when they use female-led changes, Burnouts are not making direct urban claims when they use urban-led changes. The urban–suburban sociocultural opposition was salient to suburban kids because of what they associated with urban life and urban kids. Detroit, one of the most segregated urban areas in the United States, was discussed by white kids at Belten High as a scary place dominated by African Americans. The urban kids that they identified with were white kids who knew how to cope in the dangerous urban environment – kids they saw as autonomous, tough, and street-smart. Presumably in adopting urban forms, suburban kids were affiliating with those qualities, not claiming to be urban. This presumption is further supported by an additional division between two network clusters of Burnout girls – the "regular" Burnout girls and the "burned-out" Burnout girls. The burned-out Burnout girls were quite objectively wilder, more alienated, and more urban-oriented than the regular Burnout girls; in fact, they explicitly took pride in this fact. The burned-out Burnout girls led all other Burnouts, male and female, in the use of all of the Northern Cities Shift urban variables as well as negative concord. Boys over all led in the use of negative concord in this school, as they do more generally in the population, but the burned-out Burnout girls led all boys, including the Burnout boys, in the use of negative concord. More than one academic who has heard these results has suggested that the burned-out Burnout girls were trying to talk "like boys." But talking "like a boy" is done at the level of style, not at the level of the individual variable, and these particular girls were into "femininity" in many ways, particularly the sartorial, and also led the rest of the cohort in the use of the older "female-led" changes. This embedding of a linguistic opposition between city and suburb within a community to distinguish urban or suburban orientation is a prime example of the kind of iteration that Judith Irvine and Susan Gal (2000) have called *recursiveness*. The burned-out Burnouts' even greater use of urban variants adds still another level of recursiveness.

Negative concord, of course, is a global resource in English in its stereotyped counter-standardness, and is associated everywhere with lack of education and alienation from legitimate institutions. The elements of the Northern Cities Shift are region-specific, but the spread of change outward from urban areas creates a structure in which the meanings of emerging changes have common elements across regions. An opposition between urban and suburban is common to metropolitan areas across the United States, and there is a commonality in the structure of meaning associated with urban variables across most U.S. cities. Inner cities tend to be poorer, more dangerous, and more ethnically diverse than the surrounding suburbs. Pittsburgh, New York, and Detroit urban personae no doubt share some qualities deriving from living in a poorer, more dangerous, and more diverse environment. But every city has its own character, and the specifics of associations with urban variables will depend on local characteristics of those cities. My next example, Qing Zhang's (2005) work on variation in Beijing, provides an example of the local flavor of urban variables.

Beijing Managers

Zhang's research has established a relation between particular Beijing Mandarin variables and urban personae that are associated in local ideology with Beijing as a specific urban site. Her study compared the speech of managers in foreign-owned financial businesses with that of managers in state-owned businesses. Managers in the foreign financial sector constitute the emergent "yuppie" culture. As highly paid workers in a global market, the yuppies represent an important social change in China, and are highly visible in their development

The Nature of Indexicality in Variation 151

of western styles of consumption and a generally cosmopolitan lifestyle. This cosmopolitanism characterizes their speech style as well, which contrasts quite starkly with the speech of managers in the more traditional state-owned businesses. Zhang notes, furthermore, that gender plays a different role in the two sectors. While the state sector has quite rigid policies about hiring men and women on an equal footing, the foreign businesses first hire women into front office jobs, on the basis not only of managerial qualifications but also of their linguistic decorative value: their knowledge of English and quite possibly their use of a more generally cosmopolitan Mandarin. Zhang found a significant difference in the use of two Beijing variables that have achieved the status of linguistic stereotype and are associated not simply with Beijing but with popular Beijing types.

- ***The Smooth Operator variable***. The rhotacization of syllable finals (giving vowels a retroflex quality) and the realization of retroflex initial obstruents as [ɹ] is popularly seen as giving Beijing Mandarin an "oily" quality, which in turn is associated with an oily character: the "Beijing smooth operator," *jing you-zi*, recognized in the public imagination, including the literature of Beijing writers, as a male Beijing type. This is someone who is smooth and streetwise, who can handle all kinds of situations, and who can talk his way out of situations, who has the "gift of gab." The salience of this type showed up in Zhang's conversations with managers. Referring to rhotacization as "swallowing sound," one of the managers commented, "Beijingers are glib, talk fast, like to swallow sounds, hence appear to be smooth" (Zhang 2005:443). The connection between the sound of rhotacization and oiliness and between oiliness and a specific persona is a particularly striking example of iconization (Irvine & Gal 2000). Even more striking is the comment recorded by Zhang comparing Beijing speech to southern dialects, attributing rhotacization to a physical quality or ability: "Have you ever heard anybody saying the Cantonese have 'oily accent, slippery tone'? That's because their tongues can't curl" (Zhang 2008). As shown in Figure 9.2, the yuppie style downplays local Beijing features. But while male yuppies use the smooth operator feature less than the state managers, they use it considerably more than the female yuppies – indeed, the female yuppies use it very little. It appears that this feature does not fit the persona required of a woman in the foreign sector.
- ***The Alley Saunterer variable***. Another feature studied by Zhang, the interdental pronunciation of dental sibilants, is not just a "Beijing" feature but appears to index another specific local type: the *hútòng chuànzi*, or 'alley saunterer,' a feckless character who hangs out in back streets waiting for something to happen. The managers in Zhang's study pointed specifically to the alley saunterer when discussing this variable: "Mine is not the real Beijing Mandarin, because I'm not one of those alley saunterers...They

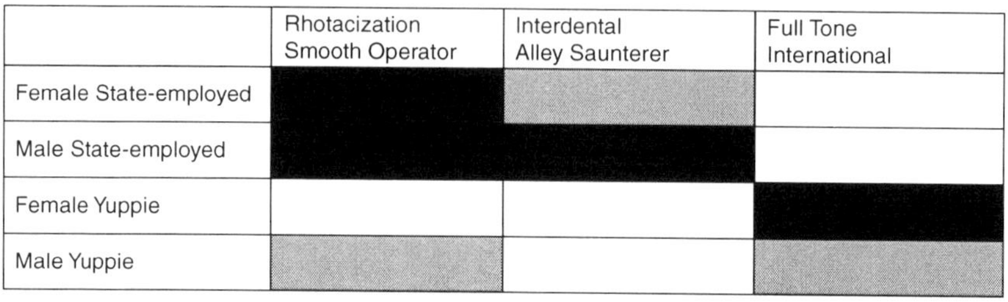

	Rhotacization Smooth Operator	Interdental Alley Saunterer	Full Tone International
Female State-employed	■	▒	
Male State-employed	■	■	
Female Yuppie			■
Male Yuppie	▒		▒

Figure 9.2 Use of Beijing and international variables by managers in state-owned and foreign-owned businesses.
Black = greatest use, gray = second greatest use.
Based on Zhang (2005).

speak the authentic Beijing speech. And they say 'big cabbage' [ta paits^{h}ai] as [ta paitθ^hai]" (Zhang 2005:443). In an example of iconization similar to that discussed above regarding the smooth operator, another manager characterized alley saunterers as "big-tongued" since they "bite their tongues when talking." While the alley saunterer image is not useful to the male or female cosmopolitan yuppie persona or to women in state-owned businesses, a little use of it works for state businessmen.

- Beijing yuppies' avoidance of these two Beijing variables builds on an association of the features with particular types and distances them from these types as part of constructing a new (yuppie) type. At the same time, this distancing process reinscribes the old types by creating a new space in the social map in opposition to them. Meanwhile, yuppies' adoption of a non-Beijing feature, full tone, projects them out into transnational space.
- *Full tone*. Unstressed syllables in Beijing Mandarin are sufficiently reduced that they lose their distinct tone, which assimilates to the preceding tone. Non-mainland dialects of Mandarin, however, retain the full tone in unstressed syllables. The yuppie use of full tone has been commented on in the media and is generally seen as evidence of a speaker's being a Hong Kong-Taiwan wannabe, or of Chinese Mainlanders' attempt to imitate the "Hong Kong-Taiwan accent." The yuppies – particularly the women – added an additional cosmopolitan flavor to their style with the occasional use of the full tone feature, which is associated with the global capitalist markets located outside the mainland – a resource that the state managers did not use at all. Of particular interest in this case is that since the use of the full tone is associated with the de-reduction of unstressed syllables, the result is a greater equality of syllable length in the stream of speech, giving the speech a more staccato sound – a crispness that one might contrast with the oily tone attributed to the typical Beijing speaker.

Studies like Labov (1963), Eckert (2000), and Zhang (2005) clearly establish that variables that historically come to distinguish geographic dialects can take on interactional meanings based in local ideology. In all three cases, the meaning is based in ideologies about what the locality is about – what kinds of people live there and what activities, beliefs, and practices make it what it is. Local identity is never an association with a generic locale but with a particular construction of that locale as distinct from some other. Local identity claims are about what it means to be from "here" as opposed to some identified "there." The Martha's Vineyard fishermen, in appropriating the centralized variant of (ay), were not simply claiming to be Vineyarders but were making a claim about what a Vineyarder is. This claim immediately raises the potential for the distinction to be activated inside the community as well, as there will be differences in the community that are construed in direct relation to differences across communities. The most salient phonological feature that distinguishes Vineyard from mainland speech came to mark opposition to mainland incursion on the island. Furthermore, the fact that the English-descent fishing community was leading in this particular linguistic opposition – not the Portuguese or the Native Americans – suggests that the English claim to authenticity on behalf of the island was inseparable from their claim to greater authenticity within the island.

Indexical Order and Indexical Fields

As the above examples suggest, "acts of identity" (Le Page & Tabouret-Keller 1985) are not primarily a matter of claiming membership in this or that group or category as opposed to another, but smaller acts that involve perceptions of individuals or categories that fall under the radar of large sociolinguistic surveys. This is not to say that these acts are independent of the larger social order; on the contrary, they are systematically related to the macrosociologist's categories and embedded in the practices that produce and reproduce them. It is in the links between the individual and the macrosociological category that we must seek the social practices in which people fashion their ways of speaking, moving their styles this way or that as they move their personae through situations from moment to moment, from day to day, and through the life course (see also Heller, this volume). In this process, they do not simply use social meaning – they produce and reproduce it. Michael Silverstein's (2003) concept of indexical order provides a crucial perspective on this process. It gives a foothold on the relation between the macrosociological facts and linguistic practice by providing a theoretical account of the role of construal in context in the process of indexical change.

In his discussion of the indexical value of variation, Silverstein engages with John Gumperz's (1968) distinction between dialectal and superposed variability and with Labov's (1971) distinction between indicators, markers, and stereotypes. In Labov's terms, *indicators* are dialectal variables that distinguish social or geographic categories but have attracted no notice and do not figure in variation across the formality continuum. *Markers* and *stereotypes* are variables that have attracted sufficient attention to emerge within those categories in stylistic variation. The difference between markers and stereotypes lies in the level of consciousness: stereotypes are subject to metapragmatic discussion, while markers are not. An indicator in variation is what Silverstein terms a *first-order index*. A first-order index simply indexes membership in a population – it designates people as Martha's Vineyarders, Beijingers, Detroiters. In the case of Labov's (1966) New York City study, which Silverstein uses as his example, the populations may be social class strata. But the social evaluation of a population is always available to become associated with the index and to be internalized in speakers' own dialectal variability to index specific elements of character.[2] At that point, the linguistic form becomes a marker, a second-order index, which figures stylistically as speakers position themselves with respect to the elements of character selected out for internal use. The difference between the notion of marker as used in variation studies and the index of Silverstein's treatment is in the ideological embedding of the process by which the link between form and meaning is made and remade. Participation in discourse involves a continual interpretation of forms in context, an in-the-moment assigning of indexical values to linguistic forms. A form with an indexical value, what Silverstein calls an *nth order* usage, is always available for reinterpretation – for the acquisition of an n + 1st value. Once established, this new value is available for further construal, and so on. While the terms *first order*, *second order*, etc. may imply a linearity,[3] this is clearly not Silverstein's intention. On the contrary, the reconstruals are "always already immanent" (2003:194) precisely because they take place within a fluid and ever-changing ideological field. The emergence of an n + 1st indexical value is the result of an ideological move, a sidestepping within an ideological field. In order to understand the meaning of variation in practice, we need to begin with this ideological field, as the continual reconstrual of the indexical value of a variable creates in the end an *indexical field*.[4] An indexical field is a constellation of meanings that are ideologically linked. As such, it is inseparable from the

---

[2] Of course, the very fact of distinction of social groups entails evaluation, and by its ideological nature, linguistic practice entails an evaluation of linguistic difference. Thus whether ideologies about groups lead to the perception of their linguistic differences or whether a perception of a linguistic difference calls for a perception of the group makes little difference: the two are indistinguishable.

[3] Johnstone, Andrus and Danielson (2006) equate indexical order with a progression from indicator (first-order index) to marker (second-order index) to stereotype (third-order index). Since the only difference between a marker and a stereotype is the level of consciousness, this distinction is orthogonal to changes in indexical value.

[4] I am a little hesitant to use the term *indexical field* for this configuration because of its mismatch with the term *semantic field*, which refers to a field of words of similar semantic content

The Nature of Indexicality in Variation 155

ideological field and can be seen as an embodiment of ideology in linguistic form. I emphasize here that this field is not a static structure, but at every moment a representation of a continuous process of reinterpretation.

The traditional view of a variable as having a fixed meaning is based in a static, non-dialectical, view of language. In this view, a variable is taken to "mean" the same regardless of the context in which it is used, and while we know, for example, that variables may change their meanings over time, the mechanism for this process is not well understood. This dilemma is reminiscent of the one that Weinreich, Labov and Herzog (1968) sought to solve by arguing that the social structuring of variability provides orderly heterogeneity in the constant process of change. The notion of the indexical field is an argument for a similar orderly heterogeneity in the ever-changing indexical value of variables. Variables have indexical fields rather than fixed meanings because speakers use variables not simply to reflect or reassert their particular pre-ordained place in the social map but to make ideological moves. The use of a variable is not simply an invocation of a pre-existing indexical value but an indexical claim which may either invoke a pre-existing value or stake a claim to a new value. As noted above, the Martha's Vineyard fishermen, in appropriating the centralized variant of /ay/, were not simply claiming to be Vineyarders but were making a claim about what a Vineyarder is. I would argue that as disagreements about the future of the island became more prominent in daily life, the terms of those disagreements entered into the local ideological field, available to be pointed to with the use of a linguistic variable already associated with Vineyarders.[5] The new construal of meaning for the re-centralization of /ay/ was no doubt not just a product of who used it, but when and how they used it. The use of the centralized variant may have been a way of asserting one's local authority and/ or loyalty in a range of utterances that gave specificity to the source of authority and the object of loyalty: an argument about the fate of the island, recounting heroic or nostalgic stories about the fishing life, taking a negative stance towards the tourist industry or towards mainland or mainland-oriented individuals etc.

It is not just the meanings of phonological variants that change in discourse – lexical change does as well. A word's denotation can absorb connotations through association with aspects of the context in which it is used and most certainly, stances. Andrew Wong (2005) has traced the development of *tongzhi* 'comrade'

---

rather than to polysemy. Indeed, it might be better to use the term *indexical field* to refer to the various variables that might have related indexical value. But at the moment it is not at all clear that this would be a profitable way to look at relations among variables since the social world is interlocked in a way that the world of the lexicon is not. (The indexical field also has no clear relation to Bourdieu's notion of *field*.)

[5] It is notable that the social correlations for (ay) and (aw) are dissimilar – the Native American community at Gay Head, which trailed in the centralization of (ay), led in the centralization of (aw). I have suggested elsewhere (Eckert 2000:23–4) that these two variables were associated with possibly competing claims to local authencity.

in Hong Kong in spoken and written discourse, from its appropriation by the local gay community as a positive term, through its pejoration at the hands of the media through the selective use of the term in news stories. The pejoration of many English words referring to females is a perfect example of the systematic absorption of ideology into the lexicon. Sally McConnell-Ginet (1989) has argued that changes such as the pejoration of *hussy*, originally meaning 'housewife,' happened over years of situated use, in which the term was used repeatedly in negative utterances about specific women or categories of women, and the utterances of those who said such negative things were registered disproportionately.

It is worthwhile at this point to return briefly to the apparent toughness of working-class men. I believe that toughness is an important social meaning – one that is a component of many styles, and that is embraced situationally, and by women as well as men. It is reasonable to guess that toughness is a common part of the indexical field for some variables originating in the working class and for urban variables. But it is important to consider the ideological work behind this connection in order to look beyond it. Working-class men are quite diverse, and while they fall everywhere on the toughness scale, toughness nonetheless remains central to the working-class stereotype. There are a variety of other qualities that one might say are characteristic of many working-class men including, for instance, egalitarianism. The process of erasure (Irvine & Gal 2000) elevates toughness by downplaying working-class men who are not tough, as well as downplaying other qualities such as egalitarianism. The fact that toughness is separated out is an ideological fact that is part of the very central construction of an opposition between working-class (physical) and middle-class (technical) masculinities (Connell 1995). In other words, the indexical values of variables are part and parcel of the ideological work of society and vice versa – and it is for this reason that the survey studies of variation have found over and over that variables correlate with the fundamental, ideologically laden experiences of class and gender. I would argue, therefore, that no trivial meanings come to be associated with variables but that any meanings that are associated with variables will be based in highly salient ideological issues.

An Example: (ING)

Kathryn Campbell-Kibler's (2007a) experimental work on (ING) provides us with a starting point for thinking about how indexical fields are configured. She has shown that listeners develop an impression of a speaker based on general speech style and the content of the utterance and interpret the particular use of (ING) on the basis of that impression.[6] Using advanced matched guise techniques

---

[6] Describing it this way implies a temporal relation between noting the style and interpreting the variable (ING), which clearly is not intended. The actual cognitive processes behind this interpretation remain to be understood.

The Nature of Indexicality in Variation

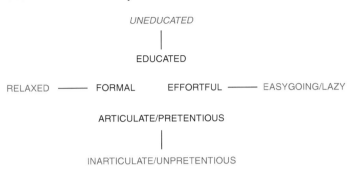

Figure 9.3 Indexical field of (ING).
Based on Campbell-Kibler (2007a, 2007b).

with college students as subjects, Campbell-Kibler demonstrates that (these) hearers associate the velar variant with education, intelligence, and articulateness. Central to this perception is a view of the velar form as a full form and therefore effortful and of the apical form as a reduced form, hence a sign of lack of effort.[7] One might then presume that this lack of effort can be further construed as a result of laziness, not caring, or even rebellion, and by extension, impoliteness. In further experiments with a broader socioeconomic range, Campbell-Kibler (2007b) found that hearers additionally interpret the apical form as casual or relaxed.

Based on these potential meanings for (ING), one could imagine an indexical field for the velar form as shown in Figure 9.3. The adjectives in black represent potential meanings for the velar variant, while those in gray represent potential meanings for the apical variant. One cannot assume that the pairs work in lockstep. Among other things, while a negative evaluation of a speaker using the apical variant might be that the speaker is inarticulate or lazy, a favorable evaluation might be that he or she is unpretentious or easygoing. Similarly, the speaker using the velar variant can be heard as simply articulate or as pretentious. Which of the meanings in the indexical field the hearer will associate with a given occurrence will depend on both the perspective of the hearer[8] and the style in which it is embedded – which includes not only the rest of the linguistic form of the utterance but the content of the utterance as well. Campbell-Kibler found that hearers judged the nature of the social move being made by the speaker based on presupposed indexicality. If their impression was that the speaker was relatively uneducated or from the South, they

---

[7] While the apical variant is not in itself initially a reduction of the velar variant, it is subject to reduction while the velar variant is not.
[8] Campbell-Kibler (2007b) has even found that hearers are more likely to give negative evaluations of speakers' (ING) production when they are feeling grouchy.

expected to hear the apical variant; if their impression was that the speaker was educated and to some extent from the North, they expected to hear the velar variant. The use of the 'wrong' variant, then, led them to interpret the speaker as pretentious, condescending, insincere, and so on.

Since the same variable will be used to make ideological moves by different people, in different situations, and to different purposes, its meaning in practice will not be uniform across the population. This is a point that Barbara Johnstone and Scott Kiesling (2008) have argued, and it cannot be overemphasized. Variability across communities is not limited to linguistic form but is present in the understanding of what that form means and ultimately in the ideologies that underlie language use (cf. Sidnell, this volume). Beatriz Lavandera (1978) argued decades ago that once we leave the level of phonology, that is, once we leave linguistic units that have no meaning of their own, we can no longer claim that class differentiation is simply differentiation of form and not of content. Suzanne Romaine (1984a) has pointed out that the correlation of syntactic variation with social categories cannot proceed before taking account of pragmatic meanings. These meanings, in turn, may be related to social differences. People at different places in the political economy see the world differently, do different things, have different preoccupations, and say different things. I would argue that this principle applies to phonological variation as well.[9] While the entire population might agree on first-order indexicality – who uses what variant – the evaluation of that differentiation can differ across the population. It is reasonable to suggest that the social stratification of variables may in fact reflect socially stratified ideological orientations. One might consider that socioeconomic differences in the use of (ING) potentially involve highly ideological choices, with the use of the velar form indexing one's association with institutions of legitimacy and the power they represent, and the use of the apical form indexing opposition to such institutions and the power that they represent. It is also reasonable to speculate that the class stratification of this form can reflect class-based ideologies about formality. Presumably the almost categorical use of the apical form by Lord Peter Wimsey in the murder mysteries of Dorothy Sayers indexes the effortlessness that comes of entitlement. And it is the embedding of this apical form in a broader upper-class style that allows it to take on this meaning. If I am correct in my assumption that class differences involve ideological differences about formality and displays of education, then one might expect working-class speakers to have the more positive evaluations of this form and middle-class speakers to have the more negative ones.

---

[9] I understand that Michael Silverstein made this point in his Collitz Lecture in 1989. I wish I'd been there to hear it.

Another Example: /t/ Release in American English

Most variables that have been studied socially have been either sound changes in progress or a relatively small set of stable linguistic stereotypes. But recent explorations of hyperarticulation in the form of /t/ release where one would normally not expect release in American English have found correlations with an oddly unconnected set of social categories: nerd girls, Orthodox Jewish boys, and gay men. In a study of the speech of high school students in northern California, Mary Bucholtz (2001, 2011) encountered a group of girls who fashioned themselves as "nerds" – a particular kind of intellectual identity stereotypically limited to boys. One might characterize these girls as intellectual mavericks, since they distanced themselves from teachers, whom they viewed as mere consumers and purveyors of standard intellectual fare. These girls developed a distinctive linguistic style through a variety of means, among them the use of /t/ release. /t/ release has also been associated with Jewishness. In a study of an orthodox Jewish school in northern California, Sarah Benor (2001) found that boys produced significantly more released /t/s than girls, and that the leaders in /t/ release among boys were those who had been formally studying Talmud in a Yeshiva. Furthermore, anecdotal evidence suggested that these boys were particularly likely to release /t/ when making a strong point in an intellectual argument. Finally, released /t/ is part of a common stereotype of gay speech. Rob Podesva, Sarah Roberts, and Kathryn Campbell-Kibler (2002) studied the speech of two lawyers in a debate about the exclusion of gays in the Boys Scouts, one a "straight" lawyer representing the Boy Scouts and the other a "gay" lawyer representing the Lambda League. (While the sexual orientation of the lawyers was not specified in the debate, each lawyer can be seen as officially representing a group defined by sexual orientation.) In this debate, the Lambda League lawyer released significantly more /t/s than the Boy Scout lawyer.

What makes this variant "nerdy," "Orthodox" or "gay" is its participation in three quite different styles. So what is the underlying potential of this variable? The use of /t/ release in the nerd girl style and in the Yeshiva boy style no doubt builds primarily on the social significance of clear speech, which in turn is associated with a school-teachery standard. (There is also the potential of Yiddish as an additional source for Orthodox Jewish /t/ release.) The contrast between the flapped intervocalic /t/ of the United States and the released /t/ of British English further evokes stereotypes of the British as cultured, refined, and articulate, and Americans as anti-intellectual and loutish. Indeed, /t/ release is a common resource for Americans imitating British English, and loutish types in the United States are commonly portrayed as using hypo-articulated /t/. Needless to say, this leads us into a broader view of language ideology – the association of hyper-articulation with care and hypo-articulation with laziness.

The combination of the North American-based association with clear speech and the international association with British speech opens up another set of possible meanings having to do with refinement and elegance. And the intersection of refinement and care opens up the terrain of politeness.

The potential of clear speech is further clarified in Rob Podesva's work (2004, 2007) on gay speech. The very notion of gay speech has been elusive, and Podesva has pursued the study of stylistic variation in the speech of several gay professionals in situations where gayness had different salience. Particularly relevant here is his study of a doctor, Heath, in several settings, including at work in the clinic and at a barbecue with friends. In the clinical setting, Heath needed to present himself as a competent, educated, and articulate professional. But at the barbecue, he was with good friends with whom he was in the habit of presenting himself as a gay "bitchy diva" – as meticulous, style-conscious, critical, and flamboyant. In keeping with the doctor image as an educated and precise professional, Heath released significantly more occurrences of /t/ in the clinic than at the barbecue. But while there were more occurrences of /t/ release in Heath's speech in the clinic, those occurrences of /t/ that he did release at the barbecue had significantly longer and stronger bursts than those in the clinic. In other words, his /t/ release at the barbecue was a parody of his /t/ release in the clinic, yielding what Podesva (2008) calls a "prissy" effect in keeping with his diva persona.

An additional aspect of stop release is its potential to express emphasis, which is related, but not identical, to clarity. Stop release commonly emerges to index exasperation and even anger – and one might consider that Heath's bitchy diva persona combines the prissiness of the teacher's pet and the expression of some kind of generalized attitude of exasperation. Figure 9.4 is an approximation of an indexical field for /t/ release. Needless to say, while Figure 9.3 is based on experimental evidence of hearers' interpretations, Figure 9.4 is based on interpretations of correlations in speech and hence is more speculative. The point, however, is to propose both a way of looking at the indexical value of variation and a goal for further analyses. For purposes of discussion, Figure 9.4 differs from Figure 9.3. While I included both variants of (ING) in Figure 9.3, Figure 9.4 does not include alternatives to /t/ release, although I will discuss alternatives below. In Figure 9.4, I have distinguished between what might be considered permanent qualities (in black) and stances (in gray). I do this not to distinguish between two distinct categories of meanings, but to emphasize the fluidity of such categories and the relation between the two in practice. While anger or cynicism may be momentary and situated stances, people who are viewed as habitually taking such stances may become 'angry' or 'cynical' people through *stance accretion* (Rauniomaa 2003, cited in Bucholtz and Hall 2005:596). By "becoming an angry or cynical person," I mean that one may come to be socially positioned as angry or cynical – that anger and cynicism

The Nature of Indexicality in Variation   161

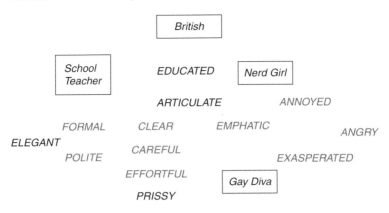

Figure 9.4 Indexical field of /t/ release.

become part of one's identity (in the sense of Bucholtz & Hall 2005) or one's habitual persona. This possibility of stance accretion is central to the fluidity of indexicality, as a mechanism for the elaboration of the indexical field. Figure 9.4 also includes, in boxes, the social types, or enregistered voices, that live at the less fluid end of the field, anchoring the process of interpretation.

The indexical field of /t/ release does not exist in a vacuum but is part of a vast system. While I have not included alternatives to /t/ release in Figure 9.4, an understanding of these alternatives is crucial to understanding this feature and ultimately they belong in this picture. In all his work, Podesva emphasizes that phonetic details are crucial to social meaning in variation, and his attention to the range of variability in stop production leads to an even broader view of the indexical value of /t/ release. Podesva did not limit his study to this form alone but included the full range of articulation of /t/, from hyperarticulation to deletion. In his study of Heath's variation, Podesva not surprisingly finds significantly more /t/ deletion in his casual speech at the barbecue than in the clinic. It is the combination of deletion with the exaggerated bursts that begins to construct the diva style. The salience of hyperarticulation goes beyond clarity and into broader ideologies associated with this trait. The prissy meaning of Heath's strong bursts is no doubt associated with the "goody-goody" image associated with purist teachers who insist on clear standard speech and with their teachers' pets. At the other extreme of the legitimacy hierarchy, the deletion of /t/ is a stigmatized feature of African American Vernacular English (AAVE). The relation between power and hyperarticulation cannot be underestimated, because it provides the basis for the depreciation – and perhaps the maintenance – of AAVE in particular as actively counter-cultural. Some of the main stereotypes of AAVE (cluster reduction, absence of plural and third singular -s) involve absence or hypoarticulation of consonants, throwing the variety directly into opposition with the hyperarticulation of the hyper-standard (Bucholtz 2001). (Andrea Kortenhoven [personal communication] recalls a humorous pronunciation of *anyway* [ɛntiweyz] developed in her African American childhood friendship group, parodying the hyperarticulation of teacher talk.) This attention to the continuum of articulation level thus can be seen as part of a broader national ideology that links hyperarticulation to clarity and clarity to education and power. I might be tempted, then, to revise the indexical field for (ING), inasmuch as in English language ideology, the velar variant is commonly seen as clearer and as hyperarticulation (in some circles), while the apical variant is seen as hypoarticulation (in some circles). Certainly (ING) and /t/ release co-occur stylistically to a great extent, but this has not to my knowledge been studied quantitatively as yet. Whether the two overlap enough that they contribute the same thing to styles is an empirical question.

So far I have examined a very limited kind of variable – hyperarticulation – which is not the kind of variable that is the subject of most variation study. It remains to be seen what kinds of indexical fields other kinds of variables have. No doubt the longer a variable is around the more nuanced meanings it can take on (Haeri 1997), so the fields of sound changes in progress may be less well defined than those of stable variables. On the other hand, they may leave more room for local interpretation. But even stable variables may have a broad potential for social meaning. While Labov's (1966) study of (DH) (commonly referred to as /dh/ stopping) in New York City focused on class differentiation, it is a common variable across immigrant communities and has been found to be ethnically salient among Germans (Rose 2006), Cajuns (Dubois & Horvath 1998a, 1998b), Poles (Edwards & Krakow 1985), and Latinos (Mendoza-Denton 2008). This variable no doubt began in all of these communities as a substratal form, providing a quite pure first-order index. This situation then made the variable available to index ideologies associated with those ethnic groups. Mary Rose's (2006) study of a farming community in Wisconsin found that this variable was overtly associated with the German farming community, although German ancestry no longer correlates with its use. Rather, it appears to have come to be linked to lack of education on the one hand and with the value of hard work associated with small farming on the other. Meanwhile, in Louisiana Cajun English (Dubois & Horvath 1998a), this variable has come to be associated with the prestigious Cajun renaissance. Students in my sociolinguistics class years ago studied this variable in Chicago's Little Italy and found a correlation between /th/ stopping and integration into the Italian community. In my own experience in suburban New Jersey, where the working class was predominantly Italian, /th/ and /dh/ stopping were highly salient, highly conscious variables that we associated overtly with certain personae in our school. These personae were boys we saw as Italian, tough in an endearing way, and not terribly bright, and people regularly used /th/ and /dh/ stopping in performances of each of these characteristics separately. The use of /th/ and /dh/ stopping usually involved emphasis of some sort, and to this day my own speech features /dh/ and sometimes /th/ stopping for emphasis. Of course, this retrospective analysis is highly suspect, but it raises, among other things, the prospect that the indexical field of /th/ stopping in my community overlapped in interesting ways with the field of /t/ release. First of all, /t/ release could be an exaggeration of /th/ stopping – one could say that /th/ stopping feeds /t/ release. But it does not have the same indexical field, for while as a fortition it is certainly emphatic, as a hypoarticulation, it is unlikely to have the indexical values associated with clarity. Thus, /th/ stopping and /t/ release are likely to co-occur stylistically only in cases in which /th/ stopping is quite explicitly indexing annoyance. Once again, this is pure speculation, but with the intention of suggesting directions to follow.

Conclusions

Labov's introduction of class into the study of language was a landmark of immense importance. But his view of the class hierarchy, and of the relation of standard and vernacular language to that hierarchy, is only the beginning of a theory of the social value of variation. The social is not just a set of *constraints* on variation – it is not simply a set of categories that determine what variants a speaker will use – it is a meaning-making enterprise. And while one's place in the political economy has an important constraining effect on how one makes meaning, and on the kinds of meanings one engages with, this place cannot be defined in terms of a simple model. A theory of variation ultimately must deal with meaning, and not only does a view of meaning in variation as predetermined and static seriously undershoot human capacity, it cannot even account in any principled way for the changes in correlations that have been observed over the lifetime of a sound change (e.g. Labov 2001, Chapter 9). Ultimately, all change unfolds in the course of day-to-day exchange, and that exchange involves constant local re-interpretation and re-positioning. Ultimately, it is in this action that we can get at the meaning-making that gives life to variation. While the larger patterns of variation can profitably be seen in terms of a static social landscape, this is only a distant reflection of what is happening moment-to-moment on the ground.

The study of style and of the meaning of variation will raise many new questions. I have focused in this paper on the indexical potential of a few variables, and claimed that variables combine to constitute styles. I have left undiscussed the question of the process of bricolage and the structure of style: Are there constructions? Is stylistic meaning compositional? And implicit in this discussion is the need to examine a far greater range of variables than is commonly done in the field. A study of style and social meaning will focus us on variables that are not apparently changes in progress, or that currently have no particular structural interest. Sadly, these variables will not have been included in large community studies, so we will not benefit from the kind of macrosociological information about them that we do for the more commonly studied variables. This study will also draw our attention to more abstract aspects of variables such as fortition–lenition, hypo–hyperarticulation, or the differential stylistic potential of different phonetic classes. And it will draw us into details of prosody and voice quality. This may also lead us to think about "edgier" issues of emotional expression in language, following Fónagy (e.g. 1971). What I have presented here is just an idea, and an expectation that others will carry the project forward.

10 What Kinds of Signs Are These?

One problem with the indexical field construct is that it isn't clear where the field lives. That is, while I have emphasized fluidity in the meaning of a variable, this field represents pretty much what's in my head. Fluidity resides in the fact that no two people are alike, so we're left with the problem of the relation between my indexical field and those of others near and far, as well as anyone's indexical field over time. For the very reason that Labov argues that the individual is not a subject of linguistic investigation, I would say that the individual is in the end the most interesting subject. Because linguistic competence, when it comes right down to it, is the ability to function as if we all lived in the same world, and as if we all had the same linguistic system. Indeed, the closest I can come to a definition of the speech community is an aggregate of people who are committed to talking the same, in the face of the fact that they don't quite.

Discourse is a continual meaning-making enterprise. The mechanism of variation is not the recognition of a pre-existing relation between variables and consensual social categories; meaning is a product rather than a condition of linguistic practice. Where the study of variation began with the view of variation as a perturbation in the signifier, it is clear now that variables are signs, and part of the larger meaning system of language.

Sociolinguistic variables are indexical signs. That is, they "point to" the immediate context – and from the speaker's perspective. Crucially, the hearer must recognize that the sign is indexical, and must construe what exactly in that context the form is pointing to. The act of construal is central to semiotics, and Peirce (1931) built it into his theory of the sign. Where de Saussure defined the sign in a static fashion – a pairing of form (*significant*) and meaning (*signifié*) – Peirce's sign is tripartite, adding the *interpretant*, or the construal of the relation between the form (*sign vehicle*) and its meaning (*object*). Every use of a sign is based on a construal, and gives rise to an act of construal, which gives rise to a new sign. The Saussurian sign allows us to view meaning as pre-existing in language, but the Peircian sign portrays language as a continual construction of meaning through continual acts of construal and use. In a moment of anger and disgust, I might frown, raise my voice a little, and utter some fortis consonants, including a strongly released /t/. In a moment of beatitude, I might smile benignly, raise my pitch and lower my amplitude a bit, and hyperarticulate some consonants, including /t/. The reader can imagine other things that go with these gestures. The latter of these is more likely to take place in an art museum or after a concert than the former. And depending on how much I raise my pitch, lower my amplitude and hyperarticulate my /t/ (etc.), my interlocutor, particularly if they know me well, might suspect that I'm mocking beatitude. In other words, a variable never occurs alone, and the construal of any verbal gesture is embedded in a larger construal of its context at every level. As Kathryn Campbell-Kibler (2007a) has shown in her experimental work, variables are not interpreted *de novo* but on the basis of the hearer's immediate social perception of the speaker and the speaker's intent. And this interpretation is swift and automatic – not usually the result of conscious thought. In her experimental work, Annette D'Onofrio (2015, 2016) has shown that information about a speaker's persona enters into processing in the very earliest milliseconds of hearing a variable, and indeed we should think of our functioning in the day-to-day world as a continuous and unconscious construal of signs of all sorts.

The following paper, based on my work in Steps Elementary, deals with the multilayered nature of construal. In this case, the issue is a variable that clearly indexes ethnicity. But ethnicity is embedded in a broader set of social meanings. Nobody is ever just Chicano, or Anglo, Brown or White. People are rich, poor, cool, uncool, nice, mean, good students, bad students, troublemakers, teacher's pets, friends, enemies and on and on. And any number of these qualities and many many more may be at play at any moment of construal.

WHERE DO ETHNOLECTS STOP?

Introduction

One day, as I was sitting in Ms Hernandez's fifth grade classroom at Steps[1] Elementary School, Susan, a European American girl, raised her hand to ask the teacher a question. Carlos, sitting beside me at the next table, turned to me with a look of disgust and said, "I hate her – why can't she talk normal?" It wasn't clear which specific feature or features of her speech particularly offended him that morning, but clearly her speech screamed "Valley Girl" to him (as it did to me). At Fields Elementary down the road in a predominantly white Anglo neighborhood, this would not have been remarkable. But at Steps, with its

---

[1] All names, of schools as well as of individuals, are pseudonyms.

small minority of white Anglos, Susan's utterance clashed with the kinds of English that dominated the scene. At Fields, her speech would have struck her classmates as affected, as an attempt to sound cool; at Steps it sounded affected and hyper-white. At Steps, in other words, her speech emerges as an ethnolect.

I recognize that the term *ethnolect* is generally reserved for varieties of a majority language that have been modified through a period of bilingualism in an immigrant community (Clyne 2000). Leaving aside the fact that white Anglos constitute a minority in California, I would argue that the status of an immigrant community's speech as an ethnic variety renders the majority language, by virtue of contrast, an ethnic variety as well. I do not say this simply to point to the fact that this terminology marginalizes minority communities, but to raise a more general issue about linguistic variability. In so doing, I follow Jürgen Jaspers (2008) in pointing out that not only can the notion of ethnolect serve to reinscribe popular ideologies, it also belies the constructed nature of linguistic varieties and of social (in this case ethnic) categories. The term *ethnolect* (like *sociolect* and the more generic *dialect*) reflects a view of language as a fixed rather than fluid entity, and of identity as compartmentalized, allowing one to think of an ethnolect as a discrete system indexical of ethnicity alone. The emphasis in this paper will be on the fact that speakers of so-called ethnolects do not live or speak in isolation, and even if the ethnolect is highly reified, its existence depends on a fairly restricted set of resources. The linguistic resources that ethnolectal speakers deploy in their day-to-day lives are not all specific to the ethnic category, and those that appear to be specifically ethnic can index far more than ethnicity. By examining one feature of "Chicano" and "Anglo" English among students in two elementary schools in Northern California, I will show how ethnically distinctive ways of speaking emerge out of shared social practices, in interaction with each other, and have indexical values that are associated not simply with ethnicity but with those shared practices as well.

Variation and Indexicality

The argument in this paper grows out of my more general view of sociolinguistic variation as a structured set of resources that speakers deploy both intentionally and automatically in their day-to-day practice. The traditional emphasis in variation studies has been to correlate linguistic variables with macro-sociological categories (e.g. class, gender, ethnicity), and to take the correlation to be a sufficient characterization of the variable's social significance. Thus people speak of "working-class" features and "female-led" sound changes. However, the statistical finding that, for instance, women lead in a particular sound change, is the outcome of an aggregate pattern, and says nothing about the kinds of behaviors and ideologies that underlie it, or what kinds of meanings the speakers in question attach to the conservative and innovative variants. The aggregate pattern says nothing about language use and gender in everyday life. It also says nothing about why the same generalization may apply to class stratification – not only women, but working-class people as well, generally lead in sound change. Quantitative generalizations of this sort are fundamental to the study of variation, but understanding the social meaning of variation requires that we examine what lies beneath those generalizations. The very fact that the same variables may stratify regularly with multiple categories indicates that their meanings are not directly related to these categories, but to something that is related to all of them (Silverstein 1985). Thus while a phonological feature might correlate with membership in an ethnic category, and be heard as indexing ethnic identity, it may also take on associations with some apparent quality – some aspect of a stereotype – of that category. And if it falls into use to index that quality, it may take on a more general utility beyond the ethnic group itself.

The study of ethnic "markers" runs the gamut from claims of a full-fledged ethnolect to treatment of small probabilistic differences in the use of individual variables in the majority dialect. In Labov's New York City study (Labov 1966), for example, Italian, Irish and Jewish speakers were shown to differ very slightly in their use of certain New York vocalic variables. Latino and African American speakers, on the other hand, are viewed as having dialects that are quite separate from the dialects of co-territorial white speakers, and their use of features of the white dialect is seen as stepping outside of their dialect – as a sign of ethnic assimilation. But just as there is no way to distinguish between a language and a dialect, there is no obvious way to distinguish between a dialect with ethnic features and an ethnolect. Furthermore, the designation "ethnolect" can be part of a more insidious practice. In the dominant discourse of American dialectology, the white Anglo variety is considered a regional dialect, while African American and Latino varieties are considered ethnic dialects. While these dialects are in fact different from their co-territorial white dialects in ways that Labov's Italian, Irish and Jewish[2] varieties of New York English are not, the dichotomy between regional and ethnic varieties and the lack of attention to regional varieties of African American and Latino speech underscores a deterritorializing discourse of subordinated racial groups. And when the white Anglo variety is given the regional designation, allowing its speakers to run the gamut from deep vernacular to hyper-standard, ethnolects are defined as non-standard, and movement away from ethnolectal features is viewed as a move away from ethnicity. I propose that we consider relations between co-territorial ethnic patterns in different terms. Like Carmen Fought (1999), I would argue

---

[2] There are varieties of "yeshivish," used by some Orthodox Jews, that are sufficiently distinctive to qualify as ethnolects (Gold 1985).

that the participation of Latinos (and African Americans) in sound changes associated with the white population should be seen not as assimilation, but as a stylistic move that deserves more careful attention. Studies of white kids using features of African American English (Bucholtz 1999) do not claim that these kids are trying to assimilate, but that they are trying to borrow specific qualities that they admire in their African American peers. This difference in interpretation lies quite directly in differences in analyses of variation more generally. If a variable is taken to index gender, class or race directly, then one can only view the use of a variable that correlates with one of those categories as constituting a claim to category membership. If, on the other hand, one views variables as indexing these categories indirectly (Ochs 1991; Silverstein 1985), by indexing more everyday stances (Kiesling 2009) and qualities such as toughness, coolness, sexual prowess, maturity, refinement, then such stylistic moves can be seen in the context of speakers' more general movement in the social landscape.

Ethnic differentiation in language is a particularly rich place to see indirect indexicality, or the development of multiple orders of indexicality, at work. The fortition of English /dh/ to [d], often referred to as /dh/ stopping, is a common feature of ethnic varieties in English. Since [ð] is a highly marked consonant, /dh/ stopping is almost a universal substratum form in English, and occurs as an ethnic feature in a variety of communities in the U.S. – Germans (Rose 2006), Cajuns (Dubois & Horvath 1998a; Dubois & Horvath 1998b), Poles (Edwards & Krakow 1985), and Latinos (Mendoza-Denton 2008). In all these cases, the feature has taken on social meanings that emerge from ideologies associated with each community. In her study of a farming community in Wisconsin, in which German ancestry is associated with small farming, Mary Rose (2006) argued that this variable indexes the value of hard work associated with small farming. In Louisiana Cajun English (Dubois & Horvath 1998a), meanwhile, this variable has come to be associated with the prestigious Cajun renaissance, and in the Chicano community in Northern California (Mendoza-Denton 2008), it has come to be associated with toughness and gang affiliation. As long as this feature was associated with non-native speech, its use simply indexed immigrant status. This simple association with a category of speakers is what Michael Silverstein (2003) has termed *first order indexicality*. First order indexicality renders the linguistic feature in question available for association with stereotypes associated with the category. The minute such an association materializes in practice – as soon as speakers begin to use a feature to signal something associated with the category – the feature becomes a *second order index*. In the Wisconsin farm, Cajun and Chicano communities, /dh/ stopping is available to all local speakers to index hard work, prestige or gang affiliation respectively, whether or not the speakers are German, Cajun, or Chicano. This process is continual, since one association tends to raise others so that a variable can move through many meanings and come to have a fairly vast indexical field (Eckert 2008a, see Chapter 9).

Chicano and Anglo Englishes in California

While ethnolects in the U.S. are commonly viewed as variants on a standard or at least regional variety of English, one can argue that the status of Chicano English is as deep as the white variety that is commonly thought of as "California English." Spanish has a deeper history in California than English, as California was originally a Spanish colony, and from Mexican independence until 1848, it was part of Mexico. Anglo American adventurers began to arrive in the early part of the nineteenth century, and groups of Anglo American settlers started arriving halfway through the century. Now, 32% of the California population is Latino, and of them, 84% are of Mexican origin. Steady immigration in the twentieth century, with a major influx since the 1940s, has yielded several robust generations of American-born Latinos – several robust generations of native speakers of English. These generations are known for their development of a distinctive native dialect of English, Chicano English, and it is over comparable generations that the white Anglo population has become sufficiently settled that a distinctive California Anglo dialect has emerged (Moonwomon 1992) as well. Thus while people generally think of Chicano English as based on some Anglo dialect, the two actually emerged over the same historical period, and in clear relation to each other.

There are features of Chicano English that are clearly substratal in origin, such as (th,dh) stopping, light /l/, an [in] variant of (ING), and patterns of intonation – particularly the rise-fall in sentence-final contours (Penfield & Ornstein-Galicia 1985). The segmental variables are quite commonly used by non-Chicanos – light /l/ is a regular feature of AAVE, and often appears in the speech of white Anglo kids, particularly those who hang out with Latino or African American kids. The [in] (as opposed to [ɪn]) pronunciation of the apical variant of (ING) appears to have spread to Anglo dialects of English more generally in California (Fought 2003). On the other hand, the intonational variant is more restricted to Latino speakers. As a prominent feature of Mock Spanish (Hill 1993), and a resource commonly used by Latino comedians to mimic a bracero stereotype, the use of this intonation pattern by an Anglo is likely to be heard as racist.[3] In fact, while one might expect to hear a good deal of crossing (Rampton 1995) at Steps, there is very little. While I have heard some instances of Chicano kids

---

[3] This may be similar to the status of distributive (BE) in African American Vernacular English (AAVE). Julie Sweetland has noted that white kids who grow up in African American peer groups, and are for all intents and purposes speakers of AAVE, will use AAVE phonology but not the distributive (BE) on the grounds that it would be presumptuous.

using bits of Vietnamese to their Vietnamese peers (and these have always been aggressive incidents), I have not heard a similar use of Spanish. The use of Mock Spanish at the national level, in fact, may well preclude such crossing by making it a potentially racist act. But more important, the status of Chicano English makes its features far more appropriate for affiliative moves.

Features of the California white Anglo dialect have been popularized, gendered, raced and classed through their media association with the male surfer and the Valley Girl – gendered icons of privilege, materialism and empty-headedness, but also national trend-setters and the embodiment of white California. I would be inclined to argue that innovations in the white California dialect, which are featured prominently in the media, are part of a setting of California apart from the rest of the country as casual, fun-loving, affluent, free, and white. And at home in California, this is part of staking a claim to California – of establishing California as the property of the casual, fun-loving, affluent, free and white Californian. This Californian exists only in distinction from Californians of color, most particularly Latino Californians, those who take care of the infrastructure and provide the services so necessary to the exercise of fun, freedom and affluence. Arising in opposition in this way, both Chicano English and white California speech could be said to constitute ethnolects, were it not for the fact that while white speech no doubt builds upon features brought here from other states, Chicano English builds upon features from another language. Both represent ways of taking possession of the resources of English to construct a linguistic identity, and the features of both index class, ethnicity, and any number of things that emerge through their lives together.

Valley Girl speech in particular is an extreme stereotype involving distinctive lexical, prosodic, and discourse features, some idiosyncratic consonantal realizations, and an exaggerated use of the California vowel shift. This shift, which will be discussed below, is a series of counter-clockwise vowel changes. Among them, the most prominently recognized as "California" are the fronting of /uw/ and /ow/. The surfer stereotype involves a regular use of *dude*, featuring a simple fronted variant of /uw/ – [dyd]. The Valley Girl pronunciation of both /uw/ and /ow/ involves diphthongization and fronting of the nucleus ([fɪwd] for *food*, [gɛwz] for *goes*). These two features are uncommon in Chicano English. Carmen Fought (1999) has shown, however, that resistance to /uw/ fronting is primarily characteristic of young people who affiliate with Latino gangs, while other Chicanos are likely to show some fronting. She argues, as I will, that this is not a sign of assimilation to white Anglo culture, but a way of being Chicano.

Susan, Carlos, Ethnicity, and the Heterosexual Market

Returning to the classroom, Carlos' reaction to Susan's utterance was not simply to her speech, but to her as an individual. Susan was a very unpopular girl – unhappy, unattractive, without friends, and sometimes overbearing. Her unpopularity had nothing to do with ethnicity – she was equally unpopular with all groups of kids in the school. Nonetheless, she was part of the white minority at Steps, and while some of the other white kids fit in with the diverse student population, their Latino and African American peers generally viewed white kids as privileged in the school and out. For Carlos, Susan's utterance sounded snotty[4] – but white Valley Girl snotty, not Chicano snotty. And as such, it embodied the white claim to favor, approval and privilege – all important commodities in an elementary school. In this way, societal discourses of race and ethnicity unfold on the ground, in day-to-day practice. Susan's unpopularity, her whiteness, her snotty-sounding use of a Valley Girl feature are inseparable, and this tiny incident contributed to Carlos' participation in discourses of race and ethnicity in the school more generally, and in his life outside of school – in his family, his neighborhood, and the media.

I was sitting with Carlos in the course of my ethnographic study of his age cohort's social and linguistic move from childhood to adolescence. I followed this age cohort in two schools through fifth and sixth grades in elementary school, and into seventh grade in junior high school[5] (roughly from the ages of 10 to 14). In both schools, I watched the cohort develop a peer-based social order, with an emerging popular crowd as its focus. This crowd was a community of practice based in the activity of constructing a heterosexual market. The similarities in the events in both schools are striking, and I will focus in what follows on the ways in which these similarities interact with ethnic difference. In this context, ethnic differences in language are deployed not simply in the service of ethnic differentiation, but in the service of other kinds of social differences within the cohort that crosscut – and interact with – ethnicity.

The two schools are in the same district in Northern California, just a ten-minute ride from one another, but they could be in different worlds. Fields Elementary serves a predominantly white Anglo, relatively middle-class student population, while Carlos' school, Steps, serves a poor and ethnically heterogeneous population. The ethnic landscape at Steps is complex. Many kids are second generation, and most of these are bilingual. While there are African Americans, Pacific Islanders, East Indians, Eastern Europeans, and White Anglos, the Latinos and Asian Americans tend to dominate in numbers, hence in visibility. Where the student makeup is similar in the three classrooms serving the age cohort at Fields, there are three quite distinct classrooms at

---

[4] This is not simply speculation. Carlos was quite articulate about language and race.
[5] I was accompanied at Fields Elementary by Christi Cervantes, who was at the time a doctoral candidate at the University of California at Santa Cruz and is now on the faculty at California State University at Sacramento. I am grateful to Christi for her very wonderful ethnographic skills, and her excellent company.

Steps – a Spanish bilingual class, a sheltered English class, and a "regular" class. The majority of the Chicano kids are in the bilingual classroom. Since bilingual education is underfunded in the public schools, the bilingual class can not be a truly bilingual environment, but it provides support to Spanish-speaking kids whose English is not strong, some Spanish literacy to kids who speak Spanish, and a small amount of exposure to Spanish for kids who do not already know the language. The sheltered English class contains many native speakers of English, but also a number of kids who need some extra support in English. The third classroom has no label, and is generally considered to be somewhat accelerated.

With their considerable differences, the kids at Steps and Fields are engaged in a common enterprise – the cohort-wide collaborative move from childhood to adolescence, which involves the construction of a peer-based social order. In childhood, kids belong to friendship groups, they engage in norm enforcement, and some kids are more popular than others. But ultimately, organized social control lies in the hands of adults. In general, friendships are determined by neighborhood and classroom assignment, and it is parents and teachers who discipline kids for social transgressions, enforcing adult norms for the age group. As a cohort approaches adolescence, it appropriates social control from adults and creates norms and a structured social system and norms to support them. This is the first time that kids begin to see themselves as part of a structure beyond the family, and to view themselves as having value on a social market. In both Fields and Steps (as in my own postwar elementary school on the east coast), the social order emerges in the course of fifth and sixth grades in the form of a heterosocial crowd, which is an alliance of smaller friendship groups of kids who have emerged as popular through early elementary school. The crowd brings boys' and girls' networks into a collaboration, combining social status and resources and yielding a sufficiently large social aggregate to dominate the local scene and to contrast with the other kids' small friendship groups. The crowd stands out not simply as popular people, but as above the everyday friendship business of "ordinary" kids. The crowd draws from all classrooms, and while their business unfolds primarily on the playground, they bring crowd business noisily back into their respective classrooms in a constant display of their transcendence of adult arrangements.

Crowd business is above all concerned with building alliances both among girls and between girls and boys, most crucially in the construction of a heterosexual market. Anyone knows that kids experience a good deal of heterosexual boyfriend–girlfriend talk from almost toddlerhood. However, it is in the preadolescent social market that heterosexuality becomes organized, as it underlies the emerging peer social order. It begins in late elementary school (age 10) with a frantic and highly visible activity of pairing up of male–female pairs. The pairs generally last as little as a day and a week, and the boy and girl who make up a pair do not interact much – in fact, mutual avoidance is the norm. This is not just a result of shyness and the newness of the situation, but because the pairing is not about a relationship between a girl and a boy. What is at stake in this activity is the integration of the peer social order. The pairs are negotiated, not by the two individuals involved, but by the crowd as a whole, and the short duration of the pairs allows for fast trading, and the creation of value both for those who are traded and for those who accumulate the power to do the trading. This process involves a crucial change in the gender order as male and female become complementary constituencies in the heterosexual enterprise. Overwhelmingly, girls decide who should be paired, and approach the boys to facilitate with the male side of the pair. The process of negotiation comes to be not only central to their own activity, but the focus of public performances that engage the entire cohort in one way or another. The events in the crowd become news, and the actual activities take center stage on school grounds so that the school becomes a stage for the crowd's public performances. In this way, the crowd gains the power, coherence and visibility to dominate the social market, giving everyone else the status of onlooker.

The trading process itself creates a new gender order, as the crowd girls become social engineers, seeking excitement in negotiation, the technology of beauty, the construction of a "cute" personality, and drama. The crowd girls enter into flamboyant stylistic activity, including – even perhaps particularly – speech activity. And it is at this point that the social market spawns a linguistic market. Bourdieu's notion (e.g. 1977) of the linguistic market is a monolithic market at the national level. Institutions of power are the locus of the construction of legitimacy, including the construction and maintenance of the legitimate linguistic variety. Put quite simply, ideas expressed in the legitimate variety will have greater legitimacy in the social market. In the elementary school, the heterosexual crowd is in the business of constructing local legitimacy. Like a national elite, the crowd generates and commodifies access (e.g. birthday party invitations; participation in games), and knowledge (e.g. who's who and who's with whom in the new social order; who's fighting with whom). Most crucial is knowledge of ever-changing stylistic information of all sorts – new ways of dressing, moving, saying things. It is in this context, I would argue, that gender differences emerge in many aspects of language, as the boys take on ways of moving and speaking that create an appearance of bulk and containment, while the girls become flamboyant in motion, posture, adornment, and speech.

While the bones of these activities are the same at Fields and Steps, there are important differences. The paired girls and boys at Fields show a level of avoidance that one does not find at Steps – while the Steps pairs do not spend time together, there is a discourse of romance that is noticeably absent at Fields. The crowd is quite monolithic at Fields – although there are African Americans and a Latina in the Fields crowd, the crowd is dominated by white Anglos and there is no discourse of diversity. The main crowd at Steps is predominantly Latino. While there is something resembling an Asian American crowd that involves some heterosexual pairing, none of this is done in public to the extent that it is done in the Latino or the Fields Anglo crowd. This means that while it isn't the only game in town, the Latino crowd dominates public spaces, and it is the voices of the Latino crowd that get heard on the playground. While this crowd is dominated by Latino kids, it is quite consciously diverse, involving not only Latinos, but a few white Anglos, Asians and African Americans, and it perceives itself as an alliance of kids of color.

The hub of activity for the crowd is the bilingual classroom, and the classroom buzzes with social activity, almost exclusively in English. There is tremendous class pride, and the students in this classroom express competition with, and contempt for, the sheltered English class, whose students they consider uncool. The relation between ethnicity and coolness is key to social dynamics at Steps. The Chicano community has a deep history in California and in this community, whereas the other populations are relative newcomers. Like the Anglos at Fields, the Chicano kids at Steps have older siblings, and many of them have parents and aunts and uncles who have gone through the American school system. Thus they have a sense of tradition, of following others like them through a time-worn process and into an established adolescent culture. While this adolescent culture is in many ways similar to the adolescent culture that is emerging at Fields, it is also grounded in a strong ethnic community that is solidly based in the area, with family ties and activities that are grounded in the local area. This community is also steeped in violence – many of the kids at Steps have had relatives who were threatened, injured or killed, making the danger extremely personal. This violence connects kids to gang orientation – both because the gangs bring violence, and because they provide protection in the face of violence. Most of the Chicano kids claim a Norteño identity[6] while entering quite sincerely into school anti-gang rhetoric. For them, the anti-gang rhetoric is about gang violence – which they see as separate from the association of ethnic identity with protection, support and loyalty that are the positive side of gangs. Some of the boys have older siblings, cousins, or uncles who socialize them into gang culture, and in concrete situations, one can see this tutelage emerging as pressure to maintain their pride through violent means. At the same time, kids will entertain themselves by playfully practicing "dogging" each other in preparation for confronting Sureños in public places. This stage, this entrance into adolescence, therefore, is the beginning of the end of innocence. Bravado – like the heterosexual market – becomes a kind of play, but with a clear serious future.

---

[6] A U.S.-based gang that emerges in opposition to Sureños, who are more oriented to Mexico (see Mendoza-Denton 2008).

176   The Third Wave

At Fields, there is much talk of gangs, but only a handful of students have had any personal contact with gangs. The kids in Steps and Fields are aware of each other's schools, and of their ethnic and socioeconomic makeup. And just as the Steps kids are aware of them, the Fields kids are aware of the poor Latino presence around them. To the kids at Fields, Latino means tough, gang, threat, disenfranchisement. It is to a great extent in contrast to the disenfranchisement of the Latino population that the white kid social order achieves local hegemony. At Fields, there is a sense of historical entitlement. They have just walked into a school that was made for them – a school just like the ones their parents and older siblings went to, a school that feels like a smooth extension of home – a school made in their image. The school is there for them to do what they're going to do. At Steps, the school is preoccupied with the real danger from others that Steps kids face in their neighborhoods, and with the potentially harmful actions of the kids themselves – gang affiliation, sexual activity, violence. As a result, activities that are generally smiled upon at Fields are closely watched at Steps. At Fields, teachers watch the beginnings of heterosexual activity with amusement, while at Steps, teachers watch it with trepidation.

Linguistic Resources

In both schools, the crowds represent social advance, sophistication, coolness. Their activities amount to a production of legitimacy, as they become the arbiters of all things social, including style of all sorts. As they become the stylistic movers and shakers of the cohort, their linguistic practice takes on a particularly public character, and it is their social market that allows for the development of a local, cohort-wide, linguistic market. A discussion of these two linguistic markets begins with the obvious observation that California Anglo English is the symbolic capital of the crowd at Fields, while Chicano English is capital in the crowd at Steps. And while each crowd – and the school it dominates – has a clear ethnic character, the relation between speakers' ethnicity and place in the social market is not simple.

The California vowel shift shown in Figure 10.1 involves, in addition to the well-known fronting of back vowels, a counter-clockwise rotation of the front and low vowels. The lax vowels are lowering, and backing across the bottom of the system: [bɛt] *bit*, [bæt] *bet*, [bɑt] *bat*. The merged /o/ (*cot*) and /oh/ (*caught*) are moving into the vowel space of /oh/. Finally, /ʊ/ is fronting or lowering to yield [pʉt] or [pʌt] *put* and /ʌ/ is moving slightly forward to yield [bɛt] *but*. A particularly striking difference between Anglo and Chicano speech in California is the treatment of /ae/ (*man, cat*). Figure 10.1 shows /ae/ *bat* both lowering-backing and raising. In all regions across the U.S., in what is commonly referred to as a *nasal pattern*, /ae/ diphthongizes and the nucleus raises before nasals ([meᵊn] *man*). In the east and midwest, /ae/ raises

What Kinds of Signs Are These?

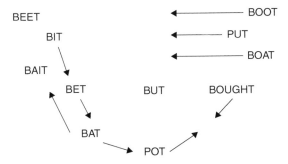

Figure 10.1 The Northern California Vowel Shift.

in other environments as well, depending on the region. California shows a pure nasal pattern, in which /ae/ diphthongizes and raises only before nasals. This combines with a more general counter-clockwise vowel shift, so that while pre-nasal occurrences are fronting and raising, other occurrences of /ae/ are lowering and backing ([mɑt] *mat*). This creates a potential split between the two sets of occurrences, and it is this development that will be of interest in what follows, for Chicano speakers tend not to show the nasal pattern. /ae/ represents a salient point of differentiation between English and Spanish, since orthographic convention links English /ae/ to Spanish /a/, and indeed, an [a] pronunciation for this phoneme is a common feature of non-native accents in English. The low Chicano pronunciation of /ae/, therefore, is commonly heard as Spanish interference. Certainly such a substratum effect in native English can provide a convenient resource for the construction of Chicano identity, analogously to /th,dh/ stopping, and this may well be an important force behind the Chicano feature. But it is now a feature of a native dialect of English, and once part of the dialectal repertoire, it is available to become a second order index, and to be used for social purposes beyond marking ethnicity.

The domination of Fields and Steps by Anglo and Latino crowds respectively, predicts that the nasal (Anglo) pattern will be the norm in the crowd at Fields, while the non-raising (Chicano) pattern will be the norm at Steps. Indeed, this is so. Figures 10.2 and 10.3 show F1–F2 plots for /ae/ for two extreme speakers of the two patterns, Rachel (from Fields Elementary) and Selena (from Steps Elementary). Rachel and Selena are central members of the crowd in their respective schools. In Figures 10.2 and 3,[7] the squares highlighted in black are the pre-nasal occurrences (aeN), while the plain squares represent /ae/ before non-nasals (ae0). The difference in the means of the two sets of occurrences is

---

[7] I have not normalized these formant values, because the speakers are pre-pubescent and show very little difference in F0 range. In the case of (ae0)-(aeN) difference, this is not even an issue since I am comparing within speakers.

178   The Third Wave

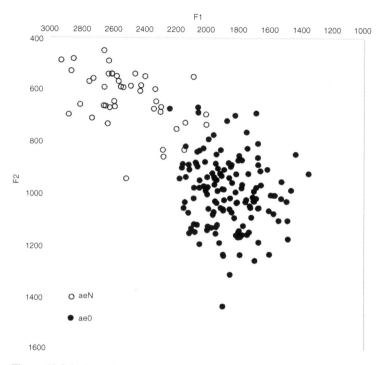

Figure 10.2 /ae/ nasal pattern (Rachel, Fields Elementary).

significant at the <.001 level in Rachel's speech, and there is no difference at all in Selena's speech. These two girls' patterns are extreme versions of the nasal and the non-raising pattern – one might say they are the stylistic norms of the two crowds – and the rest of their peers show a range of patterns in between.

Table 10.1 shows the range of vowel height, represented by the first formant, for boys and girls at each school. The overall range for all tokens of /ae/ is significantly greater at Fields than at Steps, and in both schools it is greater for girls than for boys. The gender difference in the use of this vowel reflects a generally greater stylistic activity among the girls, and reflects the more general finding that women and girls show a greater range of variation than men and boys, suggesting a gender-based difference in the tendency to use language to signal social difference (Eckert 2000; Eckert & McConnell-Ginet 1992). The evidence (Romaine, 1984b) shows that across communities, gender differences in phonological variation appear at about this age, and I would argue that the radical process of change in gender practice taking place in preadolescence is the social power behind this linguistic development.

Overall, however, the range of variation is considerably smaller at Steps than at Fields. This reflects not a lack of sociolinguistic activity, but diversity

What Kinds of Signs Are These?

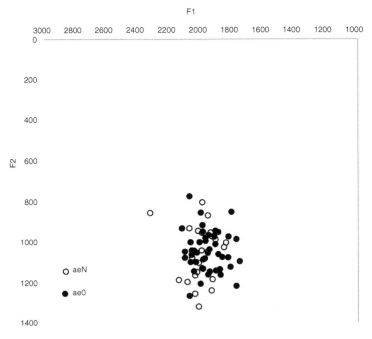

Figure 10.3 /ae/ non-raising pattern (Selena, Steps Elementary).

Table 10.1 *Range of F1 for /ae/ in Hz at Fields and Steps*

	Lowest	Highest	Range
Fields Girls	352	1377	1025
Fields Boys	507	1361	854
Steps Girls	575	1368	793
Steps Boys	660	1241	581

of a different kind, as it is the outcome of averaging speakers with and without the nasal pattern. Figures 10.4 and 10.5 are F1–F2 plots showing (aeN) (highlighted) and (ae0) for individual Fields and Steps speakers respectively. While the difference between the (aeN) and the (ae0) means is greater at Fields than at Steps, speakers in both schools show a significance of .001 for the overall difference in means between (aeN) and (ae0) in both F1 (which corresponds to vowel height) and F2 (which corresponds to vowel frontness) overall. But at Fields, this overall mean is mirrored in the speech of every individual: half the speakers at Fields show no overlap at all between the tokens of (aeN) and (ae0), and in all cases but one, the difference in the means for (aeN)

180   The Third Wave

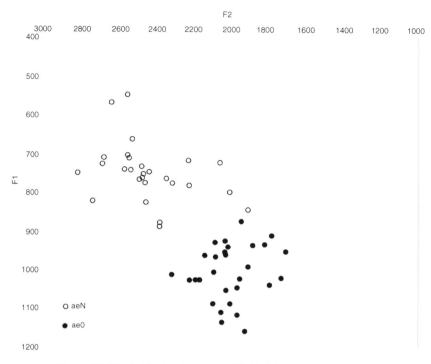

Figure 10.4 Individual (ae) means at Fields Elementary.

and (ae0) is significant for both F1 and F2. The only exception is one boy who shows a difference in F2 that is not statistically significant, but he shows a highly significant (p<.001) difference in F1. There is far greater diversity in the use of this pattern at Steps. While the difference between the aggregated (aeN) and (ae0) means is significant at the .001 level in both formants for the cohort as a whole, all but two speakers show some overlap between the tokens of (aeN) and (ae0). Half the speakers show a significant difference in F1 and half of them show a significant difference in F2, but only one third of the speakers show a significant difference in both formants, and one third of the speakers show no significant difference in either formant.

The fact that the nasal pattern is the norm at Fields but not at Steps shows up clearly in the weakness of the splits that do occur at Steps. Those people at Steps who do have the nasal pattern have a weaker pattern than is the norm at Fields. Figure 10.6 plots the values for the difference in F1 between the (ae0) and (aeN) means for students at Steps (n=22) and Fields (n=26). As this figure shows, the values at Steps are consistently lower than at Fields.

At Fields, the main social difference in the use of /ae/ is gender – girls overall show a more extreme split than boys. While the most extreme examples

What Kinds of Signs Are These? 181

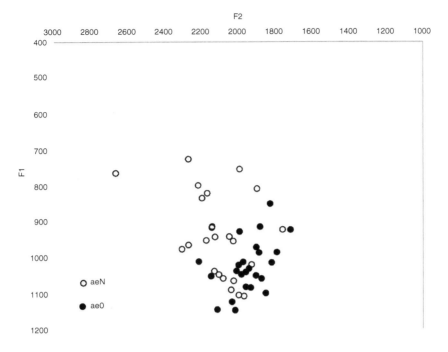

Figure 10.5 Individual (ae) means at Steps Elementary.

of the split show up in the speech of crowd girls, there is no general correlation between crowd membership and the extent of the split. The one Latina in the crowd shows the same pattern as her Anglo peers – in fact, her nasal pattern is the second strongest at Fields. This girl is from the Steps catchment area, but attends Fields because her parents consider it a better and safer school. At Steps, the non-raising pattern appears in the speech of all crowd members regardless of ethnicity, while almost all of the non-crowd people show at least some nasal pattern. Table 10.2 shows 20 speakers from Steps Elementary: 6 boys and 14 girls. Speakers are listed in ascending order of the F1 difference between (aeN) and (ae0). The crowd members cluster at the top of the table, showing no significant difference between (aeN) and (ae0), while with only one exception,[8] the non-crowd members show a significant

---

[8] Merilee, the one non-crowd member who shows no significant difference is the only exception to this pattern. While she identifies as African American, her speech shows no phonological or morphosyntactic AAVE features. One of her parents is European (hence her bilingualism), and the parent who is African American speaks standard African American English (that is, some African American phonology and standard syntax and morphology). Thus it would be a mistake to conclude that her non-adoption of the nasal pattern is due to competition from AAVE.

182   The Third Wave

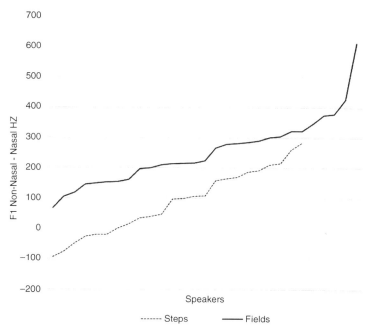

Figure 10.6 F1 (ae0) – F1 (aeN) in Hz.

difference. While the number of speakers analyzed so far (particularly boys) is somewhat small, the data nonetheless show that it is not ethnicity alone that determines whether a kid will have a nasal or a non-raising pattern. While six of the crowd members in this table are Chicano, two of them, Randolph and Trudy, are not. Similarly, two of the non-crowd members showing the nasal pattern are Chicanas. These two girls, Belinda and Carolyn, each have one Anglo parent, and one might reasonably ask if their lack of the non-raising pattern is a result of early exposure to the nasal pattern. But early exposure does not account for several other speakers. Randolph's parents are both native speakers of English, yet he has a pronounced non-raising pattern. And Purnima and Judi, both coming from non-native English speaking homes, show a clear nasal pattern. It appears from these figures that it is crowd participation, which invokes but does not equal ethnicity, that is most salient in the use of the non-raising pattern. It is important to emphasize that ethnicity is simply not a given, but is something that is claimed and contested. Belinda and Carolyn both come from families in which Chicano culture dominates, and both clearly identify as Chicana. However, their status as 'on the outs' with the crowd is intimately connected with challenges to their ethnic status, which seem to center not

What Kinds of Signs Are These?

Table 10.2 *F1(aeN) – F1(aeO) for 20 kids at Steps Elementary (Shaded rows are crowd members)*

Speaker	Ethnicity	Sp.bilingual	F1 Diff. Hz.	p
Manny	Chicano	yes	−26	n.s.
Selena	Chicana	yes	−20	n.s.
Carlos	Chicano	yes	1	n.s.
Renata	Chicana	yes	14	n.s.
Randolph	European American	no	35	n.s.
Geneva	Chicana	no	39	n.s.
Marisol	Chicana	yes	47	n.s.
Merilee	African American	yes	54	n.s.
Trudy	Asian American	yes	57	n.s.
Arthur	Indian American	yes	106	.05
Winifred	European American	no	107	.025
Purnima	Indian American	yes	187	.025
Adam	European American	yes	97	.005
Carolyn	Chicana	no	260	.005
Leslie	European American	no	284	.005
Kenneth	European American	no	216	.001
Judi	Asian American	yes	210	.001
Katya	European American	yes	192	.001
Jocelyn	European American	no	158	.001
Belinda	Chicana	no	169	.001

around the authenticity of their homes but around their inappropriate behavior as members of the peer social order.

The stylistic use of variables is of course essential to establishing indexical value. If the nasal and the non-nasal patterns are associated with crowd practice at Fields and Steps respectively, then one would expect these patterns to intensify when speakers are engaged in such practice. The beginnings of an examination of stylistic variation supports the claim being made here. Figure 10.7 shows two points for each of five speakers – one point representing the value of F1(ae0) – F1(aeN) in conversation with me alone (labelled 'serious'), and one representing the value of F1(ae0) – F1(aeN) in more excited speech with peers about cohort-related topics. The figure shows Merilee in a conversation with me about friends on the one hand, and in an interaction with friends on the playground in which she is complaining about problems in the classroom. The figure also shows Trudy's speech in a similar conversation about friends with me, and in a gossipy interaction with a friend and me. Merilee and Trudy, both of whom show the non-raising pattern, show even less raising in more peer-oriented speech. The reverse pattern shows up in Fields. Elmira, who is

184   The Third Wave

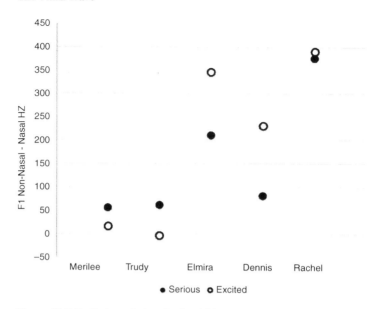

Figure 10.7 Stylistic variation for five kids.

not part of the crowd, increases the split from 210 Hz in an interview with me to 346 Hz while discussing her shopping for school clothes. Dennis, a member of the crowd, moves from a difference of 76 in an interview to 231 when he's discussing plans for the big upcoming party (most particularly, who's going to dance with whom). Finally, Rachel, the class drama queen, shows a very slight increase as she moves from talking to me about sixth grade to talking with friends about the same upcoming party that Dennis is discussing. I might note that Rachel's speech with me already shows such an extreme split that it would be difficult for her to increase it. While none of these shifts are large enough to be very significant on their own (particularly Rachel's, who is quite dramatic in all her speech), the fact that they all follow a clear pattern does suggest that these differences are meaningful.

Conclusions

Certainly many features of Chicano and Anglo English are quite distinct, and ethnic distinctness is an important force in the community and in language use. At the same time, in many places, Anglo and Chicano kids attend school together, play together, and ultimately marry each other. And while it is common for there to be ethnic divisions in school and out, these divisions are produced and reproduced in the context of day-to-day contact, and become part and parcel of a broader peer culture, in which social, cultural and linguistic resources are on the table for all to interpret, consider, and possibly use. In this context, it becomes a bit odd to view the California shift as propelled by Anglos and resisted by Chicanos; rather, one can view aspects of this shift as being propelled by identity work within and across both communities. California white Anglo English and Chicano English are constructed not simply in opposition to each other, but in conjunction with each other as well. And in communities in which Chicano and white Anglo speakers interact on a day-to-day basis, the meanings of linguistic resources may come to have a very complex relation to ethnicity. The non-raising pattern at Steps is not only associated with ethnicity, but with norms of coolness that emerge within the ethnic group, but which are about the peer-based social order at school, and which are available to those outside the ethnic group as well. If we are to focus only on larger demographic categories, the importance of what is shared across ethnic groups will appear as negligible subtleties, and the speakers whose use of (aeN) does not conform to their ethnic assignment will appear to indicate assimilation to another category. This difference will appear subtle to the sociolinguist seeking the larger patterns, and for whom the distinction between ethnic membership and ethnic practice may be just noise. But if our aim is to understand linguistic competence in practice – to understand how the individual speaker constructs a persona within a landscape in which ethnicity plays a prominent but not determining role – then the subtleties of indexicality take on supreme importance.

11 The Semiotic Landscape

So what's going on here? Are the kids in the Steps crowd resisting an Anglo pattern that's spreading through the speech of the non-crowd kids? And are they being more Chicano than their non-crowd peers? Clearly it's not that simple.

Carlos lives in a landscape inhabited by all kinds of people. The ones closest to him are the ones in his own family, neighborhood and school. But his landscape extends far beyond – to people he encounters in public places, in the media, and in conversation with teachers, friends and family. This landscape is peopled with gangsters, veterinarians, taggers, storekeepers, bullies, snobs, cute girls, clueless white teachers, a white ethnographer, and on and on. And ultimately he moves through this landscape, construing signs in the interests of seeking justice, fun, opportunity, love, friendship. And his peers at both Steps and Fields are doing the same thing, but each from a slightly different perspective and on a slightly different landscape.

One might say that macro-social categories constitute a kind of social map. What distinguishes a landscape from a map is that it embodies perspective, and persona is the means by which individuals present themselves, and identify others in, and with respect to, the social landscape. *Landscape* is a metaphor that pops up all over social science in the form of ethnoscapes, technoscapes, financescapes, mediascapes (Appadurai 1996), even selfscapes (Hollan 2014). It is a useful metaphor not only because spatializing social relations is a cognitive aid, but because every landscape embodies a perspective. In his account of the enregisterment of RP, Asif Agha (2003:232) emphasizes that "the folk-term 'accent' does not name a sound pattern alone, but a sound pattern linked to a framework of social identities." A stylistic landscape is such a framework, emphasizing the perspective of ego, the stylistic agent.

An individual's, or a community's, landscape is constructed in the interests of producing a *local* – a "who we are" – that embodies relations to the non-local. Appadurai (1996, Chap. 9) speaks of localness as an active construction, which involves what the local is not, as well as what it is. One could say that a stylistic landscape is constructed in the service of the production of locality, combining resources that are available through direct everyday exposure with resources encountered at a greater social (and geographic) distance. Stylistic

The Semiotic Landscape 187

practice picks out and arranges elements to create a "here," in relation to diverse "theres," which will be constrained, but not determined, by physical and social locality.

As an example, I go back to the case of the two Preppy girls at Palo Alto High who pegged their blue jeans as a way of incorporating what they saw as the New Wavers' independence. The New Wavers who served as the source for these girls' pegging were a community of practice of about ten people, who prided themselves on their social consciousness and their alienation from what they saw as the shallowness of the affluent adolescent community around them. One of them had a sister studying in Germany, and they had gotten into Punk and New Wave through her. Their style, thus, came not from direct contact or from their own community. In fact, reaching beyond their immediate community was part and parcel of their claim to alienation from, and transcendence of, the local high school culture. They pointed out to us that they recognized the irony that they drove BMWs to school, while real Punks "live in garbage cans." But they bought their clothes at second-hand stores and countermanded local stylistic norms as an expression of their alienation from what they saw as a local elitist hierarchy, and from the conformism that they saw as maintaining that hierarchy. In other words, these kids were reaching beyond their immediate social landscape, basing their style on their locally based perception of a distant figure.

The Punk in this story is a characterological figure (Agha 2003),[1] an abstract and widely consensual social type. The *Punk*, the *Valley Girl*, the *Cholo*, the *Hippy* and the *Preppy* all stand out as reference points – as time-specific social types stereotypically identified with specific ways of looking, acting and speaking. They give shape to the stylistic landscape, marking important and timely social distinctions. While characterological figures articulate the landscape, persona relates each individual to the landscape and to those figures. The Paly High New Wavers had no personal knowledge of Punks or even of the British social scene in which the Punks figured. But they imagined the Punks in terms of their own local concerns, selecting aspects of the Punks' counter-cultural stance to align with their own. Thus while characterological figures may be present in the imaginations of a large component of the population, the perception of what those figures mean is part of the construction of the local. The New Wavers in turn offered a local counter-cultural style as a resource for the Preppy girls. The Preppy girls knew little of the New Wavers' ideology but admired their resistance to the high school establishment, which was what they

---

[1] Both the term *social type* and the term *character type* are problematic, to the extent that they were coined by Simmel and Reich respectively, to refer to types within specific theories. I adopt Agha's (2003) characterological figure to refer to the social construct associated with linguistic register.

borrowed by pegging their jeans. They constructed a persona that placed them in a distinctive position within the Preppy community, carving out that position as part of what it meant to be Preppy, thus shifting the entire community of practice just a bit. If their move had been more extreme – for example, if they had chosen to wear black – they would have risked moving too far to still be Preppies, because black had a more enregistered meaning that was in clear conflict with Preppie-hood.

Spreading vs. Circulation

Landscape is an important way to see variation in the social world because it allows us to see meaning arrayed in the world. Differences in material style call out social differences, and so do differences in linguistic style. The two go hand in hand to locate social meaning in its multidimensional context. Sociolinguists talk about the movement of change as *spread*, while Linguistic Anthropologists use the term *circulate*. The notion of spread carries a connotation of moving across a continuous area in a continuous direction, arriving at each new place once and for all. Circulation, on the other hand, involves passing from person to person or place to place, but not necessarily in a predetermined direction, and can involve returning to the starting point. While structure constrains circulation, circulation emphasizes the fact that the movement and construal of a sign is not a once-and-for-all thing, but it continues to move around in the places to which it has spread.

The *spread* metaphor surfaces when linguists speak of kids as developing patterns of variation by imitating older kids, providing a straight line of transmission from individual to individual. But while small children do imitate older people, this is a very childlike thing to do, and imitation is stigmatized among older children. Imitation implies that the variable is taken on not as a sign, but just as a way of speaking that's more like an admired person's way of speaking. I would guess that imitation of individuals ceases and engagement with social meaning takes over at a fairly early age.

Our ability, indeed our need, to recognize, parse and produce patterns underlies language development, which has to begin with the recognition of the patterning of linguistic form with non-linguistic happenings. The development of variation is part of the child's development of social distinctions, and there is every reason to believe that their first perceptions of social patterns are in emotional displays – quite possibly beginning in infancy with prosodic patterns (Fernald 1989). The earliest household social relations expand beyond. Small kids' use of variability in role playing (Andersen 1990) involves character types in family life – doctors, fathers, mothers – and shows clearly that kids are systematically attentive to style from the start. Probably some of the earliest socially significant variables are features

The Semiotic Landscape

of "baby talk," since being or not being a baby is a central social concern for kids from an early age. (Features of baby talk also figure prominently in adult stylistic practice, used to express both belittlement and intimacy.) Studies of small children's acquisition of variation so far (e.g. Foulkes, Docherty & Watt 2005; Smith, Durham & Fortune 2009) have focused on parent–child interactions rather than on interactions with siblings and peers, so for the moment we can only speculate about the way in which small children's indexical systems expand as their social landscapes expand. And linguistic variability is built into that landscape.

I have argued (Eckert 1994, 2000) that children are driven by a "developmental imperative," that is, a focus on moving to the next stage, developing new abilities, knowledge, freedoms, constructing an older persona. But kids are not necessarily looking to take on the same older persona as their elders. Rather, asserting oneself involves differentiation. As I approached each life stage, I did not move into it in the way my mother did – or even my older sister. As a child, I was aware that my mother came from an "old-fashioned" era, and part of my emerging sense of self was based in what I saw as a native understanding of the contemporary world. My differentiation of myself from my mother was embedded in ongoing social changes as I strived to be a "more advanced" kind of person. When I reached adolescence, adolescent life was already different than it had been for my sister. We are indeed quite different from each other, but some of those differences are a result of historical circumstance. My sister and I spent our adolescences in very different social-semiotic landscapes: Benny Goodman vs. Elvis, and my developmental imperative at that point encompassed the need to be "more modern." In other words, we do not just imitate our elders – we also move away from them, and we compete with them.

Archaeologist Ian Hodder (1982) has argued that stylistic distinction "may relate not so much to the existence of social categories but to a concern with those categories ... to ideologies and strategies of legitimation" (p. 193). The fact that global engagement emerged in the construction of Beijing Yuppie personae is an indication of the need for a stylistic resource at that time and in that place. The north–south difference in Mandarin tone structure acquired new meaning in a particular place in a particular moment in the course of changes in the nature and locus of economic power. The Yuppies' cosmopolitan style was a prerequisite for their role in foreign financial institutions, but also contributed to the success of those institutions. And as they brought this new kind of persona into being, they drew the cosmopolitan milieu into young Beijing society. The Yuppie style, thus, was not simply an outcome of massive economic and social change, but part of, and essential to, that change. The small stylistic moves that participate in the construction of new personae are micro-moments of social change. This is the crux of the performative nature of variation. It creates, in the moment, that which it indexes – a persona, and it is in that creation that change happens.

Like linguistic change, social change must take place in small enough increments to maintain interpretability. Innovative personae are the more immediately accessible manifestations – indeed agents – of change. Valley Girls and Yoga Moms, for example, represent change in our daily landscape, and this in turn indicates change in the social order. Age, class and gender are basic and enduring systems of social distinction to society, but they are not static – they have changed in my lifetime, and we can expect to find changes in their broader correlations with variation over the long term. Most Yoga Moms did not have mothers who were Yoga Moms, and the fact that they are Yoga Moms is part of their place in society and in history.

Where Do We Go From Here?

Approaching variation from the perspective of meaning raises questions about the range of meanings variables can carry, and about how variation interacts with other meaning systems in language. Variables are a heterogeneous bunch, ranging in form from morphosyntax to voice quality, and in meaning from social class to emotion in the moment. I would venture that variables constitute a continuum of interiority – that is, a continuum from the public to the personal, from the exterior to the interior self – a continuum of increasing performativity, iconicity and embodiment.

Morphosyntactic variables, I would argue, define the public, exterior end of the continuum. The constraints on their appearance are primarily propositional – that is, whether the sentence is negative or positive depends on the nature of the proposition. But once negation occurs, the choice of whether to use the standard or the non-standard form is purely indexical. Segmental size, sporadic availability and referential components raise morphosyntactic variables to such a level of awareness that they become the focus of standard ideology and educational attention. It is no doubt for this reason that variables like negative concord, non-standard subject–verb agreement, and the lexical variant *ain't* are highly enregistered, functioning as shibboleths, with quite fixed social meanings associated with external facts like class and particularly education. In situated discourse, orders of indexicality that emerge from these external facts are generally consciously and ideologically related to class, such as toughness and alienation.

Phonological variables are indexically more reliable than morphosyntactic ones since they occur regularly and frequently. Some of them have structural origins, such as components of chain shifts, while others may emerge from contact – such as the non-English origins of th/dh stopping. These seem to enter into orders of indexicality that depart from the populations in which they originate, specifically to the social distinctions that set those populations apart.

Then there are phonological variables that involve sound symbolism. Annette D'Onofrio and I have begun to work on sound symbolism in segmental variation, based on my preliminary finding (Eckert 2011) of the use of the frequency code (Ohala 1994) in expressions of affect. Sound symbolic resources are recruited into affective expression precisely because they seem natural – because speakers feel that they are not specific to social groups or categories but are what we share as humans. At the sound-symbolic level, it is the very materiality of phonetic features that takes on meaning, which brings us into the realm of embodiment. When we move beyond the segmental to prosody, we get into territory that people commonly think of as even less under the speaker's control – as in some sense betraying emotional states. And finally, voice quality is the ultimate embodied resource, commonly believed to reflect the person's inner self.

While we may find co-variation between sound change and morphosyntactic variables such as negative concord at the macro-social level, they do not necessarily co-vary at the individual level. I would argue that this is due to their only partially intersecting indexicality – the sound change related primarily to place and negative concord primarily to class. And this is no doubt behind the fact that women at the macro level lead in sound change but lag in the use of non-standard morphosyntactic variables. But how about affect? Macro-social structures shape social contact, so they play a fundamental role in shaping linguistic patterns. But they also shape living conditions, which in turn shape practice, ideology and affect. And of course, these turn around and reproduce the macro-social structures. Affective ideology was central to the Jock–Burnout distinction in my Detroit study – kids in both categories focused on the fact that the Jocks did *happy* and the Burnouts did *serious* and *oppressed*. If we were to follow many of our affective variables up to the macro-social level, we'd no doubt find correlations. I wouldn't even be surprised to find that amplitude is class and gender stratified, at least controlling for situated use. Peasants in Soulan considered that talking loudly was a sign of honesty – that the bourgeoisie talked softly because they had something to hide. And while /t/ release has been studied as an affective variable, I would imagine that it is class stratified. This cline of interiority is, of course, purely speculative at this point, and it is up to sociolinguists to see whether it's crazy or not.

Variation is special for its lack of reference, which frees it up to be purely indexical. It layers "social meaning" on the content of utterances. The social meanings of variables could, of course, be rendered semantically as well – or instead. But saying "I'm cool," "I'm kind" or "I'm educated" would have a very different effect when enunciated than when signaled stylistically. Some such utterances would backfire, but above all, performances of qualities are more believable than verbal claims. First of all, one can deny making a claim, or one can deny being sufficiently preoccupied with coolness to make such a claim. At the same time, while the meaning of an utterance like "I'm cool" is pretty explicit, the stylistic performance of coolness does not explicitly set out coolness from the rest of the persona.

The space between variation and semantics lies in the balance of performativity, indexicality and reference. All of language is performative to some extent, as well as indexical, but while variation is exclusively indexical and performative, sentential propositions are primarily referential. In between, there is an array of resources that semanticists are only beginning to explore. Conversational implicatures can carry affective meaning on top of semantic content. For example, Sarah Palin's use of demonstratives in utterances like "I think Americans are craving something new and different and that new energy and that new commitment that's going to come with reform" serves to indicate – or coerce – shared perspective (Acton & Potts 2014). Eric Acton has also shown that referring to a group with a definite article rather than a bare plural (e.g. Americans vs. the Americans) has the effect of depicting the group as "a monolith of which the speaker is not part" (Acton 2014:iv), with the effect of "othering" the group.

At the edge of indexical and semantic meaning are the discourse resources that have been treated as variables, such as intensifiers (e.g. Tagliamonte 2005) and quotatives (e.g. Tagliamonte & D'Arcy 2004; Buchstaller 2006). While these have clear indexical meanings by association with the speakers who use them, their indexical potential lies in their semantics. The quotative and discourse marker uses of *like*, for example, were originally based in its approximative meaning. Andrea Beltrama has shown that the innovative use of *totally* as an intensifier does both pragmatic (Beltrama forthcoming) and indexical (Beltrama & Staum 2017) work.

Expressives (e.g. *damn*, *bastard*, *friggin'*), meanwhile, share important properties with variables. Chris Potts (2007) enumerates six characteristics that set expressives apart from the normal semantic realm, and all of these characteristics are shared with sociolinguistic variables. Both express the speaker's perspective in the utterance situation, their meanings are "ineffable," and they share the iconic quality by which intensification can be achieved by repetition. Variables, in other words, are not alone in language, but blend into a heterogeneous system ranging from the primarily referential to the primarily performative and indexical. And this is because language is not simply a referential system, but also quite fundamentally an expressive system. Linguistics until now has focused on the referential, and for good reason. But at this point, we have learned enough about the expressive realm that to ignore it is to doze off in the snow and die.

This book hereby ends fairly abruptly, because there is no end. We are always at a beginning. Naming the Third Wave seemed like a beginning ten years ago, as it drew attention to new ways of viewing the meaning of variation. But in some ways the reification of waves has created a monster by increasing the risk of constructing intellectual and social boundaries where there can be none. To the extent that this reification has attracted people to the study of meaning, I'm proud; to the extent that it has created boundaries, not so much.

Postscript

Writing this "intellectual memoir" has often been an awkward exercise. At times I've thought I was being unbelievably arrogant, at other times I've thought I was just embarrassing myself. But, like the rest of my life, I've just done it and I'll live with the consequences.

References

Acton, Eric. (2014). *Pragmatics and the Social Meaning of Determiners*. PhD thesis, Stanford University.
Acton, Eric and Christopher Potts. (2014). That straight talk: Sarah Palin and the sociolinguistics of demonstratives. *Journal of Sociolinguistics* 18:3–31.
Agha, Asif. (2003). The social life of a cultural value. *Language and Communication* 23:231–73.
(2005). Voice, footing, enregisterment. *Journal of Linguistic Anthropology* 15:38–59.
Andersen, Elaine. (1990). *Speaking with Style: The Sociolinguistic Skills of Children*. London: Routledge.
Appadurai, Arjun. (1996). *Modernity at Large*. Minneapolis, MN: University of Minnesota Press.
Baby, François. (1972). *La Guerre des Demoiselles en Ariège (1829–1872)*. Laroque d'Olmes: Montbel.
Bakhtin, Mikhail. (1981). *The Dialogic Imagination*. Austin, TX: University of Texas Press.
Baroni, Maria Rosa and Valentina d'Urso. (1984). Some experimental findings about the question of politeness and women's speech. *Language in Society* 13:67–72.
Bec, Pierre. (1968). *Les Interférences Linguistiques entre Gascon et Languedocien dans les Parlers du Comminges et du Couserans*. Paris: Presses Universitaires de France.
Bell, Alan. (1984). Language style as audience design. *Language in Society* 13:145–204.
Beltrama, Andrea. (forthcoming). *Totally* between discourse and subjectivity. Exploring the pragmatic side of intensification. *Journal of Semantics*.
Beltrama, Andrea and Laura Staum. (2017). *Totally* tall sounds *totally* younger: Intensification at the socio-semantics interface. *Journal of Sociolinguistics* 21:154–82.
Benor, Sarah Bunin. (2001). Sounding learned: Phonological variation in Orthodox Jewish English. In T. Sanchez and D. E. Johnson (eds.) *Penn Working Papers in Linguistics: Selected Papers from the 29th Annual Conference on New Ways of Analyzing Variation*. Philadelphia, PA: University of Pennsylvania, Department of Linguistics, 1–16.
Bereiter, Carl and Siegfried Engelmann. (1966). *Teaching Disadvantaged Children in the Preschool*. Englewood Cliffs, NJ: Prentice Hall.
Blom, Jan-Petter and John Gumperz. (1972). Social meaning in linguistic structure: Code-switching in Norway. In John Gumperz and Dell Hymes (eds.) *Directions in Sociolinguistics*. New York: Holt, Rinehart & Winston, 407–34.

References

Bourdieu, Pierre. (1977). The economics of linguistic exchanges. *Social Science Information* 16(6):645–68.
  (1990). *The Logic of Practice*, tr. Richard Nice. Stanford, CA: Stanford University Press.
Bourdieu, Pierre and Luc Boltanski. (1975). Le fétichisme de la langue. *Actes de la Recherche en Sciences Sociales* 4:2–32.
Brown, Penelope. (1980). How and why women are more polite: Some evidence from a Mayan community. In Sally McConnell-Ginet, Ruth A. Borker and Nelly Furman (eds.) *Women and Language in Literature and Society*. New York: Praeger, 111–36.
Brown, Penelope and Steven Levinson. (1979). Social structure, groups and interaction. In Klaus R. Scherer and Howard Giles (eds.) *Social Markers in Speech*. Cambridge University Press, 291–341.
  (1987). *Politeness*. Cambridge University Press.
Brun, Auguste. (1923). *Recherches Historiques sur l'Introduction du Français dans les Provinces du Midi*. Paris: E. Champion.
Bucholtz, Mary. (1996). Geek the girl: Language, femininity and female nerds. In Natasha Warner, Jocelyn Ahlers, Leela Bilmes, Monica Oliver, Suzanne Wertheim and Melinda Chen (eds.) *Gender and Belief Systems*. Berkeley, CA: Berkeley Women and Language Group, 119–31.
  (1999). You da man: Narrating the racial other in the production of white masculinity. *Journal of Sociolinguistics* 3:443–60.
  (2001). The whiteness of nerds: Superstandard English and racial markedness. *Journal of Linguistic Anthropology* 11:84–100.
  (2011). *White Kids: Language, Race, and Styles of Youth Identity*. Cambridge University Press.
Bucholtz, Mary and Kira Hall. (2005). Identity and interaction: A sociocultural linguistic approach. *Discourse Studies* 7:585–614.
Buchstaller, Isa. (2006). Diagnostics of age-graded behavior: The case of the quotative system. *Journal of Sociolinguistics* 10:3–30.
Butler, Judith. (1988). Performative acts and gender constitution: An essay in phenomenology and feminist theory. *Theatre Journal* 40:519–31.
  (1993). *Bodies That Matter*. Abingdon: Routledge.
California Style Collective. (1993). Personal and group style. Paper presented at the 22nd annual conference on New Ways of Analyzing Variation in English, Ottawa.
Callary, Robert E. (1975). Phonological change and the development of an urban dialect in Illinois. *Language in Society* 4:155–70.
Campbell-Kibler, Kathryn. (2007a). Accent, (ING) and the social logic of listener perceptions. *American Speech* 82:32–64.
  (2007b). What did you think she'd say?: Expectations and sociolinguistic perception. Paper presented at the 36th annual conference on New Ways of Analyzing Variation, Philadelphia.
Campbell-Kibler, Kathryn, Robert Podesva, Sarah Roberts and Andrew Wong (2002). *Language and Sexuality: Contesting Meaning in Theory and Practice*. Stanford, CA: CSLI Publications.
Cedergren, Henrietta. (1973). *The Interplay of Social and Linguistic Factors in Panama*. PhD thesis, Cornell University.
Chambers, Jack and Peter Trudgill. (1980). *Dialectology*. Cambridge University Press.
Cheshire, Jenny. (1982). *Variation in an English Dialect*. Cambridge University Press.

References

Chevalier, Michel. (1956). *La Vie Humaine dans les Pyrénées Ariègeoises*. Paris: Editions M.-Th. Genin.
Chomsky, Noam. (1957). *Syntactic Structures*. The Hague: Mouton.
Cicourel, Aaron V. and John I. Kitsuse. (1963). *The Educational Decision-Makers*. New York: Bobbs Merrill.
Clark, Eve. (2000). *First Language Acquisition*. Cambridge University Press.
Clermont, Jean and Henrietta Cedergren. (1978). Les "R" de ma mère sont perdus dans l'air. In Pierrette Thibault (ed.) *Le Français Parlé: Etudes Sociolinguistiques*. Edmonton, Alberta: Linguistic Research, 13–28.
Clyne, Michael. (2000). Lingua franca and ethnolects. *Sociolinguistica* 14:83–9.
Coleman, James S. (1961). *The Adolescent Society*. New York: The Free Press of Glencoe.
   (1966). *Equality of Educational Opportunity*. Washington, DC: U.S. Government Printing Office.
Connell, Robert. (1995). *Masculinities*. Berkeley, CA: University of California Press.
Coupland, Nikolas. (1985). 'Hark, Hark, the Lark': Social motivations for phonological style-shifting. *Language and Communication* 5:153–71.
   (2000). Language, situation and the relational self: Theorizing dialect-style in sociolinguistics. In Penelope Eckert and John Rickford (eds.) *Stylistic Variation in Language*. Cambridge University Press, 185–210.
   (2007). *Style: Language Variation and Identity*. New York: Cambridge University Press.
Deuchar, Margaret. (1988). A pragmatic account of women's use of standard speech. In Jennifer Coates and Deborah Cameron (eds.) *Women in their Speech Communities*. London: Longman, 27–32.
D'Onofrio, Annette. (2015). Persona-based information shapes linguistic perception: Valley girls and California vowels. *Journal of Sociolinguistics* 19(2):241–56.
   (2016). *Social Meaning in Linguistic Perception*. PhD thesis, Stanford University.
Dubois, Sylvie and Barbara Horvath. (1998a). From accent to marker in Cajun English: A study of dialect formation in progress. *English World Wide* 19:161–88.
   (1998b). Let's tink about dat: Interdental fricatives in Cajun English. *Language Variation and Change* 10:245–61.
Eckert, Penelope. (1978). Bilingual strategies of assimilation in Southern France. Paper presented at conference on Ethnicity and Economic Development: East and West, University of Michigan.
Eckert, Penelope. (1980a). Diglossia: Separate and unequal. *Linguistics* 18:1053–64.
   (1980b). The structure of a long-term phonological process: The back vowel chain shift in Soulatan Gascon. In William Labov (ed.) *Locating Language in Time and Space*. New York: Academic Press, 179–220.
   (1982). Clothing and geography in a suburban school. In Conrad P. Kottak (ed.) *Researching American Culture*. Ann Arbor, MI: University of Michigan Press, 139–44.
   (1983). Beyond the statistics of adolescent smoking. *American Journal of Public Health* 73:439–41.
   (1984). Age and linguistic change. In Jennie Keith and David I. Kertzer (eds.) *Age and Anthropological Theory*. Ithaca, NY: Cornell University Press, 219–33.
   (1985). Grammatical constraints in phonological change: Unstressed *a in Southern France. *Orbis* 31:169–89.

(1986). The development of social meaning in sound change. Paper presented at the Annual Meeting of the Linguistic Society of America, New York.
(1987). The relative values of variables. In Keith Denning, Sharon Inkelas, Faye McNair-Knox and John Rickford (eds.) *Variation in Language: Papers Presented at the Fifteenth Annual Conference on New Ways of Analyzing Variation*. Stanford, CA, Department of Linguistics, 101–10.
(1988). Adolescent social structure and the spread of linguistic change. *Language in Society* 17:183–207.
(1989a). *Jocks and Burnouts: Social Categories and Identity in the High School*. New York: Teachers College Press.
(1989b). Social membership and linguistic variation. Paper presented at the eighteenth annual conference on New Ways of Analyzing Variation in English, Duke University.
(1989c). The whole woman: Sex and gender differences in variation. *Language Variation and Change* 1:245–67.
(1990). Cooperative competition in adolescent "girl talk." *Discourse Processes* 13:91–122.
(1994). *Identities of Subordination as a Developmental Imperative*. Working Papers on Learning and Identity, Vol. 2. Palo Alto, CA: Institute for Research on Learning.
(1996). Vowels and nailpolish: The emergence of linguistic style in the preadolescent heterosexual marketplace. In Natasha Warner, Jocelyn Ahlers, Leela Bilmes, Monica Oliver, Suzanne Wertheim and Melinda Chen (eds.) *Gender and Belief Systems*. Berkeley, CA: Berkeley Women and Language Group, 183–90.
(2000). *Linguistic Variation as Social Practice*. Oxford: Blackwell.
(2004). Elephants in the room. *Journal of Sociolinguistics* 7:392–7.
(2008a). Variation and the indexical field. *Journal of Sociolinguistics* 12:453–76.
(2008b). Where do ethnolects stop? *International Journal of Bilingualism* 12(1):25–42.
(2011). Where does the social stop? In Frans Gregersen, Jeffrey Parrott and Pia Quist (eds.) *Language Variation – European Perspectives III*. Selected Papers from the Fifth International Conference on Language Variation in Europe (ICLaVE 5). Amsterdam: John Benjamins.
(2012). Three waves of variation study: The emergence of meaning in the study of variation. *Annual Review of Anthropology* 41:87–100.
Eckert, Penelope and Sally McConnell-Ginet. (1992). Think practically and look locally: Language and gender as community–based practice. *Annual Review of Anthropology* 21:461–90.
Eckert, Penelope, Alison Edwards and Lynne Robins. (1985). Biological categories in linguistic variation. Paper presented at the fourteenth annual conference on New Ways of Analyzing Variation in English, Georgetown University.
Edwards, Walter and Cheryl Krakow. (1985). Polish-American English in Hamtramck: A sociolinguistic study. Paper presented at the fourteenth annual conference on New Ways of Analyzing Variation in English, Georgetown University.
Eisenstadt, Shmuel N. (1956). *From Generation to Generation*. New York: The Free Press of Glencoe.
Elshtain, Jean Bethke. (1981). *Public Man, Private Woman*. Princeton, NJ: Princeton University Press.

References

Ferguson, Charles A. (1959). Diglossia. *Word* 15:325–40.
Fernald, Anne. (1989). Intonation and communicative intent in mothers' speech to infants: Is the melody the message? *Child Development* 60:1497–1510.
Fishman, Joshua. (1971). *Sociolinguistics*. Rowley, MA: Newbury House.
  (1973). *Language and Nationalism*. Rowley, MA: Newbury House.
Fónagy, Ivan. (1971). The functions of vocal style. In Seymour Chatman (ed.) *Literary Style: A Symposium*. London and New York: Oxford University Press, 159–74.
Fought, Carmen. (1999). A majority sound change in a minority community: /u/-fronting in Chicano English. *Journal of Sociolinguistics* 3:5–23.
  (2003). *Chicano English in Context*. New York: Macmillan.
Foulkes, Paul, Gerard Docherty and Dominic Watt. (2005). Phonological variation in child-directed speech. *Language* 81:177–206.
Fox-Genovese, Elizabeth. (1988). *Within the Plantation Household*. Chapel Hill: University of North Carolina Press.
Gal, Susan. (1979). *Language Shift: Social Determinants of Linguistic Change in Bilingual Austria*. New York: Academic Press.
Gal, Susan and Judith T. Irvine. (1995). The boundaries of languages and disciplines: How ideologies construct difference. *Social Research* 62:967–1001.
Gauchat, Louis. (1905). L'unité phonétique dans le patois d'une commune. In *Festshrift Heinrich Morf*. Halle: Max Niemeyer, 175–232.
Gaudio, Rudolf P. (1997). Not talking straight in Hausa. In Kira Hall (ed.) *Queerly Phrased: Language, Gender and Sexuality*. New York: Oxford University Press, 642–62.
Giddens, Anthony. (1979). *Central Problems in Social Theory: Action, Structure and Contradiction in Social Analysis*. Berkeley, CA: University of California Press.
Gilliéron, Jules. (1902–10). *Atlas Linguistique de la France*. Paris: H. Champion.
Goffman, Erving. (1981). Response cries. In Erving Goffman *Forms of Talk*. Philadelphia, PA: University of Pennsylvania Press, 78–122.
Gold, David. (1985). Jewish English. In Joshua A. Fishman (ed.) *Readings in the Sociology of Jewish Languages*. Leiden: Brill, 3–21.
Gumperz, John. (1968). The speech community. In David L. Sills (ed.) *International Encyclopedia of the Social Sciences*. London: Macmillan, 381–6.
Guy, Gregory, Barbara Horvath, Julia Vonwiller, Elaine Daisley and Inge Rogers. (1986). An intonational change in progress in Australian English. *Language in Society* 15:23–52.
Haeri, Niloofar. (1989). Synchronic variation in Cairene Arabic: The case of palatalization. Paper presented at Linguistic Society of America Annual Meeting, Washington DC.
  (1997). *The Sociolinguistic Market of Cairo: Gender, Class and Education*. London: Kegan Paul International.
Hall, Kira and Veronica O'Donovan. (1997). Shifting gender positions among Hindi-speaking Hijras. In Alice Freed (ed.) *Language and Gender Research: Theory and Method*. London: Longman, 223–66.
Hebdige, Dick. (1984). *Subculture: The Meaning of Style*. New York: Methuen.
Hill, Jane. (1987). Women's speech in modern Mexicano. In Susan U. Philips (ed.) *Language, Gender and Sex in Comparative Perspective*. New York: Cambridge University Press, 121–60.

References

(1993). Hasta la vista, baby: Anglo Spanish in the American Southwest. *Critique of Anthropology* 13:145–76.

Hindle, Donald. (1979). *The Social and Situational Conditioning of Phonetic Variation*. PhD thesis, University of Pennsylvania.

Hodder, Ian. (1982). *The Present Past*. London: Batsford

Hollan, Douglas. (2014). From ghosts to ancestors (and back again): On the cultural and psychodynamic mediation of selfscapes. *Ethos* 42:175–97.

Hollingshead, A. B. (1949). *Elmtown's Youth*. New York: John Wiley & Sons.

Holmquist, Jonathan. (1985). Social correlates of a linguistic variable: A study in a Spanish village. *Language in Society* 14:191–203.

Horvath, Barbara and David Sankoff. (1987). Delimiting the Sydney speech community. *Language in Society* 16:179–204.

Hymes, Dell. (1972). Models of the interaction of language and social life. In John Gumperz and Dell Hymes (eds.) *Directions in Sociolinguistics: The Ethnography of Communication*. New York: Holt, Rinehart & Winston, 35–71.

Irvine, Judith. (2001). Style as distinctiveness: The culture and ideology of linguistic differentiation. In Penelope Eckert and John Rickford (eds.) *Style and Sociolinguistic Variation*. Cambridge University Press, 21–43.

Irvine, Judith and Susan Gal. (2000). Language ideology and linguistic differentiation. In Paul V. Kroskrity (ed.) *Regimes of Language: Ideologies, Polities, and Identities*. Santa Fe, NM: School of American Research Press, 35–83.

Jaspers, Jürgen. (2008). Problematizing ethnolects: Naming linguistic practices in an Antwerp secondary school. *International Journal of Bilingualism* 12:85–103.

Johnstone, Barbara, Jennifer Andrus and Andrew E. Danielson. (2006). Mobility, indexicality, and the enregisterment of 'Pittsburghese'. *Journal of English Linguistics* 34:77–104.

Johnstone, Barbara and Scott F. Kiesling. (2008). Indexicality and experience: Exploring the meanings of /aw/-monophthongization in Pittsburgh. *Journal of Sociolinguistics* 12:5–33.

Kanter, Rosabeth M. (1977). *Men and Women of the Corporation*. New York: Basic Books.

Kiesling, Scott. (2009). Style as stance: Can stance be the primary explanation for patterns of sociolinguistic variation? In Alexandra Jaffe (ed.) *Sociolinguistic Perspectives on Stance*. Oxford University Press, 171–94.

Knappert, Jan. (1978). The state and the languages spoken in it. *Linguistics* 214:69–76.

Kulick, Don. (2000). Gay and lesbian language. In Annual Review of Anthropology. *Mountain View: Annual Reviews*:243–85.

Labov, William. (1963). The social motivation of a sound change. *Word* 18:1–42.

(1966). *The Social Stratification of English in New York City*. Washington: Center for Applied Linguistics.

(1971). The study of language in its social context. In Joshua A. Fishman (ed.) *Advances in the Sociology of Language*, Vol. 1. The Hague: Mouton, 152–216.

(1972a). Hypercorrection by the lower middle class as a factor in linguistic change. In William Labov (ed.) *Sociolinguistic Patterns*. Philadelphia, PA: University of Pennsylvania Press, 122–42.

(1972b). *Language in the Inner City*. Philadelphia, PA: University of Pennsylvania Press.

(1972c). Some principles of linguistic methodology. *Language in Society* 1:97–120.

(1973). The linguistic consequences of being a lame. *Language in Society* 2:81–115.

   (1980). The social origins of sound change. In William Labov (ed.) *Locating Language in Time and Space*. New York: Academic Press, 251–65.

   (1984). The intersection of sex and social factors in the course of language change. Paper presented at the thirteenth annual conference on New Ways of Analyzing Variation in English, University of Pennsylvania.

   (1990). The intersection of sex and social class in the course of linguistic change. *Language Variation and Change* 2:205–51.

   (1994). *Principles of Linguistic Change: Internal Factors*. Oxford: Basil Blackwell.

   (2001). *Principles of Linguistic Change: Social Factors*. Cambridge: Blackwell.

   (2002). Review of Penelope Eckert, Linguistic variation as social practice. *Language in Society* 31:277–84.

Labov, William, Malcah Yaeger and Richard Steiner. (1972). *A Quantitative Study of Sound Change in Progress*. Philadelphia, PA: US Regional Survey.

Laferriere, Martha. (1979). Ethnicity in phonological variation and change. *Language* 55:603–17.

Lafont, Robert. (1971). Un problème de culpabilité sociologique: La diglossie franco-occitane. *Langue Française* 9:93–100.

Larkin, Ralph W. (1979). *Suburban Youth in Cultural Crisis*. New York: Oxford University Press.

Latour, Bruno. (1993). *We Have Never Been Modern*, trans. Catherine Porter. Cambridge, MA: Harvard University Press.

Lavandera, Beatriz R. (1978). Where does the sociolinguistic variable stop? *Language in Society* 7:171–82.

Lave, Jean and Etienne Wenger. (1991). *Situated Learning: Legitimate Peripheral Participation*. Cambridge University Press.

Le Page, Robert B. and Andrée Tabouret-Keller. (1985). *Acts of Identity*. Cambridge University Press.

Macaulay, Ronald K. S. (1977). *Language, Social Class and Education: A Glasgow Study*. University of Edinburgh Press.

Martinet, André. (1952). Function, structure and sound change. *Word* 8:1–32.

   (1963). *Eléments de Linguistique Générale*. Paris: A. Colin

Maltz, Daniel and Ruth Borker. (1982). A cultural approach to male-female miscommunication. In John J. Gumperz (ed.) *Language and Social Identity*. Cambridge University Press, 195–216.

McConnell-Ginet, Sally. (1989). The sexual (re)production of meaning: A discourse–based theory. In Francine W. Frank and Paula A. Treichler (eds.) *Language, Gender and Professional Writing: Theoretical Approaches and Guidelines for Nonsexist Usage*. New York: MLA, 35–50.

Mendoza-Denton, Norma. (2008). *Home Girls*. New York: Blackwell.

Meyer, Leonard B. (1979). Toward a theory of style. In Berel Lang (ed.) *The Concept of Style*. Philadelphia, PA: University of Pennsylvania Press, 3–44.

Milroy, James and Lesley Milroy. (1985). Linguistic change, social network and speaker innovation. *Journal of Linguistics*. 21:339–84.

Milroy, Lesley. (1980). *Language and Social Networks*. Oxford: Basil Blackwell.

   (1982). Social network and linguistic focusing. In Suzanne Romaine (ed.) *Sociolinguistic Variation in Speech Communities*. London: Edward Arnold, 141–52.

Moonwomon, Birch. (1992). *Sound Change in San Francisco English*. PhD thesis, University of California, Berkeley.

Nichols, Patricia C. (1983). Linguistic options and choices for black women in the rural south. In Barrie Thorne, Cheris Kramarae and Nancy Henley (eds.) *Language, Gender and Society*. Rowley, MA: Newbury House, 54–68.

Ochs, Elinor. (1991). Indexing gender. In Alessandro Duranti and Charles Goodwin (eds.) *Rethinking Context*. Cambridge University Press, 336–58.

Ohala, John. (1994). The biological bases of sound symbolism. In Leanne Hinton, Johanna Nichols and John J. Ohala (eds.) *Sound Symbolism*. Cambridge University Press, 222–36.

Paunonen, Heikki. (1994). Language change in apparent time and in real time. Paper presented at the 23rd Annual Conference on New Ways of Analyzing Variation, Stanford University.

Peirce, Charles. S. (1931). *The Collected Papers of Charles S. Peirce*, 8 vols. eds. C. Hartshorne, P. Weiss and A. W. Burks. Cambridge, MA: Harvard University Press.

Penfield, Joyce and Jacob L. Ornstein-Galicia. (1985). *Chicano English: An Ethnic Contact Dialect*. Amsterdam: John Benjamins.

Piaget, Jean. (1954). *The Construction of Reality in the Child*. New York: Basic Books.

Podesva, Robert. (2004). On constructing social meaning with stop release bursts. Paper presented at Sociolinguistics Symposium 15, Newcastle upon Tyne, UK.

  (2007). Phonation type as a stylistic variable: The use of falsetto in constructing a persona. *Journal of Sociolinguistics* 11:478–504.

Podesva, Robert. (2008). Three sources of stylistic meaning. *Texas Linguistic Forum* 51:134–43.

Podesva, Robert, Sarah J. Roberts and Kathryn Campbell-Kibler. (2002). Sharing resources and indexing meanings in the production of gay styles. In Kathryn Campbell-Kibler, Robert J. Podesva, Sarah J. Roberts and Andrew Wong (eds.) *Language and Sexuality: Contesting Meaning in Theory and Practice*. Stanford, CA: CSLI Press, 175–90.

Potts, Christopher. (2007). The expressive dimension. *Theoretical Linguistics* 33:165–98.

Pratt, Mary Louise. (1988). Linguistic utopias. In Colin MacCabe, Nigel Fabb, Derek Attridge and Alan Durant (eds.) *The Linguistics of Writing: Arguments Between Language and Literature*. New York: Methuen, 48–66.

Pullum, Geoffrey K. and Barbara C. Scholz. (2001). Language: More than words. *Nature* 413(6854):367.

Rampton, Ben. (1995). *Crossing: Language and Ethnicity among Adolescents*. London: Longman.

Rauniomaa, Mirka. (2003). Stance accretion. Paper presented at the Language, Interaction, and Social Organization Research Focus Group, University of California, Santa Barbara, February.

Rich, Adrienne. (1980). Compulsory heterosexuality and lesbian existence. *Signs* 5:631–60.

Rickford, John. (1986a). Concord and contrast in the characterization of the speech community. *Sheffield Working Papers in Language and Linguistics* 3:87–119.

  (1986b). The need for new approaches to class analysis in sociolinguistics. *Language and Communication* 6:215–21.

References

Romaine, Suzanne. (1984a). On the problem of syntactic varation and pragmatic meaning in sociolinguistic theory. *Folia Linguistica* 18:409–39.
Romaine, Suzanne. (1984b). *The Language of Children and Adolescents*. Oxford: Basil Blackwell.
Rose, Mary. (2006). *Language, Place and Identity in Later Life*. PhD thesis, Stanford University.
Sacks, Karen. (1974). Engels revisited. In Michelle Rosaldo and Louise Lamphere (eds.) *Women, Culture and Society*. Stanford, CA: Stanford University Press, 207–22.
Sankoff, David and Suzanne Laberge. (1978). The linguistic market and the statistical explanation of variability. In David Sankoff (ed.) *Linguistic Variation: Models and Methods*. New York: Academic Press, 239–50.
Sattel, Jack W. (1983). Men, inexpressiveness, and power. In Barrie Thorne, Cheris Kramarae and Nancy Henley (eds.) *Language, Gender and Society*. Rowley, MA: Newbury House, 119–24.
Schieffelin, Bambi and Don Kulick. (2003). Language socialization. In Alessandro Duranti (ed.) *A Companion to Linguistic Anthropology*. Malden, MA and Oxford: Wiley-Blackwell, 349–68.
Silverstein, Michael. (1985). Language and the culture of gender: At the intersection of structure, usage and ideology. In Elizabeth Mertz and Richard J. Parmentier (eds.) *Semiotic Mediation*. New York: Academic Press, 219–59.
 (2003). Indexical order and the dialectics of sociolinguistic life. *Language and Communication* 23:193–229.
Smith, Edward E. and Stephen M. Kosslyn. (2007). *Cognitive Psychology: Mind and Brain*. London: Pearson.
Smith, Jennifer, Mercedes Durham and Liane Fortune. (2009). Universal and dialect-specific pathways of acquisition: Caregivers, children, and t/d deletion. *Language Variation and Change* 21:69–95.
Stinchcombe, Arthur. (1964). *Rebellion in a High School*. Chicago, IL: Quadrangle.
Tagliamonte, Sali. (2005). So weird; so cool; so innovative: The use of intensifiers in the television series *Friends*. *American Speech* 80:280–300.
Tagliamonte, Sali and Alex D'Arcy. (2004). He's like, she's like: The quotative system in Canadian youth. *Journal of Sociolinguistics* 8:493–514.
Thibault, Pierrette. (1983). *Equivalence et grammaticalisation*. PhD thesis, Université de Montréal.
Thorne, Barrie. (1993). *Gender Play*. New Brunswick, NJ: Rutgers University Press.
Trudgill, Peter. (1972). Sex, covert prestige and linguistic change in the urban British English of Norwich. *Language in Society* 1:179–95.
 (1974a). Linguistic change and diffusion: Description and explanation in sociolinguistic dialect geography. *Language in Society* 3:215–46.
 (1974b). *The Social Differentiation of English in Norwich*. Cambridge University Press.
Veblen, Thorstein. (1931). *The Theory of the Leisure Class*. New York: Viking.
Walters, Keith. (2003). Gender, nationalism and language ideology: The Tunisian case. Paper presented at Conference on Language, Identity and Change in the Modern Arab World: Implications for the study of language and culture, Berkeley, CA: University of California.

Weinreich, Uriel, William Labov and Marvin Herzog. (1968). Empirical foundations for a theory of language change. In Winfred Lehmann and Yakov Malkiel (eds.) *Directions for Historical Linguistics*. Austin, TX: University of Texas Press, 95–188.

Wenger, Etienne. (2000). *Communities of Practice*. Cambridge Univesrity Press.

Wexler, Paul. (1971). Diglossia, language standardization and purism. *Lingua* 27: 330–54.

Wolfram, Walt. (1969). *A Sociolinguistic Description of Detroit Negro Speech*. Washington, DC: Center for Applied Linguistics.

Wong, Andrew. (2005). The re-appropriation of Tongzhi. *Language in Society* 34:763–93.

Zhang, Qing. (2001). *Changing Economics, Changing Markets: A Sociolinguistic Study of Chinese Yuppies*. PhD thesis, Stanford University.

   (2005). A Chinese yuppie in Beijing: Phonological variation and the construction of a new professional identity. *Language in Society* 34:431–66.

   (2008). Rhotacization and the "Beijing Smooth Operator": The social meaning of a linguistic variable. *Journal of Sociolinguistics* 12:201–22.

Index

AAVE, 15, 137, 161, 170, 170n.3
accommodation, 92
Acton, Eric, 192
acts of identity, 153
adolescence (as life stage), 44–5
affect, 131, 132, 164, 191, 192
African American Vernacular English, *see* AAVE
age, *see also* life stage
    segregation in school, 51
    and social change, 87, 189
    and sound change, 139
agency, 33, 136–40, 145
    and awareness, 84–5, 136, 141–2
Agha, Asif, 146, 186
Andersen, Elaine, 188
Appadurai, Arjun, 186
Arnold, Jennifer, 110
attention, *see* awareness
Australian Question Intonation, 92
authenticity, 136–40, 144, 153
    and gender, 137
    of Occitan, 7, 9–11
authority (and gender), 97, 99
autonomy
    adolescent, 51, 52, 56, 72
    regional, in France, 6
awareness, 136–40, 141–2, 154
    as a continuum, 138, 140

baby talk (as stylistic resource), 189
Bell, Allan, 138
Beltrama, Andrea, 192
Benor, Sarah, 125, 128, 159
Blake, Renee, 110
Blum, Susan, 38n.2
borrowing, *see* Gascon: French borrowing in
Bourdieu, Pierre, 83, 155n.4, 174
bricolage, 112, 113, 118, 147
Brown, Penelope, 90, 91
Bucholtz, Mary, 108, 125, 129, 136, 137, 138, 143, 159
Burling, Robbins, 81
burned-out Burnouts, 64, 141, 150

Butler, Judith, 122
BWLG (Berkeley Women and Language Group), 108

California (as imagined), 171
California vowel shift, 166–85
Campbell-Kibler, Kathryn, 125, 128, 156–8, 159, 166
categories, *see* social categories
Cau, Anna, 3
Cervantes, Christi, 113
change
    indexical, 155, 163
    in later life, 139
channel cues, 140
Chapin, Paul, 81
characterological figure, 187
Chicano English, 135, 166–85
child development, *see* development and variation
Chomsky, Noam, 85
circulation (vs. spread of change), 188
Clark, Eve, 139n.6
class, 156
    and gender, 89
    and high school social categories, 33, 42–4, 45
    and ideology, 158
    and linguistic change, 89
    reproduction of, 72, 84–5
    and urban geography, 72
clothing, *see* style: clothing
cognitive science (sociolinguistics as), 143, 146
community of practice, 83, 85, 115, 116, 121, 123, 128, 149
cosmopolitan Mandarin, 77, 150–2, 189–90
Coupland, Nikolas, 125, 135, 136, 138
Covert, Jane, 38n.2
covert prestige, 90, 203
crossing, 170
cruising, 73, 79
curvilinear pattern (and gender), 92

205

Index

D'Onofrio, Annette, 166
de Saussure, Ferdinand, 165
deDuve, Christian, 2
demonstratives, 192
Deo, Ashwini, 138n.5
desire, 126, 134
Detroit conurbation, *see* urban/suburban geography
Deuchar, Margaret, 90
development and variation, 188–9
developmental imperative, 189
Diemer, Larry, 38n.2
Diglossia
 definitions, 16–17
 and language shift, 15–18
Diver, William, 1
double voicing, 141

Edwards, Alison, 38n.2, 85
elementary school, *see* heterosexual market, preadolescence
embodiment, *see* style and the body
emotion, *see* affect
enregistered voices, 161
enregisterment, 146
erasure, 74, 156
ethnicity, 66, 86, 101, 115, 166–85
ethnography, 65, 78–9, 80, 81, 85, 113–14, 172
ethnolect, 166–85
 as a construct, 167
 and deterritorializing discourse, 168
expressives, 192

femininity, 98
Fields Elementary, 113, 166, 172
First Wave, *see* Waves of variation study
Fishman, Joshua, 6, 17
flamboyance, 119, 120, 121
Fought, Carmen, 107, 168, 171
Francez, Itamar, 138n.5

Gal, Susan, 31, 74, 125, 147, 150
gangs, 117, 175–6
Gascon, *see also* Occitan
 French borrowing in, 4, 11, 25–7
 stigma, 3, 27
gay speech, 128, 160
gender, 80, 85, 87
 and authenticity, 137
 and authority, 97, 99
 as binary, 85, 91–5
 and class, 89
 differentiation in preadolescence, 114–22, 178
 and power, 97–8, 99–100
 and variation, 63–4, 101–7, 145, 178, 191

Giddens, Anthony, 83
Gifford, Bernard, 82
Goffman, Erving, 131
Greeno, Jim, 82
Gumperz, John, 31, 153

habitus, 84–5
Haeri, Niloofar, 93
Hall, Kira, 108, 125, 143
Herzog, Marvin, 3, 140, 155
heterosexual market (in elementary school), 113, 114–22, 133–5, 173–5
 couples in, 133, 173
 and heteronormativity, 115
 and popular crowd, 116, 133, 173, 176
high school
 as institution, 48, 71
  peer-based social order in, 44–56, 71–3, 109
 social categories in, *see* Jocks and Burnouts
 territories in, 36, 75–6
Hill, Jane, 137
Hindle, Don, 91
Hodder, Ian, 189
Holmquist, Jonathan, 70

iconicity, 93, 191
iconization, 75, 151
ideology
 and class, 158
 and stylistic practice, 113
 and variation, 144, 147, 154, 156, 158, 159
IGALA, 126
impostor syndrome, xi, 1, 2, 107, 125
In-betweens, 34, 37, 40, 55, 58, 62, 79
indexical field, 143–64
 and ideology, 154
 problems with, 165
indexical order, 144, 153–5, 169
indexicality, 143, 144, *see also* social meaning
 indirect, 145
 presupposed, 157
 and reference, 192
 variation as indexical system, 144
indicators, 154
individual, 165
Inkelas, Sharon, 109
Inoue, Miyako, 125, 143
Institute for Research on Learning, 82, 109, 113, 123
intensifiers, 192
interiority, 190
interpellation, 122
interpretant, 165
Irvine, Judith, 74, 125, 147, 150
Iwai, Melissa, 110

Index

Jaspers, Jürgen, 167
Jock–Burnout differences
  in autonomy, 52, 55
  in clothing, 76
  in networks, 47, 52–5, 84–5
  in style, 33, 75–6
  in urban orientation, 73–4
Jocks and Burnouts, 33–8, 44–56, 71–3, 99–100, 149
Johnstone, Barbara, 69, 158

Kiesling, Scott, 158
Knack, Rebecca, 38n.2
Kortenhoven, Andrea, 125, 162
Kottak, Conrad, 81
Kroch, Tony, 92
Kulick, Don, 122, 126, 127, 129

Labov, William, xii, 2, 15, 32, 88, 89, 90, 107, 140, 143, 154, 155, 162, 163, 165, 168
Lafont, Robert, 19, 20
landscape (social-semiotic), 146, 186–8
language shift, 8–9, 15–18
Latour, Bruno, 138
Lavandera, Beatriz, 158
Lave, Jean, 82, 115, 123
Levinson, Stephen, 91
life stage, 87, 133
  and change, 139
  Jock-Burnout difference in, 50, 52, 53
  and variation, 42–4, 113
Linguistic Institute, 107, 133, 143
local identity, 56, 71, 153
localness (as construct), 186
lower middle class crossover, 141

Macaulay, Ronald, 43, 67, 107
Mandarin, *see* cosmopolitan Mandarin
markers, 91, 154, 168
Martha's Vineyard, xi, 70, 80, 88, 144, 146, 153, 155
Martinet, André, 18
Marx, Karl, 97
masculinity, 98
McConnell-Ginet, Sally, 107, 114, 156
meaning, *see also* reference, indexicality, social meaning
meaning (as constructed in discourse), 165
meaning-making rights, 67
Mendoza-Denton, Norma, 110, 123
Meyer, Leonard, 138
Milroy, James, 67, 68
Milroy, Lesley, 31, 63, 67, 68, 83, 96, 135
Mock Spanish, 171
Moore, Emma, 125
Morgan, Carol, 110
Moyer, Melissa, 109

National Science Foundation, 31, 81
naturalization
  of desire and sexuality, 127, 130
  of identity categories, 132
New Jersey suburbs, 66–7
New Wavers, 112, 147, 187
Nichols, Patricia, 96
Northern Cities Shift, 57, 76, 101–5, 149
  gender difference in, 101–5
NWAV, 15, 81, 85, 107, 109, 136

Oberlin College, 1, 107
Occitan
  peripheralization of local dialects, 11–14
  punishments for speaking in school, 22
  regional movement, revitalization, 4, 5–14
  stigma, 3, 4–5, 8, 27

Palo Alto High School, 109, 110, 147, 187
Payne, Arvilla, 91
peer pressure, 45
peer-based social order
  emergence in elementary school, 115, 133, 172–3
  in high school, 44–56, 71–3
Pei, Mario, 2
Peirce, Charles, 165
pejoration, 156
performativity, 112, 122
  and reference, 192
persona, 99, 117, 121, 129, 131, 135, 142, 146, 150–2, 166, 187
  relation to identity categories, 132
persona style, 110, 146
Peters, Stanley, 125
Podesva, Robert, 125, 128, 140n.7, 159, 160, 161
Polanyi, Livia, 110
polarization, 44–56
popular crowd (in elementary school), *see* heterosexual market
Potts, Christopher, 192
power
  in adolescence, 99–100
  adult, 72, 133
  and gender, 90, 97–8, 99–100
Pratt, Mary Louise, 69
preadolescence
  gender differentiation in, 113, 116, 178
preppies, 112, 147, 187
prestige, xi, 89–91
  and gender, 89, 90

qualities, xi, 25, 67, 90, 98, 119, 131, 145, 149, 150, 151, 154, 156, 160, 166, 168, 169
Quist, Pia, 125
quotatives, 192

Index

Rahman, Jacqueline, 125
Rappaport, Skip, 81
recursivity, 75, 76, 150
reference, *see* indexicality and reference
regionalism, *see* Occitan
register, 146
response cries, 131
Rickford, John, 69, 82, 125
Roberts, Sarah, 125, 128, 159
Robins, Lynne, 38n.2, 85
Romaine, Suzanne, 43, 113, 158
Rose, Mary, 125, 162
Roth Gordon, Jen, 125
Rumeau family, 4

Sag, Ivan, 29, 82, 83, 143
Salomon, Marcia, 38n.2
Sankoff, David, 85, 107
Sankoff, Gillian, 139n.6
Schieffelin, Bambi, 122
Second Wave, *see* Waves of variation study
sexuality, 126, 127, 130, *see also* heterosexual market, gay speech
Sharma, Devyani, 125
Sherzer, Joel, 107
signs, 146, 147, 157, 165, 166, 186, 188
Silverstein, Michael, 144, 153, 154, 158n.9
SLIC, 125, 136
smoking, 81–2
social categories
    in high school, 44–56, 73, 109
    identity categories, 126, 129, 132
    macro-social categories, 68, 80, 83, 86–7, 107, 145, 156, 167–8, 186, 191
    problems with focus on, 78–9, 127
    sexual categories, 128
social change
    and age, 87, 189
    as change in personae, 190
    and performativity, 112
    and variation, 112, 144, 150, 190
social engineering (in preadolescence), 134
social meaning, 32, 77, 78, 112, 118, 144, 191, *see also* affect, iconization, indexicality, qualities, stance
    construal of, 142, 153–4, 155, 157, 165, 166, 188
    and macro-social categories, 144
    and pragmatics, 158, 192
    and semantics, 192
    and style, 110
social mobility, 93, 141
    and gender, 90
social networks, 83
    Jocks and Burnouts, *see* Jock–Burnout differences

and the spread of change, 40, 67
social reproduction, 72, 83, 112, 153
social types, *see* persona
social-semiotic landscape, 77, 119, 129, 141
    change in, 147
    style as movement in, 169
Solomon, Julie, 110
Soulan, 4, 66
sound change
    and adolescent autonomy, 56
    and age, 139
    and class, 42–4
    and gender, 101–7, 145, 180
    mechanisms of spread, 30, 40, 61–3, 64, 67, 145
    and social meaning, 40, 56–7, 61–3, 120
    spread from urban centers, 41, 60–1, 76
sound symbolism, *see* iconicity
speech community, 66–7, 69, 70–1, 73, 165
Spencer Foundation, 31, 113
stance, 135, 145, 155, 160, 169, 187
standardization, 5–14
Stanford University, 82, 113, 125
status
    and gender, 98
    and heterosexuality, 117, 133
    and the right to innovate, 67
Steedly, Mary, 38n.2
Steps Elementary, 113, 115, 166, 172
stereotypes, 154
stigma, *see* language shift, *see* Occitan
stop release, *see* variables
style, 33, 110–12, 118, 146–8, *see also* Jock–Burnout differences
    and the body, 67, 116, 120, 121, 191
    clothing, 33–8, 75–6, 147–8, 187
    constructions in, 136
    formality, 146
    persona style, 146
    and social category, 46, 55, 75
    and social mobility, 32
    as ways of saying the same thing, 146
stylistic icon, 118, 119, 141
stylistic landscape, *see* social-semiotic landscape
stylistic practice, 111–12, 117, 147, 148
    and ideology, 113, 147, 155
subordination (female), 122
suburbs, *see* urban/suburban geography
survey research, 80, 145
Sweetland, Julie, 125, 170n.3

tenure, 81, 82
Third Wave, 109, 125, 135, *see also* Waves of variation study
Thorne, Barrie, 115

Index

Trendy, 110–12
Trudgill, Peter, xi, 32, 63, 88, 89, 90, 145
Tyler, Leanna, 38n.2

Uhland, Sue, 109, 112
University of Illinois at Chicago, 82
urban/suburban geography, 71, 149
  and class, 72
  orientation in, 49–50, 52–5, 73–4
  and social meaning, 61, 150

Valley Girl, 171
variables
  heterogeneity of, 190–1
  as indexical signs, 165
variables, specific
  (ae) nasal pattern in California, 119, 177–84
  (ae) nasal pattern in Chicano English, 120–2
  (ay) in Detroit, 76, 149
  (eh) in Detroit, 76
  (ING), 156–8
  (ING) in Chicano English, 170
  (l) in Chicano English, 170
  (oh) in Detroit, 76
  (TH/DH) stopping, 162, 169–70
  (uh) in Detroit, 58–64, 76
  (uw),(ow) in California, 171
  full tone in Beijing, 152

interdentals in Beijing, 151
negative concord, 150
rhotacization in Beijing, 151
stop release, 159–62, 165, 191
variation
  and development, 188
  as expressive system, 192
  and ideology, 144, 158, 159
  as indexical system, 144
  and social change, 112, 144, 190
Veatch, Tom, 110
vernacular, 136–40
  as holy grail, 140
  as natural object, 138
  as source of change, 139
Vidal, André (Pépi), 4
voice quality, 33, 130, 131, 164, 190, 191
  sexy voice, 131

Walters, Keith, 137
Waves of variation study, xi–xii
Weinreich, Uriel, 2, 140, 155
Wenger, Etienne, 82, 115
white privilege, 172, 176
Wolfram, Walt, 43
Wong, Andrew, 125, 155
Woolard, Kathryn, 144

Zhang, Qing, 77, 125, 150–2

Printed in the United States
By Bookmasters